Campaigns on the Cutting Edge

Third Edition

*To our family and friends,
to whom we owe so much*

Campaigns on the Cutting Edge
Third Edition

Editor

Richard J. Semiatin

American University

Los Angeles | London | New Delhi
Singapore | Washington DC | Melbourne

FOR INFORMATION:

CQ Press

An Imprint of SAGE Publications, Inc.

2455 Teller Road

Thousand Oaks, California 91320

E-mail: order@sagepub.com

SAGE Publications Ltd.

1 Oliver's Yard

55 City Road

London EC1Y 1SP

United Kingdom

SAGE Publications India Pvt. Ltd.

B 1/I 1 Mohan Cooperative Industrial Area

Mathura Road, New Delhi 110 044

India

SAGE Publications Asia-Pacific Pte. Ltd.

3 Church Street

#10-04 Samsung Hub

Singapore 049483

Printed in the United States of America.

ISBN 978-1-5063-1645-1

Acquisitions Editor: Michael Kerns

Development Editor: Nancy Matuszak

eLearning Editor: Allison Hughes

Editorial Assistant: Zachary Hoskins

Production Editor: Olivia Weber-Stenis

Copy Editor: Melinda Masson

Typesetter: C&M Digitals (P) Ltd.

Proofreader: Ellen Brink

Indexer: Marilyn Augst

Cover Designer: Anupama Krishnan

Marketing Manager: Amy Whitaker

This book is printed on acid-free paper.

MIX
Paper from
responsible sources
FSC® C014174

16 17 18 19 20 10 9 8 7 6 5 4 3 2 1

Contents

Part I—The New Political Campaign

A smartphone can empower a twenty-year old canvasser to know everything about you: what car you drive, what smartphone you have (iPhone vs. Droid), whether you voted in the last election, what you like to read or eat, and most of all, your voting tendencies. In a sense, technology has democratized politics to a greater extent than ever in the past—because campaigns can access information, communicate concepts and produce ads more cost effectively.

What elections since 2010 show, however, is that the law, as it relates to political fundraising, is not static, nor is the enforcement of that law. Fundraising on the "cutting edge" in contemporary politics requires that a candidate have the best technology staff and the best legal staff, and it requires that candidates continue to understand how best to appeal to all different types of donors.

For the foreseeable future, the most powerful way to reach those voters is through television advertising. To those who posit that old-fashioned political ads don't matter, that the future of political persuasion lies solely on the Internet and social media highways, perhaps the best rejoinder is the ancient chant: "The King is dead. Long live the King."

remain in continual contact with their members. This is critical not only for fundraising but for mobilization to get out the vote.

The mainstream media is not disappearing, but the Internet is having a profound effect on the superficiality of campaign news coverage, promoting a greater emphasis on personality, rumor, and infotainment. We may long for the days when the television news at least gave the voters seven-second soundbites by the presidential candidates.

The future of campaigns thus seems headed backward in time to the pre-Watergate era, or perhaps even as far back as the late-nineteenth and early-twentieth century, in which there were no meaningful restrictions on a donor giving unlimited amounts to candidates. What is different, however, is that today's system has some remnants of the past regulatory regime, giving the illusion of regulation and transparency when none really exists.

Voter identification laws proliferated in the 2000s, apparently spurred by Republican state legislatures intent on preventing voter fraud, or, more cynically, interested in keeping down the number of likely Democratic voters eligible at the polls.

Appearance and nonverbal behavior will continue to matter more to the successes of female candidates than male contenders. It makes the job of political consultants considerably more difficult, the need for female voices among their ranks more critical, and the effectiveness of microtargeting the female electorate more essential. Younger voters— the Millennials—will be wielding an "immense influence" over how parties and candidates get out the critical female vote.

Future minority campaigns will be characterized by diverse strategies and communication methods to win elective office in districts and

Preface

The cutting edge of change in campaigns was never more evident than in the first Republican presidential debate in August 2015. Some have estimated that 25 million watched the event. Whatever the exact number was, it showed that the presidential campaign now has a reality-show quality to it. With social and other digital media, we can see a candidate take a picture with a voter at an Iowa barbecue and have it appear immediately on Instagram. At the same time, canvassers are out in the summer sun five months before the first caucus that begins the process to elect a new president. Even in senate campaigns, parties seek to recruit high-level candidates two years in advance. What has changed so much since the last edition of *Campaigns on the Cutting Edge* is planning. It's almost army- or corporation-like, the degree to which presidential or major senatorial and gubernatorial candidates put into their campaigns. At least that is true of the traditional political candidates, who are not billionaires.

The third edition of this book demonstrates that campaigns have become even more complex and driven than in the past. Complex in the sense that the resources that campaigns use are becoming increasingly intertwined. Driven in the sense that each moment now has the potential to be a turning point for better or worse, given the instantaneous way information is transformed today.

This book captures that transformation and looks beyond the 2016 election. It may be the last election where the traditional phone interview takes place. Our authors make informed judgments based on information at their disposal. They are expert: academic and campaign professionals. But most of all they are seasoned and understanding of the nuances that take place in campaigns.

Thus I am going to reprise what I said in the last edition here: we cannot account for all changes that may take place over the next five or ten years, but we look through the lens of contemporary politics to see what cutting-edge changes are on the horizon. I would like to thank the colleagues who have written chapters for this manuscript, many whom I have known for years. They are true scholars.

About the Contributors

Robert G. Boatright is an associate professor of political science at Clark University. His research focuses on the effects of campaign and election laws on the behavior of politicians and interest groups, with a particular focus on primary elections and campaign finance laws and practices. He is the author or editor of six books, including *The Deregulatory Moment? A Comparative Perspective on Changing Campaign Finance Laws; Getting Primaried: The Causes and Consequences of Congressional Primary Challenges;* and *Interest Groups and Campaign Finance Reform in the United States and Canada.*

Jeffrey Crouch is an assistant professor of American politics at American University. He is the reviews and book editor for *Congress & the Presidency* journal, and his first book, *The Presidential Pardon Power,* was published by the University Press of Kansas in 2009. His research focuses primarily on the Constitution, the presidency, and the separation of powers.

Thomas A. (Tad) Devine is a Democratic media consultant who has produced political ads for candidates in the United States and around the world. He is president of Devine Mulvey, a media and strategic consulting firm in Washington, D.C. He has created media in twenty winning U.S. Senate and gubernatorial campaigns. Tad has also worked on dozens of winning races for the U.S. House of Representatives and local elected officials. He has extensive experience at the highest levels of U.S. presidential campaigns and has worked on ten winning campaigns for president or prime minister outside the United States. Devine has taught courses on campaigns and media at Boston University, at the George Washington University Graduate School of Political Management, and in 2011 as a Resident Fellow at the Institute of Politics at Harvard University's Kennedy School of Government. In October 2010, Tad was recognized as one of "the most respected media consultants" in the nation by *USA Today.*

Peter L. Francia is professor of political science and codirector of leadership studies at East Carolina University. He is coauthor (with John C. Green, Paul S. Herrnson, Lynda W. Powell, and Clyde Wilcox) of *The Financiers of Congressional Elections: Investors, Ideologues, and Intimates* (2003) and author of *The Future of Organized Labor in American Politics* (2006). His most recent work (with Burdett A. Loomis and Dara Z. Strolovitch) includes *Guide to Interest Groups and Lobbying in the United States* (2012) and (with Jody C. Baumgartner) *Conventional Wisdom and American Elections: Exploding Myths, Exploring Misconceptions*(3rd edition, 2016).

Joseph Graf is an assistant professor in the School of Communication at American University. He has published extensively in the areas of political communication and online politics, and his work is focused on the intersection of civic involvement and new media technology. Graf is the former research director for the Institute for Politics, Democracy and the Internet, which promotes Internet politics to improve civic engagement. He has been a visiting professor at the George Washington University and began his career as a newspaper reporter in Wisconsin and Pennsylvania.

Wesley Joe is an adjunct assistant professor of government at Georgetown University in Washington, D.C. He is formerly the director of research for the Campaign Finance Institute, a nonpartisan think tank that is affiliated with the George Washington University.

Nina Therese Kasniunas (PhD, Loyola University Chicago) is an associate professor of political science at Goucher College. Her research focuses on organized interests as well as the pedagogy of political science. Her current research is examining community associations in Southwest Baltimore and whether they are improving the quality of democratic life for citizens living there.

Charles N. W. Keckler (JD, University of Michigan) is a Presidential Scholar at George Mason University, where he is pursuing doctoral research on partisanship, bipartisanship, and the role of independent agencies in the federal bureaucracy. In addition to his former work as a litigator and law professor, he has served in politically appointed positions in both the George W. Bush and Barack Obama administrations.

Susan A. MacManus, who received her MA from the University of Michigan and PhD from Florida State University, is a Distinguished University Professor at the University of South Florida in the Department of Government and International Affairs. For the last six election cycles, she has served as a political analyst for

WFLA News Channel 8 (Tampa NBC affiliate). Since 2008, she has been a featured columnist on sayfiereview.com—a widely read Florida-based political website. MacManus is the coauthor of *Politics in States and Communities* with Thomas R. Dye (15th edition, 2015); *Politics in Florida* with Aubrey Jewett, Thomas R. Dye, and David J. Bonanza (4th edition, 2015); and *Florida's Politics: Ten Media Markets, One Powerful State* with Kevin Hill and Dario Moreno (2004). She is also the author of *Young v. Old: Generational Combat in the 21st Century?* (1996) and *Targeting Senior Voters* (2004), along with numerous articles on women and minorities in politics.

Jeremy D. Mayer is an associate professor in the School of Policy, Government, and International Affairs at George Mason University. He is the coauthor of *Closed Minds? Politics and Ideology in American Universities* (Brookings, 2008), coeditor of *Media Power, Media Politics* (2nd edition, Rowman and Littlefield, 2008), coauthor of *Deconstructing Reagan: A Critical Analysis of Conservative Mythology* (2006), and author of *American Media Politics in Transition* (McGraw-Hill, 2006).

Candice J. Nelson is a professor of government and academic director of the Campaign Management Institute at American University. Her most recent books are *Grant Park: The Democratization of Presidential Elections, 1968–2008* (2011) and *Campaigns and Elections American Style* (4th edition, 2013), coedited with James Thurber. Nelson is a former American Political Science Association Congressional Fellow. She received her PhD from the University of California at Berkeley.

Tari Renner is a professor of political science at Illinois Wesleyan University. He served as department chair from 1994 to 2008. Renner was elected mayor of the city of Bloomington, IL, in 2013. He served three terms as an elected member of the McLean County legislature. In 2004, he was the Democratic nominee for U.S. Congress in Illinois' Eleventh Congressional District. His research interests include U.S. electoral behavior and local government structures. Renner received his PhD from American University in 1985.

Mark J. Rozell is professor of public policy and the acting dean of the School of Policy, Government, and International Affairs at George Mason University. He is coauthor of the book *Interest Groups in American Campaigns: The New Face of Electioneering* (3rd edition, Oxford University Press).

Dick Simpson has uniquely combined a distinguished academic career with public service in government. He began his academic career in 1967 at the University of Illinois at Chicago, where he has taught for more than forty-eight years and where he currently serves as professor of political science. Simpson was alderman for Chicago's 44th Ward and leader of the opposition bloc from 1971 to 1979. He ran for Congress in 1992 and 1994 against Congressman Dan Rostenkowski. Simpson has published numerous (more than a hundred) professional journal articles, magazine articles, book chapters, documentary films, and book reviews. He is the author and coauthor of books on political action, elections, ethics, and politics, including *Rogues, Rebels, and Rubber Stamps* (2001), *Winning Elections in the Twenty-First Century* (2015), *and Twenty-First Century Chicago* (2015).

Atiya Kai Stokes-Brown is associate professor of political science at Bucknell University. Her research and teaching interests are in the areas of race, ethnicity, and gender and the politics of representation and identity in the United States. Her work has appeared in several academic journals and in various edited volumes. Her most recent work includes a book titled *The Politics of Race in Latino Communities: Walking the Color Line* (Routledge, 2012, 2014).

Michael Turk has lived at the intersection of politics, public policy, and technology— crossing from the political to the commercial and into government. He is the president of Opinion Mover Strategies, a public affairs and media consultancy focused on using converged media to tell client stories. Previously, Turk served as vice president of industry grassroots for the National Cable & Telecommunications Association, the trade association that represents the United States' largest broadband providers. He has managed Internet operations for three presidential campaigns—Fred Thompson (2008), Bush-Cheney (2004), and Quayle (2000). He served as the Republican National Committee's first eCampaign director following the 2004 campaign.

Clyde Wilcox is a professor of government at Georgetown University and is currently teaching at the Georgetown Doha Campus in Qatar. He writes on interest groups, campaign finance, religion and politics, gender politics, and science fiction and politics.

Part I

The New Political Campaign

CHAPTER 1

Introduction—
Campaigns on the Cutting Edge

Richard J. Semiatin

"I WAS TIRED. I hadn't slept eight hours in two, three years. I lived on four, five hours of sleep. You can do it during a campaign because thousands are screaming for you. You're getting adrenaline shots each day. Then the campaign ends, and there are no more shots."[1] George McGovern told this story about his losing campaign to Richard Nixon for the presidency over forty years ago. Yet this is the same feeling a candidate has after a grueling election campaign today; and it is the same feeling the candidates had 100 years ago. It is also a sentiment that the most conservative (Ted Cruz) and most liberal candidate (Bernie Sanders) will share at the end of their 2016 journeys. Some things remain constant. But some things *do* change.

A smartphone can be a campaign headquarters in someone's hands. At one's fingertips is information about the demographics of voters in every city, in every neighborhood, on every street. A smartphone can empower a twenty-year-old canvasser to know everything about you: what car you drive; what smartphone you have (iPhone vs. Droid); whether you voted in the last election; what you like to read or eat; and, most of all, your voting tendencies. In a sense, technology has democratized politics to a greater extent than ever in the past—because campaigns can access information, communicate concepts, and produce ads more cost-effectively.

Today, campaigns are similar to the rest of the world—acquiring knowledge is an instantaneous proposition. That means parries and thrusts by campaigns, which were the products of deliberate thinking over hours or days or even months in the past, are now decided in minutes or even seconds. The eighteen-month hurricane of perpetual motion we call the modern campaign is driven, in large part, by technology. All campaigns have become more mobile, which has meant that more campaign functions are integrated together to enable greater efficiencies. Those efficiencies save the precious commodity of time, which is valued beyond price. But efficiencies come with speed; and speed entails danger as well: too rapid a response can fatally injure a campaign because there isn't time for staff to think things through before they react. For better or worse, this is the world of campaigns today.

Campaigns are becoming more individualized and tailored to *you*, the voter, because of technology. For the first 150 years, campaigns were largely the domain of party organizations. The birth of television and the advent of advertising spawned personality-driven campaigns. We see the next revolution where campaigns are attempting to reach each voter individually since they can target each household. Campaigns used to be about parties and candidates. Increasingly, campaigns will become about *you*, the voter, or what Madison Avenue would call you, the customer.

The book you are about to read is neither a review of the political science literature nor a major discourse on the democratic implications of elections and campaigns, although that latter discussion remains valuable and important, and addressed in the book's conclusion. This new edition shows how campaigns are becoming increasingly integrated with overlapping functions. We call this overlap *convergence*. For example, campaign advertising now appears online as well as on the television screen. Campaigns target their audiences using "big data" or consumer information blended with voting behavior patterns much as discussed above. In a large campaign, those same data are often shared by the campaign with its consultants. The same data are used to identify donors and to target potential voters for get-out-the-vote (GOTV) operations among other tasks performed by the campaign. You will see a discussion of big data and analytics in a number of chapters because they serve multiple purposes.

This new edition also demonstrates how campaign finance decisions since 2010 have affected how political operatives and candidates run for national offices. The web of decisions is intertwined. *Super PAC* has become the new buzzword of American political campaigns. The book demonstrates that like Baskin-Robbins ice cream they (Super PACs) come in many different flavors (or forms to be more precise). Super PACs are defined as "independent political action committees which can raise unlimited sums of money from corporations, unions and individuals but [are] not permitted to contribute or coordinate directly with parties or candidates."[2] Thus, our discussion on fundraising and campaign finance issues manifests itself in three separate ways in the book: The fundraising chapter explains how candidate Super PACs serve as surrogate campaign organizations. The interest groups chapter explains how Super PACs can serve as an issue-related campaign organization. The campaign finance chapter focuses, in part, on how the Supreme Court came to the opinion that resulted in the creation of Super PACs. There is no cookie-cutter approach that puts this all in one basket.

The book explores the most important facets of campaigns (fundraising, paid advertising, new media, polling, and voter mobilization), the institutions that work in campaigns (parties and interest groups), those that report on campaigns (the press), those that govern the process of campaigns (campaign finance and voter ID laws), and emerging groups that are part of change (women and minorities). The chapter on voter ID laws is new to this edition and important because the debate whether such laws prevent voter fraud or whether they infringe on the participation of minorities or both is seminal to today's politics.

The New Political Campaign

The new political campaign demonstrates the importance of contact, communications, and feedback with voters. Part I on "The New Political Campaign" discusses the various facets of campaigns from raising money, to communicating through paid and new media, to targeting messages to mobilize citizens to vote. Campaigns not only are incorporating new technological changes but also must make them work seamlessly with the techniques of the past. Chapters examine what has worked in the past and what works in the present, and most importantly speculate what the future may hold for national and state-level campaigns.

We begin with money because as former California state legislator Jesse Unruh (D) said: "Money is the mother's milk of politics."[3] Money helps facilitate speech and amplify a candidate's message to a mass audience. Money helps to identify voters and to target them for mobilization. Candidates spend more time raising money than any other task they perform in a campaign.

Robert G. Boatright's chapter on fundraising demonstrates how various methods of traditional fundraising (direct mail, events, telemarketing) are complicated by new rules that govern how money is raised. In this edition, the author shows us how a Super PAC, such as "Right to Rise USA" for presidential contender Jeb Bush (R-FL), can serve as a surrogate fundraising and campaign operation until a candidate formerly declares for office. Then it can go off and do its own thing. As long as the independent group and candidate do not coordinate or contribute in any manner, it is legal. This is a result of major court decisions on the federal level. The complexities and implications of this are enormous. Boatright argues that campaigns, especially presidential campaigns, are now more donor-driven. Understanding what donors do, which is often outside the control of candidates and campaigns, is now having a profound effect on how races are shaped at the national and (sometimes) state level.

Most of the money expended in major campaigns goes to advertising. The percentage can range from 50 percent up to more than 80 percent of the total budget in a presidential race. Tad Devine, one of the nation's leading campaign media consultants, discusses the role of paid advertising in political campaigns in the third chapter. His career includes working as an ad maker and strategist for the presidential campaigns of Al Gore (2000), John Kerry (2004), and Bernie Sanders (2016). This time Devine not only provides insight into the work of an ad maker and strategist but also draws on recent campaigns he worked on including Joseph P. Kennedy III running for Congress in Massachusetts, Seth Magaziner running for state treasurer in Rhode Island, and Bernie Sanders's first Senate race in Vermont. The web addresses are provided so that you can watch the ads online. Devine's ad campaigns always tell the story of the candidate and draw sharp contrasts with the opposition. One of the ads (available through the web address in the text), called "People," is a compelling biographical ad of Sanders's successful election to the Senate.

The growth of online communications has exploded in the last decade. New media, as consultant Michael Turk points out in Chapter 4, changes the way voters interact with campaigns. In this edition, he shows how digital now enables the campaign to better interact with itself. He shows that some candidates such as presidential candidate Rand Paul (R-KY) are constantly on social media commenting on policies and politics. Turk draws on his experiences as a consultant working as the eCampaign director for Bush-Cheney 2004. He also served in that capacity for Fred Thompson's presidential campaign in 2008. Turk shows how the Obama reelection campaign's use of technology enabled it to maximize its efforts to contact, communicate with, and mobilize voters. This demonstrates how the growing mobility of online communications makes the impact of new and social media all the more important.

The campaign survey research world is changing where a mix of landline/cell or online samples is increasingly used for polling. This is all very challenging and cutting edge for campaigns because the response rate is so low as explained by Candice J. Nelson in the fifth chapter. Nelson shows that cell phone users who do not have landlines are a growing proportion of the population. To raise the response rate, pollsters are experimenting with using social media as a way to do survey research to reach more voters as a cost-effective way to build a representative sample. Which modality or technique, if any, will become most prominent in the future? Nelson addresses what is known, and not known, at this time. The results are alarming for campaigns because they are not always sure how they can attain the most accurate information on voter attitudes truly representing the population as a whole.

Parties and campaigns have put a concerted effort into voter mobilization, which has paid off in the last decade. The chapter on voter mobilization merges the high-profile technology of the present with the shoe leather of personal contact from the past. In a sense, technology has enabled campaigns to personally contact more of the right people (meaning those who can potentially support their candidate) than in the past either by going door-to-door or by phone. The Obama campaign did this over 100 million times in 2012 as pointed out in the chapter. The results are somewhat counterintuitive from what we hear—that, in fact, campaigns are becoming more personalized because technology enables campaigns to better identify and connect directly to voters.

The Evolving Campaign: Adaptation by Political Institutions and Groups

Part II on "The Evolving Campaign" features political parties, interest groups, and press coverage in the campaign process. Moreover, the administrative institutions that govern campaign finance and state voter registration agencies are also coping with new technologies and laws, with cutting-edge changes coming at a rapid pace. Finally, women and minority groups are utilizing these new techniques to increase participation and expand their electoral power.

Political parties have been reinvigorated according to Tari Renner in Chapter 7. Parties are potent forces that provide a full spectrum of assistance to candidates. Both parties have run successful voter turnout and fundraising operations (Democrats 2012, Republicans 2014). Even more so, they have ventured into communications where they keep constant contact with supporters—both financially and voluntarily. In a sense, Renner tells us that parties no longer go to sleep for a year between elections. Instead, they operate 365 days a year providing outreach and contact with their constituents. In many ways, they mimic large campaign organizations in the way they provide services to campaigns. The difference is that an individual campaign goes out of business the day after the election. Political parties do not. Even when party leadership changes, the organization still provides a sense of continuity for voters.

No entity has benefited more in recent years from the changing political landscape than interest groups as discussed in Chapter 8. Nina Therese Kasniunas, Mark J. Rozell, and Charles N. W. Keckler point out that U.S. Supreme Court decisions resulted in associations or interest groups having an unlimited ability to spend money in campaigns via the Super PAC. Their chapter looks at traditional interest groups and Super PACs associated not with candidates but with issues, interests, and organizations. Interest groups now have more tools at their disposal to maximize their influence in campaigns by serving as an external force that can influence the outcome. The authors argue that the change emerging from campaigns is toward group-centered politics. This contrasts to Boatright's earlier chapter where he argues that campaigns are becoming more donor centered. What they share is that both show how campaigns have moved away from the candidate-centered politics of the last forty years.

Nothing has changed more than news coverage over the last decade. Chapter 9 discusses campaign press coverage and how the decline of traditional media coverage has had a profound effect on the way campaigns operate and what really is and is not news. The authors show that the rise in hundreds of blogs, partisan websites, online videos, and so on can turn the ordinary citizen into a powerful advocate "reporting" the news. The problem is that there is no arbiter confirming the information of the citizen-reporter. Press coverage has become even more personality driven than before, particularly in the electronic media where the sensationalism of stories and people rather than substance have become fodder for discussion on cable news networks. And technology enables bloggers, and other social media "reporters," to put extravagant rumors in the public eye—very similar to the role that partisan newspapers had in the early 1800s, when John Adams was disparaged as a royalist and Thomas Jefferson as an infidel.

The repercussions of campaign finance in the five years following the *Citizens United* decision are the focus of the tenth chapter. The decision stated that limits of spending by associations of individuals violated the First Amendment because money helps amplify speech; and by limiting speech, you are limiting the voice of citizens individually or as a group. However, they may not coordinate with candidate committees or political parties. The recent case of *McCutcheon v. Federal Election Commission* (2014) eliminated the cap on the aggregate amount of contributions that citizens could give to federal campaigns, parties, and political committees. Peter L. Francia, Wesley Joe, and Clyde Wilcox argue that empirical evidence demonstrates that big donors now play a much more significant role in federal races. The authors then proceed to examine plans to reform campaign finance on the federal level, such as the Fair Elections Now Act (FENA). FENA would incentivize smaller donations to federal campaigns. However, major campaign finance reform in the near future is not likely on the federal level. Instead, campaign reform may occur by thinking "outside the box" or looking at what states are producing. One example is Montana, where the state legislature enacted a disclosure law that requires greater transparency of where money comes from—whether from individuals or from independent groups—where the disclosure of names has not been required in the past.

When we think of cutting-edge changes, we often think of techniques and tactics. But voter access has become a major issue in recent years. While court decisions have governed campaign finance (as we will see in Chapter 10), they also govern the constitutionality of voter identification laws that have been passed in a number of states. Jeffrey Crouch examines the issues associated with voter access laws in the book's eleventh chapter. He looks at what states have such laws and whether such laws are necessary, nefarious, or neither. The author peruses what states have enacted laws following the Supreme Court's decision in Indiana's *Crawford v. Marion County Election Board* (2008), which led to eleven states passing strict voter identification laws since the Supreme Court decision. The protagonists argue that it will cut voter fraud, and the opponents argue that such laws are race based since more minorities are less likely to have state-issued identifications.

The role of women, African Americans, Latino Americans, and Asian Americans has been mainstreamed in politics today. Each entity has increased its participation, not only as electoral and representational forces but also as campaign managers, campaign staff, and consultants. In 2012, Barack Obama's three deputy campaign managers (Jen O'Malley Dillon, Julianna Smoot, and Stephanie Cutter) were all women. The Romney campaign had fewer, but still many, top-level positions filled by women (Beth Myers, Katie Packer Gage, and Jackie Rooney).

Susan A. MacManus shows us that campaigns are targeting women through generational approaches, which differ according to whether one is a Millennial, a Gen-Xer, or a Baby Boomer, in the twelfth chapter. MacManus enables us to understand why this is true. She shows that there are now sophisticated efforts to get women out to vote—and that these efforts are very savvy and technologically sophisticated. Given that women represent over 50 percent of the turnout in most national campaigns for Congress, the Senate, and the presidency, the "Suzy homemaker" approach to persuade female voters is a falsehood long buried. Women are no different from men in their desire to be treated the same in the political arena whether as voters or as candidates.

Research shows that a majority of the U.S. population will be non-white and Latino by 2042.[4] Atiya Kai Stokes-Brown examines the role of minorities in campaigns. She shows us that the methods of communicating with minority groups converge with those of nonminorities. Since the last edition, the author shows us that more minority candidates are communicating via social media and that some of the most prominent minority politicians are rising outside the Democratic Party (such as Senator Ted Cruz of Texas or Tim Scott of South Carolina). The myth that social media is a white-only phenomenon is dispelled in this chapter. Stokes-Brown points out that the landscape for minority candidates in a world complicated by social media and other new technologies underscores how they must compete to attract new voters in a changing world.

The conscience of the book is still in its conclusion. Technology increases participation, but does not it also increase the ability to manipulate voters? Author Dick Simpson, who has politicked in the wards of Chicago, gives us reason to pause: the wonderful cutting-edge changes discussed in the book, no matter how inviting and exciting, have the potential for great harm as well as hope because democracy is fragile. The implications of new technology may need to be questioned when it risks rights that we hold dear. Consultants, citizens, and officeholders should understand that longtime rituals in politics are still virtuous. If they do, there is hope, and if not, the seeds of destructive politics will be sewn for the future.

But the present does have great possibilities for the future. And the future is now. Several years hence, the "now" of today may already be passé.

Notes

1. Michael Leahy, "What Might Have Been" (*The Washington Post*, February 20, 2005), W20. Accessed on June 30, 2015, from http://www.washingtonpost.com.
2. "Super PAC," Definition (Oxford Dictionaries from Oxford University Press). Accessed on July 6, 2015, from http://www.oxforddictionaries.com.
3. "The New Jess Unruh" (*Time*, September 14, 1970). Accessed on September 6, 2007, from http://time.com.
4. Sam Roberts, "Minorities in U.S. Set to Become a Majority by 2042" (*The New York Times*, August 14, 2008). Accessed on September 2, 2011, from http://www.nytimes .com.

CHAPTER 2

Fundraising — The New Rules

Robert G. Boatright

IN APRIL 2008, BARACK OBAMA announced that he would decline public financing for the general election, proclaiming that his donor base—which stood at over 1.5 million people—constituted a "parallel public financing system."[1] In retrospect, it now seems possible that Obama's 2008 campaign represented the high-water mark of a shift in the way U.S. elections were financed. During the first decade of the twenty-first century, changes in technology and campaign finance law led to a substantial increase in what candidates who might have been starved for funds in prior decades could raise. Candidates for all different types of offices became much more capable of raising large sums from small donors. This change was most visible in presidential elections, but the techniques of small donor fundraising also trickled down into congressional campaigns and campaigns for local office.

A lot has changed since 2008. For one thing, the rest of the political world caught up with Obama—his methods of raising money from smaller donors became standard practice in races for all different types of political offices. In addition, however, the law changed. Obama's 2008 success took place at a time when donors were limited in what they could give to a candidate, party, or interest group. Today, because of the Supreme Court's *Citizens United v. Federal Election Commission* decision, presidential candidates (as well as a growing number of House and Senate candidates) benefit from the fundraising activities of "Super PACs," groups that are technically separate from the candidates but can raise and spend money in unlimited amounts. When reporters spoke of fundraising in the 2012 presidential campaign, they spoke not merely of the money raised by the Obama and Romney campaigns but also of the money raised by the party committees and by Priorities USA Action and Restore Our Future, two candidate-specific Super PACs that solicited contributions from people who had already given all that they could to the candidates and the party committees. The same is true for campaigns for Senate races, House races, gubernatorial races, and even mayoral races: fundraising is not done just by the candidates. Any fundraising plan must take into account the activities of outside groups and the types of donors who contribute to them.

This chapter addresses many different types of campaigns. We shall first look at how candidate fundraising has evolved over the past decade; this evolution has featured an integration of the newer model of data-driven online fundraising with older techniques. These are techniques that increasingly can be exploited by campaigns at all levels. We will then turn our attention to the effects of Super PACs on fundraising in presidential and congressional campaigns.

These changes may strike some readers as being a step backward in regard to the theme of this book. That is, there may well be nothing "cutting edge" about a return to the sort of parallel campaigning that characterized U.S. campaigns in the first half of the twentieth century, but there have been remarkable changes in the ways in which Super PACs and political entrepreneurs have sought to cultivate donors and raise funds efficiently for these parallel campaigns. What both the "new" techniques of small donor fundraising from the first decade of the twenty-first century and the techniques of large donor cultivation from the second decade of the century have in common is a changed understanding of the role of donors in campaign politics and the ways in which these donors are reshaping the content of campaigns.

Blending New and Old Candidate Fundraising Models

There is no single way to raise money for campaigns. While some campaigns may lean more heavily on one technique than another, the best-funded campaigns of the 2000s have sought to diversify the ways in which they raise money and the types of people who contribute to them.

The New Fundraising Model of the Early 2000s

The great innovation of the first decade of the 2000s was the use of new technologies to create a sense of community among supporters. At the start of the decade, the conventional wisdom was that candidates with a large number of wealthy supporters could generally raise large enough war chests early in the campaign to scare away competitors. At the presidential level, this is what George W. Bush did in 2000, and it has been standard practice for many congressional incumbents as well. This conventional wisdom was upended by the Howard Dean presidential campaign in 2004. The Dean campaign sought to present itself as a decentralized "movement" and accordingly gave supporters much of the responsibility for fundraising. This effort had two major components. First, the campaign sought to use email to remove the barrier between fundraising and other types of campaigning. That is, people on the Dean email list would receive several messages from the campaign each month; some of these would be solicitations, but other emails would encourage supporters to attend local campaign events, to view videos the campaign had posted to its website, or to discuss aspects of the campaign online with other supporters. The Dean campaign was able to monitor the success of different fundraising pitches, modifying them to see what worked and what didn't.[2] It could tie fundraising goals to campaign events or deadlines, such as a debate, a Federal Election Commission (FEC) filing deadline, or a statement by an opponent. These frequent contacts made even small donors feel like part of the team, and as a consequence, many were encouraged to make repeated contributions, and many who casually joined the email list without donating were eventually prompted to give.

Second, the Dean campaign blurred the distinction between campaign staff and grassroots supporters. Supporters were encouraged to set goals for fundraising, set up personal fundraising pages, and send links to these pages to friends. Many Dean supporters developed their own strategies for raising money, and they communicated with one another about what they were doing. Whereas the Bush campaign had gone offline to find and cultivate a select group of bundlers who could pledge to provide $100,000 or more to the campaign, Dean was able to create an army of grassroots supporters who individually could bundle amounts in the hundreds of dollars but who collectively constituted a serious fundraising machine. For the first time, it made sense for a presidential candidate to concentrate on raising money from small donors.

The Obama Campaign Model for Fundraising

Barack Obama's campaign resembled Howard Dean's campaign in several ways. Like Dean, Obama presented himself as an outsider, and like Dean, Obama sought to present his campaign as a movement, as something larger than the candidate. Obama also encouraged supporters to set up their own fundraising pages and to combine fundraising with both online and offline activism. Obama went a step further than Dean, however. The personal pages Obama supporters set up served as a sort of internal version of Facebook, complete with blogs supporters could maintain and with ways to link to other supporters who lived nearby or who had similar interests.[3] The campaign was more assertive than the Dean campaign had been in organizing campaign events, and the fundraising success of the campaign made it easy to raise and spend money in places where Democrats had previously been unorganized. Throughout the primary and general election campaigns, the Obama campaign experimented with a variety of different email approaches, carefully monitoring what worked. And it regularly sent to support-ers videos of campaign manager David Plouffe discussing the plans for the upcoming week. These videos reassured contributors that the campaign was using their money wisely, and it gave them the sort of access that was once given to only the biggest donors.[4]

The "rock star" nature of the Obama campaign also made fundraising easy. The campaign did a brisk business selling campaign-related merchandise; this was a way of raising money while also advertising the campaign.[5] And Internet fund-raising could be effectively organized around the large campaign events Obama held as the campaign went on. Ultimately, the success of Obama's primary cam-paign in 2008 had much to do with the fact that it was fueled by small donors—people who could give again and again. This gave Obama a decisive fundraising advantage over Hillary Clinton and John McCain in 2008, and arguably over Mitt Romney in 2012 as well.

Obama's success was also due in part to an ability to manage donors and to manage perceptions of his donors. During 2004, many observers worried that Dean's campaign had insufficient control over what his donors were doing; if one seeks to empower one's contributors, then a candidate may well wind up being held responsible for "off message" comments associated with fundraising events or campaign rallies. Obama's campaign sought to exert somewhat more control over his supporters' fundraising pitches. In addition, Obama frequently spoke of the signal his small donor base sent. It was a surprise to many when after the election the Campaign Finance Institute issued a report that showed Obama had far fewer small donors than his campaign had claimed; by the end of the election season, the total contribution amounts from many of these people had added up to close to the maximum individual contribution.[6] That is, they weren't small donors; they were just people making their contributions in installments. Some of this may have been almost accidental—people got excited, and they gave more and more—but candidates also now offer contributors the option of supplying a credit card num-ber and paying by the month.

Other 2008 presidential candidates had some success with small donors as well. Mike Huckabee used his website to set fundraising goals and create the sort of "phone-a-thon" atmosphere that Dean had, and Ron Paul's supporters organized a series of "money bombs," efforts to organize large numbers of contributions to the campaign on given days. For instance, Paul raised $4.3 million on November 5, 2007 (the first day of the year leading up to the 2008 election).[7] Paul's money bombs served a dual purpose—they raised money for the campaign, and they drew media attention to the campaign. In late 2011 and early 2012, Republican presiden-tial aspirants Herman Cain, Newt Gingrich, and Rick Santorum were able to use early primary successes or debate performances to raise nearly $10 million apiece in small, mostly online contributions.[8]

Despite these candidates' successful small donor appeals, the Obama campaign's fundraising success may well have been *sui generis*—the consequence of an unconventional candidate's ability to capitalize on Democratic frustrations with the Bush presidency. Obama was a distinctive enough personality that he could expect that people he had not ever asked for money would be driven to his website merely out of curiosity. Presidential elections draw more attention than do congressional elections, so one might expect congressional candidates to have difficulty garnering enough attention to steer people to their websites. In 2006 and 2008, many congressional candidates began placing advertisements on political blogs and other websites that might draw potential supporters. These sorts of advertisements, because in many instances they were aimed at people who didn't even reside in the home state or district of the candidate, were aimed more at fundraising than at gaining votes. But some have argued that in any election there are simply too many congressional candidates competing for the same pool of dollars, so the sorts of communities created by candidates like Obama are less likely to occur.

Recent Developments (2010–Present)

During the 2010, 2012, and 2014 elections, however, many congressional candidates did manage to establish national fundraising bases. In the 2010 special election to fill the seat of deceased Senator Ted Kennedy, Republican nominee Scott Brown, for example, campaigned aggressively. Brown solicited support from a variety of conservative organizations outside of Massachusetts, telling them that although he was an underdog, the potential of a Republican winning Kennedy's seat was worth investing money. Brown raised $16 million during the election; $13 million of this came from out-of-state donors, and $14 million arrived between January 1 and January 19. In fact, Brown raised so much money so quickly that Democratic nominee Martha Coakley (who raised $9 million for the primary and general elections) was unable to respond. Brown succeeded in large part because his personality and pitch were tailor made for Internet fundraising. Brown arguably would have been far less successful in a general election, where he would have needed to campaign over several months, would have competed with other Republican candidates for money, and would have lost the element of surprise. Indeed, Brown's opponent in 2012, Democrat Elizabeth Warren, was able to run a similarly nationalized campaign, assembling a national donor base through the campaign's own efforts and through the bundling efforts of liberal groups such as MoveOn.org. Despite Brown's success in the 2010 special election, Warren outraised him in 2012 in terms of both overall contributions ($42.5 million vs. $28 million) and out-of-state contributions.

The rise of the Tea Party showed that conservatives had certainly caught up to liberals in their ability to create a movement-based politics for the twenty-first century. The Tea Party phenomenon also showed, however, that fundraising did not go hand in hand with online activism. The Tea Party was heavily dependent on Twitter and social media sites for the maintenance of activist networks, for the setting up of events, and so forth, but candidates supported by the Tea Party did not tend to raise a lot of money. The 2010 and 2012 elections featured many innovations in campaign organization, in social media use, and in other aspects of political strategy, but the fundraising model developed in 2004, 2006, and 2008 did not change substantially.

The new fundraising techniques of the 2000s arrived amidst much excitement about the way in which they would change the role of donors in politics. Campaign financing of the 1980s and 1990s was often derided as "checkbook participation"— as a way of running campaigns where donors were asked for money but were not invited to do anything else. Successful online campaigning blurred the line between giving money and taking an active volunteer role. Even if a donor gave only a token amount of money, she could take satisfaction in being part of a "team"—and her membership on this team might ultimately prompt her to give more. Although the small donor model was originally believed by some to provide an inherent advantage to left-leaning politicians, the activities of the Tea Party in 2010 and 2012 showed that many different types of politicians could cultivate a small donor base.

The Old Model Still Works

Campaigns such as Obama's certainly brought many new donors into politics, and many of these donors will undoubtedly remain active in politics for years to come. At the same time, however, tried-and-true methods of fundraising are still essential. Not all donors are online, and not all campaigns can ignore people who contributed to politics before the 2000s. Hence, successful campaigns still draw upon traditional methods, such as those summarized below.

Friends and Acquaintances. Every candidate for office begins with a network of supporters: personal and professional contacts, Facebook friends, neighbors, and so on. Those who have a history of activism within local party organizations or issue-based groups can also draw upon lists of people who have supported such organizations. And, of course, those who have held political office in the past begin with a network of those who have supported them before. As Congressman David Price (D-NC) recounts in his campaign memoir, an up-to-date Christmas card list can be an important first step in campaigning.[9] This type of campaign fundraising has probably existed for as long as there have been campaigns, but social media and other new ways we have of networking can certainly help.

It is important to note, however, that the people in this constituency are not just donors; they are ambassadors for the candidate to other groups, and this community also includes people who can provide advice for all aspects of the campaign. A candidate's friends can, in turn, introduce her to their friends, hold fundraisers in their homes, or provide in-kind support. This circle of friends and acquaintances will likely include many who have made the maximum permissible donation—$2,700 per election cycle as of 2016—but these people are valuable above and beyond the dollars they personally give to the campaign.

Bundling. While candidates will likely be personally involved in the solicitation of contributions from their friends and acquaintances, the scale of campaigning for most offices precludes having the candidate play a direct role in soliciting all, or even most, of the money that will be needed to be competitive. Once a candidate has identified his or her most connected supporters (that is, people who know a lot of other people who might give), these people may either formally or informally gather contributions for the candidate. The practice of formally doing this (that is, personally collecting checks and forwarding them to the campaign) is known as *bundling.* The FEC requires disclosure of the names of groups or lobbyists who bundle contributions. Some candidates encourage bundlers to provide other, less formal, means of letting the campaign know what they have done, such as entering lists of contacts on a campaign webpage or using a tracking number on checks they have solicited. Contributors who meet these goals are usually pleased to be recognized for their accomplishments, but campaigns have also provided various perks to these people in appreciation for their fundraising, including dinners with the candidate and other forms of recognition.[10]

Interest groups can also bundle money for candidates. In some instances, they do this without ever actually discussing their efforts with the candidates. Groups, as well, are generally pleased to give some indication of what they have done since the ability to bundle a large amount of money sends a signal about the group's goals and its financial clout. Like individuals, groups can also bundle contributions in a less formal sense, by sending letters or emails to members encouraging them to give directly to the campaigns. It can at times be difficult to distinguish between groups and fundraising tools; for instance, ActBlue, a fundraising portal for Democratic candidates, is registered as a political action committee (PAC) but does little more than provide basic information about candidates and then channel donations to them.

Campaign Events. Campaign events have always been a common way for candidates to raise money. These events range from relatively casual "meet and greet" events that may cost only $50 or $100 per person to fancier $2,700-per-person dinners. Contributors at these events get the benefit of meeting the candidate and mingling among others who share their financial means and interest in the campaign. The Democratic and Republican parties hold fundraising dinners in many parts of the country—the Jefferson-Jackson Day dinners for Democrats and the Lincoln Day dinners for Republicans—that are regular gatherings of party contributors. Holidays such as Labor Day, Saint Patrick's Day, and Columbus Day are often occasions for fundraising events. Among the most lucrative fundraising events for candidates are events featuring political "superstars." An event featuring a Hollywood celebrity, a professional athlete, or a better-known politician can yield tens of thousands, or even hundreds of thousands, of dollars.

Phone Banks and Direct Mail. Telemarketing was one of the most dependable means of fundraising during the 1980s and 1990s, and it has not entirely disappeared. Telephone calls to a candidate's prior supporters, or to people who supported a similar candidate, may simply jog the memory of someone who contributes regularly. Incumbent members of Congress engage in "dialing for dollars" regularly, keeping in contact with people who are not necessarily close acquaintances but who have some connection to the candidate. A brief script tailored to the background or issue concerns of the donor in question—for instance, a reminder that the donor attended the candidate's alma mater, or is a supporter of environmental causes—can help assure the donor that there is more to the relationship than the "ask."

Candidates can also outsource some of their telephone calls, either to professional firms or to cell phone–wielding volunteers. Telemarketing firms that have access to lists of people with strong partisan views or views on controversial issues (such as abortion or guns) have had success in using more incendiary scripts to solicit contributions from people who may have no prior connection to the candidate. Telemarketing can also be done as an event; just as colleges and charities conduct "phone-a-thons" to raise money over a few days, so candidates can hold one-day telemarketing events to reconnect with donors. Mitt Romney, for instance, raised over $10 million during a one-day phone-a-thon to start his 2012 campaign.[11]

Direct mail serves a similar purpose; a well-executed direct mail campaign can use partisan rhetoric and appealing graphic design to lure potential contributors into opening the letter and perusing the contents. Direct mail remains a staple of congressional campaigns and local campaigns, where it serves the dual purpose of soliciting contributions, mobilizing voters, and informing voters about campaign issues.

More and more, however, telemarketing and direct mail are becoming a secondary feature of campaigns—a way of reconnecting with people who are already part of the campaign, or of reaching people who cannot be reached through other methods. Good lists—of prior contributors, contributors to other candidates, or people who have supported similar causes—are paramount, yet expensive to purchase or maintain. Caller ID reduces the number of people who will even answer the phone when they see an unfamiliar number, and the volume of junk mail people receive makes it likely that even a well-designed direct mail piece will never be opened. Many campaigns have reportedly spent more money on fundraising by mail or phone than they bring in. This is no surprise—the benefits to contributors of responding to direct mail or telephone solicitations are small. Candidates can work to personalize these appeals, but there is less ability to tailor these appeals to individual donors than there is for other methods.

PACs. A final mainstay of traditional candidate fundraising is the PAC. PACs are important in part because candidates often have to do very little to build a PAC donor base. Many of the largest trade PACs, such as the National Association of Realtors, routinely give to all incumbent members of Congress. Members of the House of Representatives tend to raise approximately 40 percent of their money from PACs, and senators raise about 20 percent of their money from PACs, often with minimal effort.[12] Most individual contributors do not give without first being asked. Organized interests, on the other hand, have reasons to seek out candidates. For nonincumbents, the parties may help to line up meetings with PAC directors; a showing that the candidate is viable and sympathetic to the group's objectives may yield PAC contributions. Some PACs also send candidates questionnaires or conduct interviews with them; PACs that can help candidates in ways beyond only making a contribution are more prone to do this. PAC contributions do not constitute as large a percentage of the receipts of nonincumbent candidates, however, simply because most PACs prefer to play it safe, to prioritize gaining access to legislators who are already there. PAC support can send a message to other contributors, however; if one influential PAC is convinced to give to a candidate, other PACs or individual supporters may see this contribution as a stamp of approval and give as well.

Mixing Old and New Models of Fundraising

There is one crucial difference between new and old methods of campaign fundraising: the newer methods can catapult a candidate from being a financial also-ran into a contender very quickly. We have seen this in campaigns for nearly a decade now. In 2009, when the relatively obscure South Carolina congressman Joe Wilson shouted "you lie" during President Obama's State of the Union address, liberal bundling groups enabled Wilson's prospective opponent to raise over $900,000 as a result of appeals referencing that outburst, and Wilson himself raised over $1 million.[13] Such instant cash can be converted not only into advertising, voter contact, and other campaign outputs but also into prospecting for traditional donors.

Such techniques have filtered down to all manner of races. In the race for mayor of Calgary, Alberta, civic activist and newspaper columnist Naheed Nenshi was virtually unknown to voters four months before the election. Nenshi used social media to recruit a volunteer and donor base and then quickly converted this money into more traditional campaign fundraising and outreach as he went on to win the race.[14] Although Canada's campaign finance laws differ from U.S. ones, Nenshi's story closely parallels races for a variety of U.S. offices. It shows that candidates cannot rely merely on one fundraising method but must consider how best to raise money given the resources on hand.

The New World Order of Candidate Fundraising: Candidate Super PACs

For many—indeed most—candidates, the details provided so far in this chapter tell all that there is to tell. For presidential candidates and a growing number of congressional and gubernatorial candidates, however, that story is only the beginning. Legally, candidates cannot play a role in raising money for Super PACs, 501(c)(4) organizations, or other groups that might then turn around and support their candidacy. By law, there can be no coordination between candidates' campaigns and the ostensibly independent advocacy campaigns conducted on their behalf. Yet the past three election cycles have shown that it is not difficult for candidates and their allied Super PACs to pursue a common strategy even without formal coordination. Innovations in the ways candidates and their supporters act to harness the power of unrestricted corporate, group, and individual contributions thus will determine the outcomes of many elections over the next few years. We also note that candidate Super PACs differ from other interest group Super PACs discussed in Chapter 8.

The Complex Web of the Campaign Donation World

The details of the *Citizens United* ruling are discussed elsewhere in this book; the decision has had implications for many different political actors. For our purposes here, it is most instructive to focus upon the new choices prospective political contributors face. Citizens can still contribute money directly to candidates, parties, and PACs up to the contribution limit.[15] If they wish to spend more money in support of a candidate, they can contribute to a Super PAC. In 2012, there was a Super PAC for each of the major presidential candidates, and Super PACs were formed for the purpose of aiding some Senate candidates as well. The number of candidate-specific Super PACs expanded even further, to a total of over 100, in 2014.[16] Some of these candidates were major players and drew support from many different wealthy individuals; others were less well-known candidates who appear to have simply had one wealthy supporter who chose to establish a Super PAC. Donors can also contribute to Super PACs that spread their money out among a wider array of candidates, or to Super PACs associated with interest groups of long standing. And if donors do not care for any of the existing groups, they can simply create their own.

Fundraising Lessons to Be Learned

Campaigns are strategic about where they raise money. The difference now is that donors have far more control over how their money is spent. There are several lessons this array of group types provides for those who would raise money for political purposes. As it was for candidate contributions, different types of donors have different reasons for becoming involved in politics. Anyone who can contribute only a small amount of money is better off giving that money directly to an interest group or a candidate, and candidates are better off having this money than they are having money spent by others on their behalf. Candidates will have better information about where to spend their money wisely; incumbent candidates will have the benefit of using data gathered in prior election campaigns in order to assess their best options; candidates have the expectation that they will stay in business (that is, remain in office) in subsequent years, so they will try to lay the groundwork for future elections; and candidates also pay lower rates for advertising time on radio and television than do groups or parties. In other words, candidates can spend money more efficiently than can nonparty groups. Some have contended that this difference in spending efficiency was the cause of Barack Obama's victory in 2012—similar amounts of money were spent by the Obama and Romney sides, but more of Obama's money was spent by the campaign while more of Romney's was spent by the Super PAC allied with his campaign.

While explicit coordination between candidates and Super PACs is not permitted, candidates can still come close to coordinating with a Super PAC. The details of this de facto coordination are discussed in Chapter 10 on campaign finance reform. This new development means that candidates who expect to benefit from the efforts of Super PACs have an incentive to delay their entry into the race, and consequentially the development of their candidate fundraising efforts, for weeks or even months after they have effectively begun to campaign. This is one reason why Scott Walker and Jeb Bush, the two Republican candidates widely expected to have Super PACs that could raise money from a diverse array of donors, did not join the Republican field until late June 2015. It is also arguably a reason why the earliest entrants into the race included Ted Cruz, Rand Paul, and Marco Rubio, candidates who could expect success among small donors but who did not necessarily anticipate extensive Super PAC support.

Surrogate Fundraising Committees
for Republican Presidential Candidates in 2016

Sources close to the Cruz campaign announced shortly after Cruz's March 23, 2015, entry into the race that four different Super PACs, all with similar names (variations on "Keep the Promise"), would work in tandem to advocate for Cruz's election; the groups announced a combined initial fundraising tally of $31 million—or more than any 2012 presidential primary candidate other than the two nominees and Ron Paul raised.[17] The treasurer for three of the four PACs, a friend of Cruz's, suggested that having more than one Super PAC would allow donors some choice in how they wanted their money to be spent; however, at the time the groups were established, all of the money came from one source, hedge fund investor Robert Mercer. Cruz's early entry into the race meant that he could no longer play a personal role in setting up these groups or speaking with donors, but the announcement so soon after his formal declaration of candidacy meant that he had likely reached a point where the financial benefits of running outweighed those of staying out of the race, and he could now turn his attention to more conventional fundraising.

One can read other candidates' announcements with similar fundraising concerns in mind; being a candidate invites media attention (which can aid candidates struggling to attract attention), but it can also invite scrutiny. Other early candidate announcements, such as those of Ben Carson, Carly Fiorina, and Mike Huckabee, gave these candidates a burst of attention that could translate into an initial burst of fundraising. For political insiders, however, early announcements may in years to come serve as a sign of weakness—as an indication that these candidates are forced to turn their attention to courting smaller donors. There is precedent here; in 2008, as presidential candidates were beginning to turn their backs on public financing, John Edwards's announcement that he would accept public financing was read by many as a sign that Edwards was unable to raise enough money to keep pace with Obama and Clinton.

The organizational structure and fundraising techniques of Super PACs have changed radically across the past three elections, and they will no doubt continue to change in 2016 and 2018. The story told here suggests, however, that in order to understand political fundraising in upcoming elections, we will have to understand not just the ways in which candidates raise money but also the ways in which organizations that support candidates raise money.

Does Candidate Fundraising Still Matter?

For decades, political analysts have written about the relative balance of power between candidates, political parties, and interest groups. The era from roughly the late 1960s to the 2000s was often described as an era of "candidate-centered politics"—and as such, it made sense to talk about how candidates waged campaigns, how candidates raised money, and how individual politicians sought to define the political agenda. As the above discussion shows, it is possible that we have entered an era of group-centered politics, or at least one in which the distinctions between candidates, groups, and parties have blurred. Yet the sorts of groups that have come to dominate politics rely on small numbers of large contributions; in many cases, these are not really contributions at all, but expenditures made, unprompted, by wealthy individuals seeking to change the political system. At the same time, most literature on fundraising (in politics and in the world of nonprofits or other causes) emphasizes the strategies one might employ to raise money in small amounts from large numbers of contributors.[18] In the post–*Citizens United* environment, does this sort of fundraising still matter?

There are many reasons to think that it does. When a candidate courts several dozen potential contributors, she is not just raising money—she is campaigning. If the potential contributors will have the opportunity to vote for (or against) her in November, the pitch for contributions is functionally the same as the pitch for votes. Even if the contributors do not reside in her state or district, the fundraising pitch requires that the candidate make contact with a wide array of people. Information will be exchanged, the contributors will make their views on politics known, and the candidate will develop her campaigning skills. Even less personal means of soliciting money require that a campaign exercise skill in the "care and feeding" of donors. This is a particular concern in the Super PAC era—as the amount of money raised outside of the candidates' campaigns has increased, some fundraisers have worried that candidates are becoming too desperate on their own fundraising appeals.[19]

One might respond to such claims by noting that donors—even people who give small amounts—are not like regular voters. They tend, among other things, to be wealthier and more politically extreme than the average citizen. Yet they are more representative than are the wealthy funders of Super PACs, and those who give small contributions are more representative of the public than are those who give larger ones.

One might also respond that fundraising takes time away from campaigning. Some accounts of changes in Congress over the past decades have lamented the amount of time that members of Congress spend working the phones soliciting contributions or attending PAC receptions. Fundraising, in other words, can distract from campaigning, and a candidate who could rely on someone else to fund his efforts could court voters instead of donors. This is a compelling argument, but one might respond that technology had begun to solve this problem in the early 2000s: online, small donor fundraising does not require that the candidate hobnob with donors; it can be a parallel effort.

Some postmortems on the 2012 elections made reference to some alleged triumphs for the candidate-centered fundraising model, or at least to some failures of Super PACs. It is certainly possible that the larger donor base for Barack Obama's campaign contributed to his victory over Mitt Romney. In addition, some read the poor win/loss ratio for large Super PACs such as American Crossroads as a sign that Super PAC fundraising and spending were not as efficient or effective as candidate fundraising. As Super PACs continue to develop new strategies, however, they will get better at spending money wisely. If existing groups don't do this, the people who give money to them will hold them accountable and will take their money elsewhere.

From Candidate-Centered to Donor-Centered Politics?

Innovations in fundraising are not merely a matter of taking advantage of new technology. It is easy to look at changes in communication techniques, data processing, or the U.S. media over the past few decades and map these onto changes in how candidates raise money. This process will certainly continue. What elections since 2010 show, however, is that the law, as it relates to political fundraising, is not static, nor is the enforcement of that law. Innovations in campaign fundraising are, and will continue to be, dependent on creative ways of understanding how one can push the boundaries of campaign finance law. This may strike some readers as an uninspiring way to think about political innovation, but it is hardly new. Fundraising on the "cutting edge" in contemporary politics requires that a candidate have the best technology staff and the best legal staff, and it requires that candidates continue to understand how best to appeal to all different types of donors.

Notes

1. Jeff Zeleny and Michael Luo, "Public Financing? Obama and McCain Appear Split" (*The New York Times*, April 10, 2008).

2. Larry Biddle, "Fund-Raising: Hitting Home Runs On and Off the Internet," in *Mousepads, Shoe Leather, and Hope: Lessons from the Howard Dean Campaign for the Future of Internet Politics*, ed. Zephyr Teachout and Thomas Streeter (Boulder, CO: Paradigm Press, 2008), 166–178; Zephyr Teachout, "Something Much Bigger Than a Candidate," in *Mousepads, Shoe Leather, and Hope: Lessons from the Howard Dean Campaign for the Future of Internet Politics*, ed. Zephyr Teachout and Thomas Streeter (Boulder, CO: Paradigm Press, 2008), 55–73.

3. Jose Antonio Vargas, "Obama's Wide Web" (*The Washington Post*, August 20, 2008).

4. Ryan Lizza, "Battle Plans: Finding the Right Way to Run" (*The New Yorker*, November 17, 2008), 46–55.

5. David Plouffe, *The Audacity to Win* (New York: Penguin, 2009), 51.

6. Campaign Finance Institute, *Reality Check: Obama Received about the Same Percentage from Small Donors in 2008 as Bush in 2004.* Accessed on November 24, 2008, from http://www.cfinst.org/press/PReleases/08-11-24/Realty_Check_-_Obama_Small_Donors.aspx.

7. Jose Antonio Vargas, "Ron Paul Beats Own Fundraising Record" (*The Washington Post*, December 17, 2007).

8. This, and all other campaign finance data in this chapter, is drawn from FEC reports unless otherwise noted.

9. David E. Price, *The Congressional Experience*, 3rd ed. (Boulder, CO: Westview Press, 2004), 16.

10. John C. Green and Nathan S. Bigelow, "The 2000 Presidential Nominations: The Costs of Innovation," in *Financing the 2000 Election*, ed. David B. Magleby (Washington, DC: Brookings Institution Press, 2001).

11. Jonathan Martin, "Mitt Romney's Money Machine Cranks Up" (*Politico*, May 17, 2011).

12. Campaign Finance Institute, *Campaign Funding Sources: House and Senate Major Party General Election Candidates, 1984–2014*. Accessed on June 30, 2015, from http://www.cfinst.org/pdf/vital/VitalStats_t8.pdf.

13. Ben Smith, "Wilson Breaks $1 Million" (*Politico*, September 12, 2009).

14. Tom Flanagan, *Winning Power* (Montreal: McGill-Queen's University Press, 2014), 105–106.

15. A recent Supreme Court decision, *McCutcheon v. FEC* (572 U.S. ___ [2014]), invalidated aggregate contribution limits. Donors still have a limit on what they can give to any one candidate, PAC, or party committee, but there is no longer a limit on what they can give in total.

16. Robert G. Boatright, Michael J. Malbin, and Brendan Glavin, *Independent Expenditures in Congressional Primaries after* Citizens United (Paper presented at the annual meeting of the Midwest Political Science Association, April 16–19, 2015).

17. For detail on the Cruz Super PAC, see Nicholas Confessore, "Network of 'Super PACs' Says That It Has Raised $31 Million for Ted Cruz Bid" (*The New York Times*, April 8, 2015), A20; for detail on 2012 candidate fundraising, see Robert G. Boatright, "Can Public Funding and *Citizens United* Coexist?" in *Corruption in the Contemporary World: Theory, Practice, and Hotspots*, ed. Jonathan Mendilow and Ilan Peleg (Lanham, MD: Rowman and Littlefield, 2014), 69–98.

18. Gail Perry, "Top 10 Major Gift Fundraising Trends for 2014–15" (*Fired-Up Fundraising*, June 2014). Accessed on October 6, 2015, from http://www.gailperry.com/2014/06/top-10-major-donor-trends-2014-15/.

19. Melissa Ryan, "Begging for Dollars" (*Campaigns and Elections*, November 10, 2014).

CHAPTER 3

Paid Media in Campaigns—Now and in the Future

Tad Devine

POLITICAL ADVERTISING IS CHANGING as quickly as the weather in New England. After decades of continuity, advertising is changing in terms of its content and especially its delivery. As new forums for delivery become available in this age of instantaneous online communication, campaigns are finding new ways to talk to and persuade voters.

And it's not just campaigns that are finding new ways to do the talking to voters. Now anyone with a laptop computer, some editing software, and a high-speed Internet connection can become part of the political dialogue through home-made advertising that is viewed online and through rebroadcast in the free media. Paid political advertising, which has been the centerpiece of campaign communication in the United States for decades, is in the midst of a period of consequential and ongoing change. Campaigns are communicating with voters in ways that were not available or hardly conceivable only a generation ago.

For more than five decades, political advertising has been the most powerful vehicle for a candidate to deliver an unfettered message directly to voters. From the landmark "Daisy" ad in 1964 to the high-definition and interactive ads of today, political advertising has fundamentally changed. Advances in research, technology, and the sophistication of targeting are leading ad makers to develop increasingly individualized advertising tailored to niche audiences. With these innovations, campaigns are using paid media to communicate their message to a more diverse cross section of the voting electorate than ever before.

The purpose of this chapter is to review paid media in political campaigns, to show how it became powerful and how it is changing. The chapter begins with an examination of the role of media consultants and then looks at the way research-based message development informs ad making. It then reviews message development by looking at specific campaigns and ads. Finally, the chapter looks ahead at the cutting edge of campaign advertising, focusing on the way digital technology, the Internet, conversion technology, and media targeting are affecting the way political ad makers craft and deliver messages to voters on behalf of campaigns and candidates.

Most of the examples, and all of the case studies, are ads that I have made or worked on with my business partners. My perspective is that of a practitioner spending the last two decades writing, directing, and producing television ads in the United States and around the world. That perspective is undoubtedly biased toward the power of television advertising. But until campaigns—from presidential races to statewide and even local elections—begin to concentrate the bulk of their resources on paid communication other than television advertising, the primacy of television advertising as the means of communicating with voters will remain intact. And while rapidly evolving technologies may soon fundamentally change this calculation (as the first screen of television is rivaled, and perhaps someday eclipsed, by the second and third screens of the computer and the smartphone), for today at least, television advertising is still the most powerful way to persuade large numbers of voters.

Paid Television Advertising

Campaign television ads are the most powerful tool in modern U.S. politics.[1] That is why major statewide and national campaigns spend more on paid media than on anything else.[2] Some may dispute the conclusion on television advertising primacy, and with the emergence of the Internet and other means of communication, it is a legitimate debate. But until statewide and national campaigns start spending up to half or more of their resources in areas other than television advertising, it is difficult to dispute that paid ads are viewed by most consultants and candidates as being more powerful than any other tool in a campaign's arsenal.[3] Given the power of television advertising and the strategic imperative of a campaign to reach so many voters in a short time, paid television ads will likely remain the dominant communications medium in campaigns through this next decade. In many ways, alternative media will enhance the power of television advertising, but it has not yet replaced it.

Paid advertising can have an impact that ripples throughout a race. In 2014, Seth Magaziner was a thirty-year-old first-time candidate for general treasurer in Rhode Island. He was running against Frank Caprio, the former general treasurer who had won 77 percent of the vote in the general election the last time he ran for that office in 2006. Caprio started with a huge lead in the 2014 Democratic primary, but by Election Day, that lead had become a huge deficit on the heels of a paid media campaign that depicted Caprio as the epitome of "insider politics" and Magaziner as a new leader who could help Rhode Island get "a fresh start."[4]

Increased Internet fundraising is already providing campaigns the resources needed to buy more television time, and there is now the possibility of interactivity between television advertising and campaigns. Ads now drive viewers to campaign websites to do everything from contributing money to "friending" the candidate on Facebook. Finally, as more and more people have access to faster Internet connections, and as those faster connections extend to handheld devices beyond computers, the likelihood increases that voters will one day watch ads, or even longer-format communications, as they commute to work on a train or sit in a doctor's waiting room. Perhaps one day truly undecided voters will make up their minds while standing in line at a crowded polling place and watching an ad on a handheld device.

The Role of Media Consultants

Media consultants have two principal roles in campaigns: First, as creators of television ads, we write, direct, produce, and deliver campaign advertising. We team up with other skilled professionals, such as film crews, producers, editors, and media time buyers. These production and delivery specialists typically work not only on political campaigns but on other kinds of advertising as well. They bring their skills in editing and filmmaking, as well as media placement and targeted time buying, to political campaigns under the direction of media consultants, who are the people who work most closely with the candidates and campaigns. In order for

Becoming a Political Media Consultant

Political consulting is a niche field. I did not move into my current career full-time until I was almost forty. That is not to say I wasn't involved in politics or campaigns. I got my start in politics as a delegate counter for President Jimmy Carter's 1980 reelection campaign while I was a law student on summer break. I then stayed involved with the Democratic Party, working on other presidential elections, before joining a political advertising firm in the early 1990s. Many media consultants enter the field from political campaign backgrounds like mine, but another established route is working on television production. The first political advertising consultants were real-life "Mad Men" from agencies in New York. In 1952, the Republican National Committee hired the Madison Avenue firm of Batten, Barton, Durstine & Osborn (BBDO) to help polish the image of presidential candidate Dwight Eisenhower.[5] Pursuing a degree in filmmaking, or working as a television producer, is now a popular and viable path to becoming a political media consultant.

everything to run smoothly, successful media consultants need the political know-how to read and interpret polls, understand demographics, and assimilate voting patterns, as well as the artistic and people skills to create ads and communicate personally to voters with substance, passion, and/or humor.

The second main role of media consultants is as campaign strategists. In that capacity, consultants are among the architects of a campaign's message. Media consultants collaborate with pollsters, campaign managers, candidates, and others to develop a message. For example, when Joseph P. Kennedy III ran for Congress in Massachusetts in 2012, our research showed us that the most powerful issues with voters in the Fourth Congressional District were jobs and tax fairness. The voters supported plans to raise revenue by asking the wealthiest to pay their fair share so that government could have the resources to make investments in infrastructure and education to help create jobs. Jobs and fairness became the centerpiece of Joe Kennedy's winning message.[6]

In addition to research, media consultants use their experience in campaigns to anticipate likely lines of attack and to react quickly to changing circumstances. After many years and many campaigns, situations that have occurred previously inevitably reemerge. Experience can be useful in making the quick decisions necessary in the short time frame of a typical campaign. For example, in 1998, my firm made the ads for John Edwards's winning Senate campaign in North Carolina and Parris Glendening's winning campaign for governor in Maryland. The Edwards campaign advertising was almost entirely positive and upbeat, while the Glendening ads were viciously negative. Our experience and the research from those contemporaneous races led us to produce entirely positive ads in North

Joe Kennedy for Congress—Massachusetts, 2012.

Carolina and many tough, negative ads in Maryland. This kind of battle-tested experience is particularly useful because campaigns frequently involve changing circumstances. Decisions have to be made quickly and decisively for candidates to win or to deal with fast-unfolding events.[7]

Writing Campaign Ads

Writing is the essential starting point of almost all television, radio, and online advertising. Political consultants write scripts that are typically made into thirty- or sixty-second ads read by a narrator, a third party in a testimonial ad (such as a person who knows the candidate), or the candidate.

Scripts provide a focal point at which strategy and research converge to create a deliverable message. Scripts also embody the reality that television ads are typically limited to a very short format—in the United States, almost always thirty seconds.

Sometimes ads are not scripted and are the result of a "cinema verité" technique of filming the candidate. These ads are typically made by filming a live event, such as a speech; by simply following the candidate around as he or she campaigns; or by interviewing the candidate and using his or her unscripted responses to questions asked by an interviewer. Cinema verité provides a way of communicating with voters that tends to depict the candidate in a more real and less formal light. The message discipline required for making these ads usually is applied not at the front end (as when the candidate reads a script), but at the back end when the consultant must cut and assemble the candidate's (or third party's) words and phrases in the studio. The ad maker then uses the tools of editing to ensure that the spot makes the intended point in the short time allotted. Cinema verité is the technique I have used for many years with one of my clients, Bernie Sanders, the U.S. senator from Vermont who is also a candidate for the Democratic Party nomination for president in 2016.[8] That technique allows us to communicate his authentic qualities, which are part of his message.

As of 2002, ad makers actually have less than thirty or sixty seconds due to regulations in the Bipartisan Campaign Reform Act (BCRA), which requires federal candidates to "stand by their ads." That requirement means that a candidate must "disclaim" the ad by saying something like "I am Jane Jones, and I approve this message," which can take up to four seconds. The consequence for media consultants is that ads have less time to present persuasive information and content to voters, truncating not only the visual aspects of the ads but the written aspects as well. Interestingly, media consultants have gotten creative with this constraint, adding personalized statements that fit within BCRA's rules. For example, in Kentucky's hotly contested 2010 Senate race, Rand Paul (R) ended the ad "Rand's Plan" with "I'm Rand Raul, and I approve this message because government is the servant, not the master."[9]

The Importance of Audio and Video

Other powerful tools used by media consultants are the images and sounds at the heart of television advertising. Television is primarily a visual medium, and television ad makers look for strong visuals and credible sources of authority to make their cases. Television and radio are also auditory media, in which everything from the sound of the candidate's voice to the soundtrack behind an ad can have a powerful impact on voters. In many ways, music is the secret weapon of television political advertising, since it can evoke a mood or underline the message being delivered through words and images.

Research-Based Message Development

One of the keys to media production in political campaigns is the use of research to develop a message. Campaigns and consultants review the research and based on that research develop concepts for television, radio, and other forms of advertising.[10] Typically, this takes the form of converting short narrative statements about a candidate or set of issues from the poll into an ad. The statements are road tested in polls before they are written as a script for broadcast ads.[11] Successful political campaigns almost always emanate from a disciplined regime of research, where tools such as polls, focus groups, people-metered ad testing, opposition research, and issue or candidate record research provide the basis for a message.

At the presidential level, where the resources and the stakes are most high, almost all advertisements are subjected to both pre- and postproduction research. Research includes polling that occurs prior to the development of scripts and detailed focus group testing of ads after preliminary versions of an ad has been produced. Campaigns also use online media testing of ads: preselected online groups see the advertising and are asked to comment on its impact. In almost every major U.S. campaign today at the statewide level, advertising is tested in one way or another prior to broadcast. Although there are exceptions to the rule, pre- and postproduction testing is the industry standard. By gauging the impact of messages on voters in preproduction polls, or by showing preliminary versions of a commercial to focus groups, ad makers can get a good sense of the impact on potential voters before making the costly commitment to broadcasting the spot.

Projective Research

Perhaps the most important development in the last four decades in U.S. political campaigns is the use of "projective research" in the production of television advertising and in message development. This technique, pioneered in the United States and used extensively in political campaigns around the world,[12] allows researchers to push and probe respondents with a variety of questions to gauge how voters will respond to issues and arguments. By determining whether voters are impacted, either positively or negatively, by a particular message, projective research can inform media consultants about what ads are likely to be most powerful in moving the voters who emerge as the primary targets of campaign communication strategies. If the research is well conceived and executed, campaigns can avoid the costly mistake of putting enormous resources behind messages that do not have a good chance of succeeding with voters. Developing winning messages in a poll and successfully testing the depictions of those messages in a qualitative focus group setting are the best way to ensure success in the real world of elections.

Quantitative and Qualitative Research

Polling is the form of quantitative research that campaigns use the most. Polls—either a random survey of respondents or a discrete "panel back" survey of the members of a previously identified group who are contacted more than once—are at the heart of modern research.[13] Campaigns essentially play out the election in polls, testing to see not just where the electorate is today but also how voters will be impacted by issues and new information.

Focus groups and other forms of qualitative research are the tools that media consultants use to determine which ads will work and why. Focus group research typically occurs after television ad production, when at least a preliminary version of an ad has been made. By letting a selected group of target voters evaluate an ad prior to broadcast, campaigns likely can avoid running an ad that may not produce the desired effect.

Communicating the Message through Different Ads

The skills and tools of experience, writing, and research enable the media adviser to craft a message for a campaign. Political ads communicate that message to voters in a number of forms: biographical, issue, accomplishment/vision, and negative ads to name the most prevalent.

Biographical Ads

Typically in a campaign, candidates introduce themselves to the voting public in terms of their biographies. One of the most important qualities that they can communicate is shared values. Biographical advertising opens a window into the lives of candidates so that voters can better understand and relate to them on the basis of shared values. Biographical ads help to frame the narrative of a campaign. Sometimes the biographical ads are deeply personal, and sometimes the narrative is directed toward accomplishment, agenda, or vision. The first case study illustrates how a biographical ad from Bernie Sanders's first Senate race in 2006 uses biography, accomplishment, and agenda to communicate the candidate's shared values with voters. (See the Bernie Sanders ad "People" at https://vimeo .com/12264914.)

Issue Ads

Issue ads tend to be more focused on policies. The issues may be important to a particular place or demographic group. These ads are typically informational, supplying voters with facts and the position of a candidate or the interest group who sponsored the ad on issues that are at the center of the campaign. For example, Americans United for Safe Streets made an independent expenditure ad produced by my firm after the tragic shootings in Aurora, Colorado. Stephen Barton was one of the victims of that tragedy. He was a young recent college graduate who was traveling cross-country by bike on July 20, 2012, when he and a friend decided to see the midnight showing of the movie *The Dark Knight Rises*. Stephen survived, and his testimonial ad about that night provided a powerful call to action for voters to "demand a plan" from both candidates for president to end the wave of gun violence in the United States. (See the Americans United for Safe Streets ad "Demand a Plan" at https://vimeo.com/56698626.)

Accomplishment and Agenda Ads

Another category of advertising focuses on the accomplishments of candidates, and looks ahead to future achievements and the candidate's vision and agenda. I believe that every winning campaign is about the future. It is critical for candidates, particularly incumbents seeking reelection, to remind voters of what they have done and of the bonds that exist between the candidate and the electorate but also to focus on future battles. Accomplishment and vision ads are critical to inoculating incumbents against attacks from challengers and are useful in introducing political outsiders with experience from the private sector who are running for office. In 1994, I was part of the team that produced ads for Senator Ted Kennedy's victory over Mitt Romney in the U.S. Senate race in Massachusetts. Our final ad in that race, called "Ahead," looked to "the fights that lie ahead" and the victories for working people that could be achieved if Senator Kennedy was returned to office. (See Ted Kennedy's ad "Ahead" at https://vimeo.com/12243831.)

Negative Ads

The final category of political ads is the most famous (or infamous): negative ads. If television ads are the most powerful force in politics, then negative ads may be a campaign's most powerful weapon. The most notorious negative ad was, and still is, the "Daisy" spot, televised on September 7, 1964.[14] In that ad, President Johnson's campaign showed a young girl plucking petals from a daisy juxtaposed with a countdown to a nuclear explosion. The spot left the impression that if Johnson's opponent, Senator Barry Goldwater (R-AZ), was elected president, he might actually lead the United States into a nuclear confrontation with the Soviet Union. Even though the ad aired only once during the 1964 presidential race, it had a tremendous impact, an impact felt even to this day. Indeed, some advocacy groups are still using remakes of that ad to make points on issues such as the 2010 New Strategic Arms Reduction Treaty (New START).[15]

Negative ads can be harsh, and they can be subtle. I have included two negative ads that my firm produced in recent years to demonstrate that point. The first is from Seth Magaziner's race for general treasurer of Rhode Island (referred to above). At the time the ad was filmed, Magaziner was running against two opponents in the Democratic primary—Frank Caprio (the former general treasurer and past Democratic Party nominee for governor) and Ernie Almonte (the former state auditor general). Both of Magaziner's opponents were more experienced in the public sector, but that experience also left them open to charges of insider politics and mismanagement. The ad depicts two typical politicians at a restaurant feasting, embodying the insider political culture that our campaign research told us voters were sick of in Rhode Island. The ad is not so tough and hard-edged as to alienate Democratic primary voters who might be turned off by a vicious negative ad against a fellow Democrat. (See Seth Magaziner's ad "Fresh Start" at https://vimeo.com/109967151.)

Seth Magaziner for Treasurer—Rhode Island, 2014.

The other case study negative ad, however, pulls no punches. In that ad, first-time candidate Bobby McKenzie attacks his opponent Dave Trott as the "foreclosure king" of Michigan. The ad depicts the late-night eviction of a 101-year-old African American woman in a wheelchair, and it was recognized by numerous accolades for being a brutal negative ad.[16]

Cutting-Edge Changes in Advertising

Technological changes that will affect paid advertising in the 2016 presidential election will transform the way candidates communicate with voters in the next decade. Not only is the digital process changing the quality of the product, but also the means of communicating information are becoming more and more diverse. Media consultants no longer make ads just for television and radio; they also make them for a new screen—the Internet. And they make them for distinct audiences of potential supporters and persuadable voters.

Digital Technology

Advances in digital technology have fundamentally changed the political consulting business in recent years. In the last ten years, political ad makers have moved from producing television ads in either videotape or film to using high-definition (HD) video for most production. HD video allows media consultants to have high-quality, clear images. It is also much more convenient for producing and editing ads. Instead of shooting in film, where there is a time-consuming physical demand of changing the film cartridge after only several minutes of filming, an HD camera will usually run for an hour of continuous filming. The image quality of HD is superior to lower grades of video, and new digital cameras allow filming in less light, also saving precious time on expensive shoots. That is important when you consider that political ads must compete not only against other political ads for audience attention but also against the more expensive production value of ads for financial institutions, automakers, and other high-end consumer marketers. Those corporate ads run before and after political ads in front of the same audience, and a drop in production quality can adversely affect the way viewers perceive the lower-quality ad.

The change in editing in recent years has been as dramatic as the change in filming. Political ad makers moved from large-scale online editing, which typically occurred in big studios, to PC/Avid digital editing, which can be done on hardware as small as a laptop computer. Similarly, ads can now be delivered to television and radio stations anywhere almost instantly using digital transfers. An ad can go from concept to execution, to delivery, to broadcast, all in the same day. And in many senatorial or gubernatorial campaigns today, particularly at the end of a closely fought race, that is precisely what happens.

Technology is also making big changes in the content of advertising. Ads can direct viewers to campaign websites and create the potential for interactive communication driven by the power of paid media. Once this interactivity occurs—when a viewer responds to a call to action by going to a website as directed in an ad—campaigns can capture the email addresses of people who are interested in candidates or causes, allowing them to continue to speak directly to those voters at will and for little or no cost.[17]

As digital technology changes the way ads are filmed, edited, and delivered to voters, media consultants and campaigns must adjust to a faster and more efficient process. As more and more people have access to editing technology, the process of making political ads may become even more homegrown. We've already seen competitions in which ad makers working at home have sent in ads for various causes.[18] It is not surprising that Madison Avenue is following suit, with ads made by amateurs featured in the Super Bowl and entire agencies, such as Idea Bounty and Victors & Spoils, built on the principles of "crowdsourcing," which utilizes the inexhaustible supply of eager Internet users, on a per-contract basis, instead of hiring full-time employees.[19]

In the future, the media consultant in some campaigns may become the volunteer with a laptop, a creative person who has the ability to edit images either captured by personal digital video cameras or selected from the vast expanse of imagery available now to almost anyone, anywhere, at the click of a mouse.

The Internet and Advertising

The powerful connection between the Internet and campaign advertising has been established in modern campaigns, and that connection is only likely to be enhanced in the future. Announcement videos released online have now become the norm for campaign kickoffs as opposed to press conferences and set-piece events. When Joseph P. Kennedy III announced his candidacy for the U.S. Congress, he did so with a video that laid out the parameters of his campaign and message and invited voters to email him or get in touch through social media.[20] Additionally, campaigns looking to make a splash are now harnessing the power of the Internet to spread video at lightning speed by creating advertisements that they hope will "go viral." With social networking sites like Facebook and Twitter encouraging users to share video through easy uploading systems, political ads can now reach an unprecedented number of viewers in record time. In order for an ad to be "forwarded," it must strike a special chord with viewers, oftentimes being quirky, funny, or just plain ridiculous. It is the job of the media consultant to incorporate the candidate's message into the ad, while still maintaining a viral appeal. This type of viral video was used heavily in the 2014 election cycle. Republican candidates in particular and the Super PACs supporting them used these videos extensively and successfully in that election cycle.[21]

Reaching Niche Markets

As the delivery of television advertising and the research behind campaigns become more and more sophisticated, the demand to reach niche voters will grow. As campaigns identify voters and categorize them, it has become easier to reach them with television advertising, just as direct mail has been delivered to voters on a highly segmented basis for many years. In the future, more campaigns will use niche marketing for advertising on television and the Internet.

Cable channels, with their multitude of format and geographical options, are already giving political advertisers ways to reach different groups of people in a more targeted strategic environment. For example, an ad can be delivered on a cable system that broadcasts only in a specific geographic area. This type of geographic niche advertising is important in campaigns where media markets spill over from smaller states to larger states. For campaigns in New Hampshire, where so much advertising occurs every four years in presidential races, the Boston media market (of which southern New Hampshire is a part) is much more expensive than the Manchester market. As cable systems become pervasive, political ad makers use them to deliver messages to voters who live in places like New Hampshire or Delaware, at a fraction of a larger adjacent broadcast market's cost. The ability to penetrate only New Hampshire counties, instead of paying for Massachusetts's voters to see an ad intended for the New Hampshire primary, saves enormous amounts of money for campaigns. Likewise, groups of voters may congregate around certain television shows or television channels. If the research for a campaign shows that a certain demographic of voters lines up with particular television venues, then the campaign not only can deliver messages to all voters through broader advertising on network television but also can tailor discrete messages to be delivered to a target audience via cable.

The Next Wave: The Future of Media Advertising

Television advertising in the future will have to adjust to a more rapid pace of delivery. It's simply a faster world, in which ads on television compete with other forms of communication—such as the Internet, direct mail, and paid telephone banks— to deliver and amplify the message of a campaign. Perhaps the biggest adjustment that television ad makers will make is moving to "convergence technology" (i.e., the combination of two or more technologies in a single device such as using a cell phone as a camera). Advertising in the new political campaigns is not likely to be limited to the single screen of television but may appear on the second screen (the computer) and the third screen (the smartphone) and elsewhere (like a wristwatch with a screen).

The Smartphone as a Precursor?

Smartphones and tablets are precursors to what may become an everyday means of firsthand communication with voters. Now that voters can easily view videos through their telephones, and the images are so clear that they can have the kind of powerful impact that television advertising first had forty years ago, political ad makers may decide they need to move to these screens even more. If so, it will create an interesting new way of communicating with voters. Campaigns have already begun to use text services to disseminate videos to subscribers. We've seen campaigns use texting to reach voters and the press, such as in 2008 when the Obama campaign chose to text Obama's vice presidential pick, rather than use a traditional media outlet to release the breaking news. Campaigns used to go door-to-door with candidates and ground troops. Now they may go hand to hand with video images and sound bites.

Tablets are also contributing to the changing landscape. The iPad and similar devices have revolutionized the way media consultants do business. We are now able to carry around high-tech presentations, embedded with quality video, which can transform a business meeting into an advertising pitch at the drop of a hat.

Independent Expenditures

One of the most important developments in political advertising in recent years has been the growth of "independent expenditure" advertising in political campaigns. While this phenomenon has existed for many years (examples include the "Willie Horton" spot from 1988 and the "Swift Boat" ads from 2004), the series of Supreme Court rulings that liberalized how independent groups have spent money for advertising has increased markedly since 2010.[22]

Independent expenditure advertising is something engaged in not only by groups distinct from campaigns but also by political parties and by the political party committees established at a national level to support candidates for the House and Senate. At the heart of independent expenditure advertising are firm rules and laws that forbid the independent groups and committees from coordinating, or even communicating in many cases, with political campaigns. This division between campaigns and the independent actions of groups choosing to exercise their right to political free speech in U.S. constitutional democracy is making it more difficult for political campaigns to control the message being delivered to voters.

Voters naturally attribute or impute any political advertising they see (whether or not it contains a particular disclaimer) to a campaign and not to an independent expenditure group to which the candidate has no connection. Thus, a campaign that may have decided strategically to pursue positive advertising to introduce a candidate may have to engage in a battle over tone, and groups mounting their own highly negative campaigns may undermine the content of the campaign's message. Unfortunately, the campaign, and not the independent expenditure group, may pay the price because many voters believe that candidates control everything that is being said by their side.

Conclusion

Political advertising remains the most powerful tool in a campaign's arsenal of communication, but as technology changes the way we communicate, political advertising is also changing. Soon political ads' main venue may be pop-ups on your smartphone or newscasts on your iPad. Whatever the future holds, one thing is certain: As long as we have political campaigns, we are likely to have political ads. Others will debate the impact of that reality on U.S. democracy. For now, those who want to win campaigns will try to understand and exploit the power of political ads.

For now, the future of political campaigns is not just on the Web. Even the Internet giant Google continues to advertise itself not just in cyberspace but on television as well.[23] This is because the Internet requires motivation by the user to seek out information in a way that television does not. In politics, people who consume news on the Internet tend to have much higher political interest, awareness, and participation. Political advertisers, however, must still reach that enormous segment of voters who are less involved than activists but still believe that the act of voting and the choices made for political offices are critical. For the foreseeable future, the most powerful way to reach those voters is through television advertising. To those who posit that old-fashioned political ads don't matter, that the future of political persuasion lies solely on the Internet and social media highways, perhaps the best rejoinder is the ancient chant: "The King is dead. Long live the King."

Notes

1. See Edwin Diamond and Stephen Bates, *The Spot: The Rise of Political Advertising on Television* (Cambridge, MA: MIT Press, 1992).
2. Federal Election Commission, Campaign Disclosure Reports, cir. 2014, 2012, 2010, 2008, and 2006, Accessed on June 20, 2015, from www.fec.gov/finance/disclosure/disclosure_data_search.shtml.
3. In 2012, the Obama presidential campaign spent $483.8 million on media, including $397.9 million on the media buy and $8 million on production. It also spent $74.5 million on digital advertising—about three times what it spent on digital ads in 2008. See Stephanie Stamm, "How Do Presidential Candidates Spend $1 Billion" (*National Journal*, June 8, 2015). Accessed on June 22, 2015, from http://www.nationaljournal.com/2016-elections/how-do-presidential-candidates-spend-1-billion-20150608.
4. See Alex Kuffner, "Magaziner Ends Caprio's Comeback for General Treasurer" (*The Providence Journal*, September 9, 2014). Accessed on June 22, 2015, from http://www.providencejournal.com/article/20140909/NEWS/309099867.
5. See Herbert S. Parmet, *Eisenhower and the American Crusades* (New Brunswick, NJ: Transaction, 1999).

6. See Emily Cataneo, "Kennedy in Needham: Job Creation Most Important Issue" (*The Needham Times*, May 22, 2012). Accessed on June 21, 2015, from http://needham .wickedlocal.com/article/20120522/News/305229701/?Start=1.

7. See Robert J. Huckshorn and Robert C. Spencer, *The Politics of Defeat: Campaigning for Congress* (Amherst: University of Massachusetts Press, 1971).

8. See the cinema verité Sanders ads. Accessed on June 21, 2015, from https://vimeo.com/ channels/744985.

9. The Strategy Group for Media produced Rand Paul's advertisements. "Rand's Plan" was uploaded to YouTube by randpaul on September 21, 2010. Accessed on June 13, 2011, from http://www.youtube.com/user/RandPaul-p/u/8/uVorVi8gCJM.

10. For more information about the use of research in campaigns, see Douglas E. Schoen, *The Power of the Vote* (New York: William Morrow, 2007); and Frank Luntz, *Words That Work* (New York: Hyperion, 2007).

11. Ivor Crewe, Brian Gosschalk, and John Bartle, *Political Communications: Why Labour Won the General Election of 1997* (London: Routledge, 1998), 56–57.

12. See Stan Greenberg, *Dispatches from the War Room* (New York: Thomas Dunne Books, 2009), for details on the use of survey research and focus groups in campaigns outside the United States.

13. A "panel back" survey refers to a survey of a discrete group of voters who are established initially as a random group and who are subsequently recontacted by the same pollster and asked to give their opinions on new issues, as well as on previously asked questions such as candidate support. Panel back surveys allow pollsters and campaigns to follow the dynamic within a discrete group of respondents, which may be different from what is happening at the same time with the electorate at large.

14. See Kathiann M. Kowalski, *Campaign Politics: What's Fair? What's Foul?* (New York: Twenty-first Century Books, 2000).

15. Michael D. Shear, "New 'Daisy' Ad Warns against Delay in Arms Treaty" (*The New York Times*, "The Caucus Blog," November 19, 2010). Accessed on June 20, 2015, from http://thecaucus.blogs.nytimes.com/category/the_caucus.

16. Sean Sullivan, "Michigan Democrat Launches One of the Most Brutal Attack Ads You'll Ever See" (*The Washington Post*, October 22, 2014). Accessed on June 20, 2015, from http://www.washingtonpost.com/blogs/post-politics/wp/2014/10/22/michigan-democrat-launches-one-of-the-most-brutal-attack-ads-youll-ever-see/.

17. Steve Davis, Larry Elin, and Grant Reeher, *Click on Democracy: The Internet's Power to Change Political Apathy into Civic Action* (Boulder, CO: Westview Press, 2004), 30.

18. For example, MoveOn.org's "Obama in 30 Seconds Contest."

19. See Jeff Howe, "The Rise of Crowdsourcing" (*Wired*, June 2006).

20. See "Joe Kennedy for Congress" announcement video. Accessed on June 20, 2015, from https://vimeo.com/44677109.

21. Darren Samuelsohn, "Got Viral Videos?" (*Politico*, October 7, 2014). Accessed on June 22, 2015, from http://www.politico.com/story/2014/10/viral-ads-2014-elections-111639.html.

22. Independent groups have quadrupled their spending since 2006 and in 2010 funneled about $105 million more into political advertising than did party committees.

See Spencer MacColl's report, "A Center for Responsive Politics Analysis of the Effects of: *Citizens United v. Federal Election Commission,*" available at OpenSecrets .org. Independent expenditures totaled more than half a billion dollars on television ads, most of it in the presidential campaign in 2012. See *The New York Times* report on independent spending totals. Accessed on June 20, 2015, from http://elections .nytimes.com/2012/campaign-finance/independent-expenditures/totals.

23. See the Google Chrome "offline" campaign "The Web Is What You Make of It," which is profiled in Claire Cain Miller's article "Google Takes to TV to Promote Browser" (*The New York Times,* May 4, 2011). Accessed on June 19, 2015, from http:// www.nytimes.com/2011/05/04/technology/04chrome.html?_r=0.

CHAPTER 4

Social and New Media—
The Digital Present and Future

Michael Turk

JUST A FEW SHORT YEARS AGO, the digital campaign was a relatively small part of the overall campaign structure. When people talked about the digital components of the campaign, they largely meant the website, email programs, and eventually social media. The voter database was a separate component of the operation and until just 2008–2012 was often not tied to the rest of the web/digital operation. Many campaigns, when they thought of digital, focused mostly on the fundraising aspect of the online campaign. There was an understanding that the Internet made giving—and soliciting donations especially—easy to do. Most paid Internet advertising was focused on fundraising, and relatively little was done to take advantage of the Internet for persuasion messaging.

The modern digital campaign has advanced well beyond those days and is, today, a complex operation that brings together all operational aspects of marketing and advertising, data management, fundraising, and political mobilization. The tools have become much more sophisticated, and the staff and budget resources devoted to digital operations have increased dramatically.

As campaigns have evolved over the years, changing media platforms have challenged the unprepared and presented opportunities to the bold and innovative. The story of the first televised presidential debate in 1960—the clean-shaven John Kennedy sparring with the scruffy Richard Nixon—has become the stuff of legend. Those listening via radio gave the win to Nixon; those watching television scored it for Kennedy.[1] In the end, the Nixon campaign was caught flat-footed by the new technology and paid the price by a defeat of one hundred thousand votes out of sixty-eight million cast.

In the earliest days of the Internet, the media asked if the next campaign cycle would be the one in which the Internet came into its own and made the difference between winning and losing for a presidential candidate. As the media looked on with anticipation, voters looked for more information about elections and candidates—with exponentially more going online in pursuit of politics each cycle. Between 2000 and 2010, the percentage of adult Americans using the Internet to research the election grew from 18 percent to 73 percent.[2] A July 2015 Pew Research Center study found that 61 percent of Millennials get their political news from Facebook—the single largest source for their generation. Of Generation X voters, roughly half get their news from Facebook, and half get it from TV.[3]

This chapter seeks to explore the benefits that campaigns can recognize with innovative application of new and social media. The chapter will cover the rise of the Internet and new media in campaigns, how the Internet evolved into a potent communications and mobilization tool for campaigns, how new media and social media have transformed campaigns, how mobility is changing and may further change the role of communications, and what campaigns of the future may look like. The one constant in technology is change. The one constant in campaigns is the unending quest for the technology, idea, or message that will give campaigns an electoral advantage. As we look toward the 2016 campaign, we can make some educated predictions of what technology changes we will see, and how campaigns may use them.

The Rise of the Internet and New Media in Campaigns

In the mid-1990s, the Internet was a new frontier, largely unheard of by most Americans. Political use of the Internet, however, had been a staple of the nascent network since its earliest days. Usenet groups—discussion forums visited by the Internet's pioneers and academics who were frequently given access through university networks—had been a hive of political activity for nearly fifteen years before the first presidential campaign went online. Users had discussions about topics ranging from Ronald Reagan's arms control policy to a campaign to cryogenically freeze the Reagan-Bush ticket.[4]

Despite the proliferation of political discourse online, such discussions on the Internet would remain the realm of computer science students until the invention of the browser and commercialization made the network accessible to the mainstream. As companies like AOL and Prodigy opened the door to consumers, and the ease of navigation born of HTML gave way to "browsing" the web, the growth of politics online exploded.

Campaigns began taking simple steps to extend the reach of their communications efforts with the Republican National Committee (RNC) going online in 1994, followed by a handful of state political parties and grassroots organizations like Free Republic.

In the 1996 campaign, presidential websites were little more than brochure-ware with limited navigation options for things like press releases, issue papers, and campaign updates. The "advanced" features of the site included things like quizzes and a brief audio clip.[5]

As the new millennium dawned, campaigns began to recognize the Internet's ability to organize and rolled out websites with rudimentary volunteer tools like Steve Forbes's e-Precinct, George W. Bush's Team Leader, and the Gore-Lieberman iTeam and GoreNet offerings. These tools laid the framework for more sophisticated tools that would come in later cycles. Party committees began to invest in similar tools to encourage political participation. During the early years of the twentieth century, affinity programs created by political parties and campaigns rewarded activists in much the same way frequent flyer programs reward repeat business.

The RNC's Team Leader program combined political action with affinity rewards like Velcro wallets and PDA covers. For completing certain tasks, activists would receive points they could trade in for merchandise emblazoned with the Team Leader logo. The program was initially mocked but eventually recognized for the significant role it played in the party's political operation.[6] During the 2004 campaign, Team Leader, together with the Bush volunteer initiative, was tied to walk and phone programs. Campaign volunteers were no longer beholden to campaign infrastructure if they wanted to get involved.

While the Bush campaign and the RNC were focused on driving action and rewarding activists, the Dean campaign was making use of early social media platforms like blogs and Meetup.com. Supporters of Howard Dean put Meetup's fledgling service on the map by using the site to coordinate political events. The campaign used its blog to speak directly with the activists and draw inspiration from supporters. After the campaign had developed an interactive graphic of a baseball player to track online fundraising, supporters on the blog suggested the candidate go on stage carrying a big red bat, if donors could raise $1 million online. Joe Trippi, Dean's campaign manager, directed a staffer to find a red bat. When the donations rolled past the million-dollar total, Dean strolled on stage with bat in hand.[7]

In 2008, Barack Obama and John McCain both tied much of their field organizing to the same platform that powered their websites and began operating from a single, central data source. Creating a single platform allowed the campaigns to view all of their organizing activity—be it phone banks in volunteer offices or the efforts of a single activist printing walk lists at home and going door-to-door in his or her neighborhood. Tied to rich consumer data that campaigns invest in, the voter file has become a massive trove of information about voters including such things as their issue preferences; products they buy; their vote history; and, most importantly, their likelihood to support or oppose the candidate.

Campaigns have proven beyond any reasonable doubt the adage that knowledge is power. Especially compared with the relative simplicity of early campaign websites, modern presidential campaigns combine cutting-edge digital marketing tactics; best-of-breed software; and specialized, and frequently custom, call and walk programs, affinity efforts, and community engagement tools. Presidential campaigns can be as sophisticated as any *Fortune* 500 company or Silicon Valley startup in terms of the platforms they develop and innovative tactics they employ.

While campaigns previously focused on GRPs, or television's gross ratings points, and could calculate media budgets with relative ease, today's campaign has to contend with CPA (cost per acquisition), CPM (cost per thousand ad impressions delivered), CPC (cost per click), ROI (return on amount invested in campaign advertising), email list size, open rates, click-throughs, bounce and unsubscription rates, traffic metrics, friend counts, and countless other metrics. Campaigns look closely at traffic to their websites for patterns they can exploit. For instance, in the 2012 election cycle, sixty-five million unique visitors[8] contributed $525 million[9] online to the president's reelection. With an average of $8 donated per visitor, the process of driving web traffic has a direct correlation with the campaign's fundraising success.

For the campaign manager, the wide array of metrics available with web tools provides a clearer view of success and cost than do traditional media. Campaign metrics can identify ways to maximize benefits and accountability. New media investments provide a level of feedback and reporting that campaigns can count on. The ability to track outcomes does not change the fundamental goal of political campaigns—organizing a winning coalition. It does, however, make that job somewhat easier. While television advertising can tell you the number of viewers tuned to a program or channel at any point in time, it cannot tell you if the voter you are trying to reach actually saw the ad.

New media, in this way, is more sophisticated than television in that it can be targeted to specific users. Online destinations can match voter files against their registered subscribers to ensure that the voter you are attempting to reach is the one who views your ad.

As users of social networks like Facebook and Google+ share more information about themselves and their interests, political advertisers can target their messages very narrowly based on those characteristics. Social networks, and the rich information they provide, have become valuable tools for reaching voters.

New Media and Social Media

While the terms *new media* and *social media* are often used interchangeably, for the purpose of this chapter, *new media* will be used to describe communications and mobilization efforts that are delivered via the Internet. This is as opposed to traditional media like television, radio, and direct mail. Social media is technically a subset of new media and includes platforms that rely on interconnections between people to share and distribute information or coordinate activity. In the 2016 presidential election cycle, Senator Rand Paul (R-KY) earned the nickname "Troller in Chief" for the amount of time he spent trying to engage opponents in random comments and on social platforms.[10] Donald Trump, in the early days of the 2016 GOP (Grand Old Party) primary, used caustic and baiting comments to goad his rivals.[11]

In 2012 and 2014, social media continued to play a significant role in campaigns. Platforms like Facebook, Twitter, YouTube, Instagram, and Snapchat were used by campaigns to distribute messaging and coordinate supporters and were used by supporters to self-direct their own efforts independently of the campaign. The impact of social media has become so great that friends and followers of a campaign account have became a metric by which success and failure are judged. The number of people who follow candidates and elected officials is growing significantly, and not just for presidential campaigns. The number of people following candidates in the midterm election grew from 6 to 16 percent between 2010 and 2014. Older voters are even more likely to engage via social media with 21 percent of thirty- to forty-nine-year-olds following candidates on social media.[12]

While *new media* is a generic term often used for Internet-based communications, campaigns have used the web to deliver information and engage activists for some time. Indeed, political discussion and organization can be traced back before the rise of the web we know today. In fact, discussions of campaigns were taking place on bulletin board systems years before the development of the browser.

The Role of New Media in Campaigns

The technological convergence society has witnessed in recent years has made many of the distinctions between new and traditional media relatively meaningless. Cell phones and tablets are increasingly the main methods of connecting to information. Voters are using these tools to engage in politics like never before. In the spring of 2011, just 35 percent of Americans used a smartphone or tablet to go online. In 2015, that number stood at 65 percent[13] and will likely top 75 percent by the time of the 2016 elections. What's more, time spent consuming digital media now tops five and a half hours per day with 51 percent of that spent on mobile devices.[14]

Technology has changed the way voters get information as well as the way campaigns provide it. Online campaign operatives are the first to tout the benefits the Internet brings to campaigns, but they are also the first to note the organizing aspects of campaigns haven't changed; only the tools have. Campaigns are still tasked with identifying the coalition they will need to assemble in order to win. They must still develop a coherent message that appeals to the audience that makes up that coalition. They must work to identify supporters and volunteers and mobilize those individuals to give money, contact other voters, and otherwise do the heavy lifting of the campaign. The continuing shift toward online fundraising is illustrated by the 2008 and 2012 Obama campaigns. Total digital giving (including major gifts completed online as well as small dollar giving) represented 66 percent of the campaign's fundraising in 2008 and nearly 70 percent in 2012.[15]

Attracting someone who will carry your water, without tire, day in and day out, is no small task. Fortunately, it is made easier with technology. Online tools allow you to see who is doing the work and reward them. They allow you to automate the process of tracking volunteer performance and, if used correctly, to see any shortfall in your model before it becomes an issue.

In a campaign email sent during the 2008 election, Obama's campaign made the following statement: "We to need to fill 845,252 volunteer shifts in battleground states."[16] That the campaign could tell precisely how many volunteer shifts it had to fill, communicate that rapidly to supporters, and see in real time the progress toward its goal is a testament to the power of these tools.

Harnessing New Media for Advertising

Technology facilitates almost every aspect of campaign organization, from attracting new activists to turning out dedicated supporters on Election Day. Campaigns still rely on offline events, rallies, and campaign offices to attract supporters, but new media tactics like online advertising and list matching can augment organic list growth through site traffic to grow substantial rolls of supporters. Campaigns, like other advertisers, are beginning to look for creative and often overlooked ways to carry their messages to their faithful voters. Rick Santorum,[17] Rick Perry,[18] and Kendrick Meek,[19] for instance, are three candidates who have sponsored NASCAR racers in order to put their names in front of stock car racing fans.

The Obama campaign, in 2008, also targeted racing fans, but a different sort of racing. The campaign bought virtual ad space in eighteen different video games on the Xbox network including the popular *Burnout* racing game, *Madden NFL*, NASCAR racing games, and sports games featuring the National Basketball Association (NBA) and National Hockey League (NHL). The video games targeted the young gamer demographic and may have contributed to Obama's higher number of supporters among young voters.[20] The campaign repeated the buy in 2012.

In the 2016 cycle, video game platform advertisements may well increase, and ads targeted at specific apps may increase if the campaigns' examination of consumer data reflects trends in support among certain players. Also likely to increase are ads disguised as viral video. Commercial advertisers are increasingly using videos that appear to be independent or amateur clips but are specifically designed to carry a message or promote a product. Look for this trend to continue in politics, especially as third-party groups look to stand out in a competitive media environment.

Campaigns have generally tended to limit television advertising to persuasion messages, rather than recruitment. If ads contained the campaign's URL at all, it was a cursory mention, rather than prominent placement or tied to the message. In 2012, Republican Mitt Romney ran ads featuring a URL specific to campaign messaging that attacked President Obama's economic plan. The URL, ObamaIsntWorking.com,[21] drove voters to additional context, supporting materials, and registration and donation components tied to the content of the commercial. Such tactics have become widely employed, lead to significant recruitment gains, and give campaigns a way to gauge television ad effectiveness by tracking donors, supporters, and traffic originating at that URL.

Recruiting Volunteers

Email is still one of the most powerful tools for communicating with volunteers and supporters. Yet candidates have often employed questionable tactics to grow their lists. List matching previously involved matching voter information to email marketing lists and provided campaigns with large email lists with very little effort. The disadvantages of list matching are many. List matching often results in low open and response rates. Because the list is composed of people who didn't take steps to proactively request information, these "opt out" lists are quite likely people who either didn't open the list vendor's message to begin with or actively chose not to take action. Reputable vendors will provide an "opt in" basis for building your list—in which activists must affirm their desire to receive your emails. Such services are typically more expensive and result in smaller list matches but often have higher engagement rates. Another, admittedly more expensive, option is for campaigns to take their turnout data directly to social networks and advertisers who can deliver display ads to potential voters asking them to support the campaign. These efforts generally result in better list response.

Maximizing the Effectiveness of Communications

Sending supporters timely messages with relevant content will help you keep them connected to the campaign and energized to take action. For campaigns, maximizing the effectiveness of those campaign messages can mean the difference in election outcomes. Determining the best placement of donation buttons or images, and variables like text color and word choice, can increase the amount of money raised or the number of activists willing to do something on behalf of the candidate.

The tools available for mass communication allow a level of message testing and delivery that is unmatched. A/B or multivariate testing allows campaigns to try different messages, different imagery, different color schemes, and countless other variables to convey the message that will generate the highest action rate. Many commercial email platforms now allow campaigns to very easily accommodate multivariate testing. Campaigns are given template emails that are customized with different colors, copy, pictures, and subject lines. Merge fields that allow the insertion of specific text based on supporter characteristics provide campaigns with the flexibility to target their messages to specific voters, should they choose.

Campaigns can develop variations of messages. Those messages are then sent to small subsets (typically no more than a few hundred or a thousand) of the email universe. The responses to those messages—including open rate, click-through on specific links, clicks on individual images, and so on—are tracked, and the components that perform best are then compiled into a single message that is sent to the rest of the audience. An example of that was Pat Toomey's (R-PA) successful campaign for the Senate in 2010. Toomey's message was very simple: "More Jobs, Less Government."[22] Strategically, this enabled Toomey to maximize his background as a small businessman and opponent of big government.

The benefits of multivariate testing are significant. The messages received by your broadest audience have already been adjusted to ensure the best action rate. This maximizes click-through and conversion, resulting in more money raised, more actions taken, and so on. The only real disadvantage is the amount of time it takes to test and send messages. The time constraints may place multivariate testing out of reach for smaller campaigns with less staff capacity. Ironically, it's these campaigns, due to their hunger for funds and support, that would most benefit from the approach.

Campaigns are increasingly making very sophisticated use of experimentation to hone their messages to have maximum impact. In 2012, the Obama campaign made extensive use of experimentation—both in tactics and in data. The insights the campaign gathered dramatically increased its success in web traffic, volunteer recruitment, and voter activation.[23]

The Modern Campaign Website

Emails typically drive supporters to the campaign's website for further information or activism opportunities. Presidential campaign platforms have become incredibly sophisticated—providing supporters with custom tools to generate maps for walking their neighborhoods or online phone banks that allow volunteers to work from home. These platforms can also serve as sophisticated nerve centers for the entire campaign. Michael Palmer, eCampaign director for John McCain in 2008, described the web platform as the nerve center through which all of the committee's field organization was run.[24] The platform allowed volunteers and field staff to feed all voter data into a centralized database, rather than multiple different systems.

On the Democratic side, MyBarackObama.com, used in 2008 and 2012, was recognized for its ability to organize, but more importantly for its ability to allow supporters to organize themselves. The campaign gave supporters the ability to create their own groups and freely coordinate amongst themselves.

The role of the campaign website is as much to gather data on supporters as it is to inform them of campaign activities. *The New York Times* noted the increasing role of campaign "stores" in the targeting of voters.[25] While campaigns have for years sold a limited amount of sloganeering merchandise in conjunction with their campaigns, the amount and variety have increased recently. Campaigns are looking at the data collected through the checkout process and learning about their buyers. For instance, a site visitor who picks up a campaign onesie for a baby may have a new child and be open to issue messaging targeted at parents. In this way, even the merchandise aspect of the website is built with multiple purposes.

How New Media Is Changing the Role of the Voter

The very nature of the voter is changing as campaign platforms and the Internet have become open platforms through which voters can direct their own activities. The line between producer and consumer of political messaging has become blurred, if it hasn't disappeared altogether. In early 2007, a young activist named Philip de Vellis created an Internet firestorm by creating a web video called Vote Different.[26] The ad was a mashup of Apple's "1984" ad mixed with campaign video of Hillary Clinton superimposed into the ad as the "big brother" figure. The video concluded with the Obama campaign logo and became an instant hit. That de Vellis had released the video under the pseudonym ParkRidge47 and hid his identity helped drive the rapid viral spread of the video. TechPresident organized the online political community in a digital manhunt to identify the video's anonymous creator.[27]

In the earliest days of the 2008 campaign, it was not a paid campaign spot that had the largest impact but a video whose creator says it took only a few short hours to make in his apartment on a Sunday afternoon. More importantly, though, de Vellis predicted the video would be just one of a coming wave of user-generated contributions to political messaging, saying, "There are thousands of other people who could have made this ad, and I guarantee that more ads like it—by people of all political persuasions—will follow."[28]

As if to punctuate de Vellis's prediction, in the 2012 campaign, a rogue videographer at a Mitt Romney event captured the candidate's comments that 47 percent of Americans were "dependent upon government . . . believe that they are victims . . . believe that government has a responsibility to care for them." Romney concluded that he would "never convince them that they should take personal responsibility and care for their lives."[29] The amateur video was given to *Mother Jones* and became possibly the single most impactful piece of content in the 2012 campaign.

It is exactly this challenge that campaigns are now concerned with addressing. The one-way campaign was easier than a two-way campaign. Campaigns controlled the messages voters heard. Voters had little or no ability to dramatically shift the campaign dynamic by creating content that forced campaigns to respond. The process favored candidates with money who could afford to spread their message via the best media.

Video, especially, is both a powerful tool and one that is now in the hands of campaigns and a large number of content creators looking to make a political point. The rise of YouTube has contributed to the downfall of more than a few candidates. In 2009, Virginia gubernatorial candidate Creigh Deeds was caught on tape trying to equivocate on tax increases.[30] The caricature of Deeds the video created was too much to overcome, and his Republican opponent won in a rout. The power of video is hard to overstate, and it is power that is in almost everyone's hands. Challenger campaigns, for example, are increasingly making the most of viral video in a bid to upset incumbents. In 2014, the upstart challenger to House Speaker John Boehner made a widely viewed ad mocking the Ohio Republican's last name in a spoof of erectile dysfunction medications. The ad talked about "electile" difficulty among other things.[31]

An Accidental Career

Like many people involved in politics, I became a campaign operative almost completely by accident. I had always been interested in politics and technology, but it wasn't until the 1994 campaign that I decided to get off the sidelines and into the game. Because of my background building, repairing, and using computers, in 1995, a former boss at the New Mexico GOP told me, "That thing called 'The Internet'—go figure that out." A copy of a "Teach Yourself HTML" book and time spent coding my first GOP website set the stage for a life spent trying to use the power of the web to elect Republicans. It's a career choice I'll never regret, and one I would highly recommend. The power of the Internet and technology will continue to change the way we connect to our elected officials. If you are technically inclined, harnessing that power to help shape our government is an amazing feeling.

Data Analytics Helps Online Voter Contact

Data analytics or "big data" (discussed extensively in Chapters 5 and 6) helps the online campaign target audiences for communication and voter contact. Cloud hosting allowed campaigns to create their own platforms accessible to field organizers. Centralization of tools the campaign uses for voter contact and allowing uploads and direct entry of data from the field have given campaigns more and better intelligence than ever with which to make decisions. Unfortunately, technology at the highest levels is quite often custom built and experimental. This has resulted in problems for campaigns on a scale previously unheard of as well. The Romney campaign in 2012 developed a platform called ORCA that was intended to compete with the Obama campaign's "Narwhal" system (killer whales are the only natural predator of the narwhal). This was an unprecedented effort to used technology to track tens of millions of voters on Election Day. While it failed in part (as discussed in Chapter 6), it did represent a massive change integrating both technology and traditional get-out-the-vote operations.

The Rise of Social Media Platforms

Nowhere is the power of the empowered voter more apparent than in the rise of social networks. Social networks and social sharing sites allow influential voters to curate their own content—creating, aggregating, and disseminating news and information to their circles of friends and contacts.

Sites like Facebook, Twitter, and YouTube bring friends together and make the sharing of political news easier. Users of Facebook, for instance, can create events, allowing supporters to organize themselves to conduct offline events or even just to repeat important news. Twitter, originally dubbed a "microblogging" service, provides a platform for rapid distribution of short-form news. The 140-character messages can be received via a variety of desktop and smartphone applications or as text messages. As of June 25, 2015, Twitaholic, which tracks online usage of Twitter, found that Hillary Clinton had 3.7 million followers ranking her 630th in the world. No other candidate was close. The top three Twitter accounts in terms of followers were Katy Perry (71 million), Justin Bieber (65 million), and Barack Obama (61 million).[32] While the campaign has just started, no candidate is likely to reach the level of followers achieved by President Obama both in the White House and as a candidate.

Twitter messages are grouped by conversational threads using a marking standard known as hashtags. Searching Twitter for these tags yields a nearly endless flow of information, discussion, and debate. So powerful are these threads in delineating the discussion that Facebook added support for hashtags to its status messages in 2013. Most social networks now support this threading. Campaigns have used hashtags to promote issue positions, to support candidates, and even to highlight events.

Social networks provide new opportunities for voters to engage with one another and to find new networks of supporters. These social networks have had two surprising outcomes. First, they have given rise to a new type of influential—call them social media mavens. These are people who attract large groups of followers, are seen as sources of news and information, and develop reputations for the quality of the information they curate. Second, these networks draw significant audiences composed of younger voters. More and more, these younger voters are eschewing traditional media (television, direct mail, and radio) and get much of their entertainment online.

In recent years, sites like Reddit, theCHIVE, and 9GAG have combined the features of social networks and content creation. These sites have given rise to a new type of political expression using images, brief video clips, and other content to carry political, often humorous, messages. When Marco Rubio delivered the GOP response to the president's State of the Union, a brief sip of water became the subject of mockery. Memes like the one here quickly circulated, making light of the senator.

As younger audiences move away from television viewing and focus on Internet consumption of media through alternative social media and content curation platforms, they are creating, sharing, and consuming more political messaging, but often it runs counter to the campaign's preferred messages.

It is also more difficult to reach these audiences with traditional ad buys. Direct mail has consistently lost audience as more and more junk mail fills our mailboxes. Efforts to cut through the clutter are marginally effective. A study for Rock the Vote found that technologically savvy voters were significantly less likely to respond to direct mail solicitations.[33]

As more voters raised on technology come of age, and replace voters comfortable with direct mail and television, the continuing shift to mixed-media appeals will become more critical. Social media sources will become increasingly important as voters look to online influentials for political news. As a result, effective marriage of cross-platform and targeted messaging could replace direct mail and television as the norm.

While social media is making communications easier and more direct, it is also creating unique challenges for campaigns. In the 2016 election, social media updates by paid advisers proved to be distracting, and damaging, to the campaigns of Scott Walker,[34] Donald Trump,[35] and Jeb Bush,[36] who were all forced to release staffers due to things they had previously posted online.

The Mobile Voter

Further complicating the modern campaign's effort to reach voters is the increasingly mobile nature of the populace. In 2016, campaigns are likely to spend more effort testing different messages to different audience segments on an ever-wider array of technologies. Campaign messages aimed at voters on platforms like Facebook and YouTube will be dramatically different from messages delivered via telephone and the mailbox, which will differ still from appeals delivered to mobile devices.

In addition to the challenges of delivering a message due to a mobile audience, voter turnout becomes increasingly challenging. Fortunately, mobile technologies also provide a wealth of opportunities for mobilization. For instance, pairing voter data with geolocation-aware applications can enable supporters to go door-to-door on their lunch hours by using a walk app to find the closest undecided voters. Supporters can also be empowered to find and connect with one another based on location data. As mentioned, hashtags allow campaign supporters to check in from campaign events—sharing their location, involvement with the campaign, and current activities with friends. These updates can be distributed via Twitter, Facebook, Snapchat, Instagram, and other social platforms to promote the event. This can help campaigns build support networks as studies routinely show the most effective voter contact is friend-to-friend. As voters check in to events, their activism is conveyed to everyone connected to them.

Mobile technologies like near-field communications and mobile payment systems will allow campaigns to receive donations at rallies or while going door-to-door, further increasing the amount campaigns can raise by removing even the website from the donation process. Applications could also connect mobile supporters with opportunities for activism based on their current coordinates. *Given the large majority of Americans using smartphones, most voters in this country could have such capability.*

The combination of technologies available to campaigns makes it easier than ever to reach voters, and just as easy for voters to engage with the campaign. These new applications are changing the way campaigns operate today, but also hold great promise for the future of campaigns.

The Online Future

The early online campaigns of the 1990s, discussed at the beginning of this chapter, were rudimentary by today's standards but seemed revolutionary at the time. Today's online campaigns, similarly, will look relatively uninteresting by the benchmark of future campaigns.

As campaigns innovate, the continuing convergence of technologies will likely make mobile the focal point of campaigns. It's no longer enough to simply try to reach voters. It will be critical to reach voters no matter where they are. Campaign offices will be supplemented with powerful mobile apps that make supporters an office unto themselves. Voter data, and the applications they power, will significantly change the way we communicate with, mobilize, and raise funds from supporters. These changes will impact not only the Internet but the traditional media we take for granted today—things like direct mail, television, and even the web.

Personalized Direct Mail

Direct mail today is typically anything but glamorous. If voters even bother to read their mail, the messages are often irrelevant. To appeal to the lowest common denominator, direct mail is generic and may have little personal impact for the recipient.

Personalized direct mail tied to Internet landing pages is changing the way campaigns use the postal service to reach voters. These messages contain tailored messages specific to individual voters. While the mail piece still qualifies for the bulk rate preferred by campaigns, each individual piece can contain different messages, different images, and a URL for a personalized landing page customized to the voter's issue preferences. On that landing page a web video tailored to match the voter's key issues will accompany an appeal to give, get active, or spread the word.

For instance, voters living next door to one another could get a mail piece that shared the same structure, image placement, and areas for copy. The two pieces of mail, however, could not be more different. The first voter would receive a message about military spending and support for our troops while the second would receive a message on tax cuts and economic issues. Each of the voters would see a message tailored to their interests, complete with custom landing pages tailored to what each user would want to see.

The direct mail piece may even contain a QR (quick response) code the recipient could scan to reach the web component. The union of offline formats with online technologies will create more engaging and highly relevant messaging for voters and invite them into the campaign, rather than push them away.

Toward Integration—Advertising across Platforms

In much the same way, political advertisers in the future will be able to target specific voters across platforms—delivering a consistent message regardless of the platform. Like direct mail, television currently delivers a message that broadcasts the same generic appeal to all viewers at once. An ad delivery system tied to the individual set-top box or addressable TV could deliver completely different ads to different televisions during the same program.

Cable television is working on new models that will do just that. By delivering advertising based on viewing habits of each voter in the household, a person watching the TV in the bedroom could be identified as a female over forty-five, while watching the TV in the bedroom is her nineteen-year-old son. If both are registered to vote, they may see completely different appeals—even if watching the same program on different televisions. By delivering specific messages to different members of the household, even as they consume the same content, campaigns will be able to target specific voters, while ignoring all others. If voter data indicate the mom in question is likely to vote Republican while her son would vote Democrat, the GOP candidate could reach the mom without potentially mobilizing her son to vote against him or her.

New developments in Internet-connected televisions could also allow viewers to "click through" from television programming to web-based content on the TV. The content would load alongside the program, allowing the viewers to browse information about the campaign without having to step away from their favorite shows.

Campaign communication strategies will be driven no longer by the media but by the audience. Voters will be matched to the media they consume. Young people, who are increasingly turning away from linear television, will be reached on platforms like Hulu or Facebook, while older voters may get highly targeted mail. More likely, the media used to reach voters will vary widely across archaic notions of age group, gender, or even party affiliation. All voters identified as likely supporters of a particular candidate, however, will see consistent messaging across all channels, tied to their personal profiles of interests. Through the marriage of big data and increasingly targetable ad and content platforms, campaigns are beginning to speak to the single voter rather than arbitrary groupings.

Will Candidate Websites Become Obsolete?

In the previous edition of this book, this question was posed, and the answer was a bit more optimistic. As social networks like Facebook continue to connect audiences on platforms that allow for fundraising, voter mobilization applications, and content sharing, some wonder whether candidates should even bother investing money in a website of their own. Given the adage "Go where the people are," it seemed that candidates might forgo the expense of developing and hosting (even through the cloud) their own platforms. The Pew Research Center estimates that 71 percent of Americans now use Facebook and 52 percent of online adults now use two or more social platforms.[37] With that many potential voters in one place, is there a need to drive them to a competing site?

While campaigns may be able to spend less time and money trying to attract supporters and more time working with supporters on centralized platforms to build networks of people to carry their messages, it is unlikely that campaigns will make the move to a social-only approach. In the past few years, many organizations have found their ability to control the messages on social sites often runs afoul of platform terms and conditions. Conservative pundit (and former congressman) Allen West went so far as suggesting that Facebook was actively censoring conservative messaging.[38] With open platforms connected to millions of voters, the possibilities are almost endless, but the possibility of an intermediary influencing your content will likely be too much for bigger organizations to bear.

Conclusion

While the role of digital has changed significantly over several cycles—moving from an added bonus for the campaign to an integrated piece of the operation—the importance of digital has grown exponentially. The modern campaign cannot exist without a strong digital effort that includes a number of disciplines. Marketing, analytics, voter mobilization, fundraising, and communications now rely heavily on staff with an understanding of, and appreciation for, digital tactics and tools. As campaigns continue to become more sophisticated, data-driven operations, this role will only continue to increase. Staff will be expected to know more about, and have experience with, digital skills. The level of knowledge about voters, their preferences, and what those preferences indicate about their propensity to vote will increase dramatically, as will efforts to find new and interesting ways to reach them.

Notes

1. Theodore H. White, *The Making of the President 1960* (New York: Atheneum House, 1961), 348.
2. "Youth Vote Influenced by Online Information" (Pew Internet and American Life Project, December 3, 2000); "The Internet and Campaign 2010" (Pew Internet and American Life Project, March 17, 2001). Accessed on May 24, 2011, from pewinternet.org.
3. Amy Mitchell, Jeffrey Gottfried, and Katerina Eva Matsa, "Millennials and Political News" (Pew Research Center Journalism Project, June 1, 2015).
4. Search of Usenet's net.politics thread courtesy of Google Archive at groups.google .com. Accessed on May 30, 2011.
5. 1996 presidential websites. Accessed on June 1, 2011, from 4president.us/1996websites .htm.
6. Paul Boutin, "Grand Old Protest: A Republican Web Site Even Bush-bashers Can Love" (*Slate*, January 24, 2003). Accessed on June 1, 2011, from www.slate.com.
7. Garrett Graf, "The Dean Campaign Finds Treasure on the Internet: Lessons for the Social Sector Change" (November 2004). Accessed on June 2, 2011, from proxied .changemakers.net/journal.
8. "2012 Election: Visitors to Barack Obama's Campaign Site 2011–2012" (*Statista*, August 2, 2015).
9. Byron Tau, "Obama Campaign Final Fundraising Total: $1.1 Billion" (*Politico*, January 19, 2013).

10. Arlette Sands, "Rand Paul Is Turning Out to Be 2016's Troller-in-Chief" (*ABC News,* January 29, 2015). Accessed on June 24, 2015, from abcnews.go.com.

11. Donald J. Trump tweet (August 2, 2015). Accessed on October 9, 2015, from https://twitter.com/realdonaldtrump/status/627841345789558788.

12. Aaron Smith, "Cell Phones, Social Media and Campaign 2014" (Pew Research Center Internet, Science & Technology Project, November 3, 2014).

13. Aaron Smith, "U.S. Smartphone Use in 2015" (Pew Research Center Internet & American Life Project, April 1, 2015).

14. Danyl Bosomworth, "Mobile Marketing Statistics 2015" (*Smart Insights,* July 22, 2015).

15. Michael Scherer, "Exclusive: Obama's 2012 Digital Fundraising Outperformed 2008" (*Time,* November 15, 2012). Accessed August 2, 2015, from http://swampland.time.com/2012/11/15/exclusive-obamas-2012-digital-fundraising-outperformed-2008/.

16. Obama Campaign email (October 22, 2008). Accessed on June 2, 2011, from barackobama.com.

17. Nate Ryan, "Rick Santorum Campaign to Sponsor Daytona 500 Underdog" (*USA Today,* February 25, 2012) Accessed August 2, 2015, from http://usatoday30.usatoday.com/sports/motor/nascar/story/2012-02-25/Rick-Santorum-campaign-to-be-Daytona-500-sponsor/53241258/1.

18. Nick Wing, "Rick Perry Sponsors NASCAR Driver: Texas Governor's Campaign Teams Up with Bobby Labonte" (*The Huffington Post,* June 6, 2010). Accessed August 2 2015, from http://www.huffingtonpost.com/2010/04/06/rick-perry-sponsors-nasca_n_527248.html.

19. Francisco Alvarado, "Kendrick Meek Supports NASCAR, but Speedway Owners Back Charlie Crist" (*Miami New Times,* February 9, 2010). Accessed August 2, 2015, from http://www.miaminewtimes.com/news/kendrick-meek-supports-nascar-but-speedway-owners-back-charlie-crist-6523276.

20. Declan McCullagh, "Obama Ad Appears in Xbox 360 Car Racing Game" (*CNET,* October 14, 2008). Accessed August 2, 2015, from http://www.cnet.com/news/obama-ad-appears-in-xbox-360-car-racing-game/.

21. Ed Kilgore, "Obama Isn't Working" (*The Washington Monthly,* April 20, 2012). Accessed August 2, 2015), from http://www.washingtonmonthly.com/political-animal-a/2012_04/obama_isnt_working036812.php.

22. See toomeyforsenate.com. Accessed on August 3, 2011.

23. Sasha Issenberg, "The Definitive Story of How President Obama Mined Voter Data to Win a Second Term" (*MIT Technology Review,* December 19, 2012). Accessed August 2, 2015, from http://www.technologyreview.com/featuredstory/509026/how-obamas-team-used-big-data-to-rally-voters/.

24. Michael Palmer, Director, Intell360. Interview conducted April 11, 2011, Washington, D.C.

25. Vanessa Friedman, "Presidential Hopefuls Sell Swag and Collect Data" (*The New York Times,* June 24, 2015). Accessed August 2, 2015, from http://www.nytimes.com/2015/06/25/fashion/presidential-campaign-stores-voter-data.html.

26. Phillip de Vellis, "Vote Different" (March 5, 2007). Accessed on May 27, 2011, from youtube.com.

27. Micah L. Sifry, "Who Is ParkRidge47?" (March 7, 2007). Accessed on June 2, 2011, from techpresident.com.

28. Phillip de Vellis, "I Made the 'Vote Different' Ad" (*The Huffington Post*, March 21, 2007). Accessed on August 3, 2011, from huffingtonpost.com.

29. David Corn, "SECRET VIDEO: Romney Tells Millionaire Donors What He REALLY Thinks of Obama Voters" (*Mother Jones*, September 17, 2012). Accessed August 2, 2015, from http://www.motherjones.com/politics/2012/09/secret-video-romney-private-fundraiser.

30. Vagoptv.com, "Deeds on the Ropes on Taxes" (September 17, 2009). Accessed on June 4, 2011, from youtube.com.

31. Darren Samuelsohn, "Got Viral Videos?" (*Politico*, October 7, 2014). Accessed August 2, 2015, from http://www.politico.com/story/2014/10/viral-ads-2014-elections-111639.html.

32. Twitaholic.com. Accessed on June 25, 2015.

33. "Keeping Young Voters Engaged: 2007–2008 Re-Registration Test Program." Accessed on June 3, 2011, from rockthevote.org.

34. Nick Gass, "Walker Digital Strategist Quits after Tweets Critical of Iowa" (*Politico*, March 18, 2015). Accessed August 2, 2015, from http://www.politico.com/story/2015/03/liz-mair-scott-walker-iowa-116174.html.

35. Igor Bobic, "Donald Trump Campaign Fires Staffer after Racially Charged Posts Surface: The GOP Front-runner Suffers a Setback" (*The Huffington Post*, August 2, 2015). Accessed August 2, 2015, from http%3A%2F%2Fwww.huffingtonpost.com%2Fentry%2Fdonald-trump-sam-nunberg_55be3bd0e4b06363d5a27f5a.

36. Philip Rucker, "Jeb Bush's Chief Technology Officer Resigns after Racially Insensitive Comments" (*The Washington Post*, February 10, 2015). Accessed August 2, 2015, from http://www.washingtonpost.com/news/post-politics/wp/2015/02/10/jeb-bushs-chief-technology-officer-resigns-after-racially-insensitive-comments/.

37. Maeve Duggan, Nicole B. Ellison, Cliff Lampe, Amanda Lenhart, and Mary Madden, "Social Media Update 2014" (Pew Research Center Internet, Science & Technology Project, January 9, 2015). Accessed August 2, 2015, from http://www.pewinternet.org/2015/01/09/social-media-update-2014/.

38. Allen West, "Is Facebook Censoring Conservative Content?" (March 10, 2014). Accessed on August 2, 2015, from http://allenbwest.com/2014/03/facebook-censoring-conservative-content/.

CHAPTER 5

Survey Research and Campaigns— Getting to the Future

Candice J. Nelson

IT IS PERHAPS IRONIC THAT A PROFESSION that asks questions for a living is struggling with what questions to ask about its future. Survey research continues to confront questions it has faced for now almost a decade. How to incorporate cell phones into a practice that has relied on landline phones for over forty years? Should survey respondents be contacted by random digit dialing, again, the practice for decades, or should voter files be used? What is the role of online surveys? Should interactive voice response surveys, often referred to as robocalls, be incorporated into surveys? In addition to these ongoing questions, new questions have arisen. How do modeling and "big data" fit into survey research? What is the role of social media? With more and more people using mobile devices as their basic mode of communication, how do mobile devices mesh with survey research?

The Role of Phones in Survey Research

Phones have long been the basic means by which survey research has been conducted. While most campaign pollsters still agree that phones are preferable to online surveys, the use of phones for campaign surveys has become more complicated over the past decade. As cell phones, answering machines, and caller ID have proliferated, respondents have become increasingly difficult to reach by phone. As a result, survey research has become more expensive for campaigns, which start with, in most instances, limited resources. This is especially difficult for congressional candidates, particularly challengers, on tight budgets.

According to the most recent national health interview survey by the National Center for Health Statistics, 45 percent of Americans live in households that are cell phone only, and another 42 percent of Americans have both a landline and a cell phone.[1] Only 8 percent of Americans have only a landline phone.[2] The percentage of Americans with only cell phones increased 4.4 percent between December 2013 and December 2014,[3] and every indication is that the cell-only population will continue to grow.[4]

Moreover, cell phone ownership varies by demographic group, including two demographic groups particularly important to campaigns: younger people and Latinos. In December 2014, 58 percent of eighteen- to twenty-four-year-olds and almost 70 percent (69.2) of twenty-five- to twenty-nine-year-olds were cell only, compared to just 17 percent of Americans sixty-five and older. Fifty-eight percent of Latinos were cell-only users, compared to 40 percent of whites.[5]

Campaign pollsters need to include cell-only or cell-mostly users in surveys to get a complete picture of the electorate, but the question pollsters face is what percentage of the survey should be cell phone users. Some campaign pollsters did not begin to include cell phone use until 2012, and then in some cases the percentage of cell users included in the survey was only 20 percent, which some pollsters concede was too low,[6] and might explain why some campaign pollsters thought the presidential election was closer going into Election Day than the actual results of the election. Expectations are that in 2016, cell phones will need to be 40–45 percent of any sample.[7]

Polling organizations apart from campaigns are including cell phone users as even larger parts of their samples. The Pew Research Center announced in January 2015 that 65 percent of its national telephone surveys in 2015 would be cell phone based, compared to 60 percent in 2014 and just 25 percent when Pew first started including cell phones in its surveys in 2008.[8] The University of Michigan's Surveys of Consumers are 100 percent cell only as of 2015.[9]

Challenges with Phone Surveys

Pollsters face increasing challenges in using phones in survey research. First, the proliferation of answering machines and caller ID has greatly increased the number of calls pollsters need to get a completed sample. With a typical response rate of between 8 and 12 percent,[10] estimates are that pollsters need to call ten times the number of phones needed to get a sufficient sample size. This only increases the expense of using phones. The problem for campaigns is this increases the costs of survey research, a needed part of any campaign.

The increasing use of cell phones in surveys also increases the costs of surveys. Landline phones may be called using automated dialing mechanisms, so-called computer-assisted telephone interviews (CATI). However, federal law prohibits automated dialing of cell phone numbers, so calling cell phones is 50 percent more expensive than calling landline phones.[11] Also, cell phones are the most efficient way to reach younger survey respondents, but it can be hard to get their cell phone numbers. Often they are still on their parents' family plan, so the only name available to survey researchers belongs to the primary plan holder, not the younger people also on the plan.[12]

Cell phones provide other complications. With landline phones, when a respondent answers a call, the pollster knows the respondent is at his or her residence. A cell phone respondent could be anywhere. While callers are trained to ask respondents if they are someplace where they can safely or conveniently answer the call, there is no way to measure what distractions may be affecting the respondent.

Additional problems with cell phones are that area codes of cell phone numbers do not necessarily match particular geographic jurisdictions. Landline area codes represent specific physical geographies, but cell phone numbers migrate as individuals move from one area of the country to another. Again, this is a particular problem for reaching younger respondents, as the area codes of their cell phones may be the area codes where they grew up, but not where they currently reside.

Finally, cell phones pose problems for the survey instrument itself. Cell phone calls are difficult for message testing, a key part of campaign surveys. Cell phone calls need to be shorter, and often message testing involves longer and more complicated questions.

Random Digit Dialing or Voter Files

Since phone surveys became the primary means by which surveys were conducted, random digit dialing (RDD) was the practice by which pollsters reached voters. However, given the problems with reaching voters by phone, campaign pollsters have increasingly turned to voter files. Voter files are lists of registered voters that are compiled by state election officials and then enhanced to include information about past voting history and other available information about voters. The consensus among most campaign pollsters is that, with the possible exception of national surveys, voter files are the best practice for reaching survey respondents. First, by definition, only those eligible to vote—registered voters—are on the voter file. One caveat to this, of course, is that in states that allow Election Day registration, voters who register on Election Day are not on the voter file. Second, because information on past vote history—has the voter participated in both primary and general elections, or is he or she a less frequent voter?—is on the file, those questions do not need to be asked in the survey itself. Also, voter files contain demographic information, such as date of birth (age), often gender, and in some states race and ethnicity, so again these are questions that don't need to be asked in the survey. Increasingly, consumer data are also appended to the voter file. Finally, starting with the Help America Vote Act in 2002, voter lists have generally[13] become more accurate and are updated frequently,[14] making voter files a more efficient way to reach potential voters.

Interactive Voice Response Surveys

Interactive voice response (IVR) surveys, so-called robocalls, have become more prevalent, and campaign pollsters are divided on whether or not to use them for campaign purposes. One argument against IVR surveys is that because they are entirely computer generated, there is no way to know who is actually responding to the survey. Another problem is that with live surveys, interviewers can use techniques to keep respondents on the phone. With a computer-generated survey, that is not possible. Further, because IVR calls are by definition computer generated, they cannot be used to call cell phones, thus excluding the increasing cell-only population from the surveys. IVR surveys also do not work well for message testing. However, some campaign pollsters think that there is a role for IVR surveys in campaigns, particularly for a short survey with only a few questions.[15] IVR surveys are less expensive than live surveys, so, given the increasing costs of surveys, campaign pollsters are giving increasing consideration to what role they might play in campaigns.

Mobile Devices

As more and more Americans receive information on mobile devices, the question arises as to what role mobile devices will play in campaign surveys. Surveys by the Pew Research Center found that in 2015, 64 percent of American adults owned a smartphone—almost double the percentage of Americans, 35 percent, who owned a smartphone just four years before.[16] Moreover, 7 percent of Americans have a smartphone but no broadband service or other readily available means to access the Internet.[17] Those Americans most reliant on smartphones tend to be younger and non-white. Fifteen percent of Americans eighteen to twenty-nine are heavily reliant on smartphones, and 12 percent of African Americans and 13 percent of Latinos are heavily dependent on smartphones, compared with 4 percent of whites.[18]

While the percentage of the population that is dependent on smartphones for Internet access is still relatively small, the fact that those most reliant on mobile devices are younger and minorities poses challenges for campaigns. Just as cell phone–only use has increased over time, it is likely that smartphone-only use will also increase in the next few years. To the extent that some parts of the population can be reached only on a smartphone, this poses logistical challenges for campaigns. For example, different mobile devices have different platforms, so surveys have to be tested to make sure they work across platforms. Also, some of the questions that plague calling cell phones also apply to mobile devices. An American Association for Public Opinion Research (AAPOR) task force on mobile technologies points out suggestions for dealing with surveys on mobile devices: "[e]nsuring that the respondent is in a safe location (i.e, not driving) and that they are able to speak or utilize the data entry features of mobile data-collection privately."[19] Even then, there are still questions about what distractions respondents answering a survey on a mobile device might face. Another challenge facing surveys on mobile devices is that they need to be short, given the limitations presented by a smaller screen. "Respondents are used to making regular but brief uses of their smartphones (e.g., texting, looking up directions, scrolling through apps). Thus shorter surveys fit more naturally with the way in which the devices are normally utilized."[20] There are also ethical considerations in the use of mobile devices, particularly with respect to privacy. The AAPOR task force highlights some of these—for example, "[t]he use of GPS to identify a respondent's location and track their movements. Location is a form of personally identifying information because it is a part of the respondent's physical context. Likewise, the collection of visual data via mobile devices raises some new challenges for researchers, such as the risk of inadvertent exposure of personally identifiable information; location identification via geotags embedded in many digital picture files these days; or, the chance that others, who have not given consent for the study, are captured directly or indirectly in the background of the photo."[21] A recent study commissioned by the AAPOR concluded that "the mobile world is a messy one from a measurement perspective, with differential coverage and usage across the population and various platforms being accessed by these individuals."[22]

Online Surveys

As Internet usage has become almost ubiquitous, the question of using online surveys for campaign research has become more and more of an issue. Eighty-seven percent of American adults use the Internet, and for some populations—those living in households that earn $75,000 or more, eighteen- to twenty-nine-year-olds, and those with college degrees—Internet usage is virtually universal.[23] However, most campaign pollsters are still hesitant to use online surveys, for two main reasons. One, online surveys are not random, and two, the size of online panels for anything other than national surveys is too small. While some online survey companies such as GfK and YouGov have made great strides in trying to randomize online surveys, campaign pollsters are still not convinced that online surveys are random enough for their needs. Online surveys involve panels of people who have agreed to participate in the surveys, usually for some token material compensation. The lack of randomness and the concerns about "professional panel respondents" continue to concern campaign pollsters. Also, campaign surveys need quick turnarounds, and that is not necessarily the case with Internet surveys. In addition, despite the prevalence of Internet access for most Americans, there are still concerns that some populations, particularly those who are poorer or older, are still not online in large enough proportions to be represented accurately in a survey.[24]

It is also not clear how responses may vary to questions asked in online surveys and questions asked in phone surveys. For example, online surveys may provide a don't know/not sure option, but phone surveys typically do not. Longer questions with multiple responses may be easier to understand in an online survey, where the respondent has time to read and think about the question and responses, than in a phone survey. Alternatively, without an interviewer asking questions, respondents may go through an online survey quickly, without taking time to consider their responses, a practice known as speeding.[25] To guard against the latter, some pollsters discard online surveys completed in less than the expected time.[26] To do this, a survey research firm would pretest the interview internally to get a mean and a range for time, to set researchers' expectations, and then put the survey in "soft launch" (the same sample is used, and the interviews "count," but a cutoff/temporary stop is set at perhaps fifty interviews). If the total number of respondents is 500, it is typical for a soft launch to be 5–10 percent of the total. Then the researcher reviews the partial data from those fifty soft launch interviews. The mean and range for time in the soft launch would be compared to the internal pretest for consistency. That provides some hard data to establish what constitutes a "speeder" for a particular project. While there is no hard rule, it is typical to define a speeder as anyone who takes less than 50–60 percent of the mean. So, for example, if the mean is eighteen minutes, a speeder might be defined as anyone who completes the survey in less than ten minutes (55 percent of the mean).[27]

During the summer of 2014, the Pew Research Center conducted a study to see if the mode of the interview—self-administered (online) or interviewer-administered (phones)—affected responses. The results showed significant differences in responses for two types of questions important to campaigns: responses to questions about discrimination faced by blacks, Latinos, and gays and lesbians, and responses to ratings of political figures. For both sets of questions, "social desirability" responses were more prevalent in phone surveys than in online surveys.

Ratings of political figures were more negative in online surveys than in phone surveys. For example, among online respondents, 53 percent who identified themselves as Republican or leaning Republican had a very unfavorable view of Hillary Clinton, compared with 36 percent of phone respondents.[28] Mode differences existed for other political figures, such as Michelle Obama, Sarah Palin, George W. Bush, and Harry Reid. In all instances, online respondents were more likely than phone respondents to report viewing the political figures unfavorably.[29]

These mode differences also existed in questions about discrimination against blacks, Latinos, and gays and lesbians. In all cases, phone respondents were more likely to say that each group faced a lot of discrimination.[30] The differences between phone and online respondents were 14 percent for gays and lesbians, 12 percent for Latinos, and 10 percent for blacks.[31] As campaigns consider the relative advantages and disadvantages of online and phone surveys, the differences in online and phone responses to questions, which may seem to have politically correct answers, may be important in assessing the accuracy of the responses.

One area of survey research where some campaign pollsters feel more comfortable venturing online is focus groups. A typical focus group involves recruiting ten to twelve potential voters, usually a targeted voting group for a campaign, to meet for a few hours to discuss issues of importance to the campaign. In-person focus groups involve the costs of recruiting and reimbursing participants, the travel expenses of the focus group moderator, and the cost of the focus group facility itself. Online focus groups are less expensive, often one-third the cost of an in-person focus group,[32] thus saving the campaign valuable resources. Yet some campaign pollsters still prefer in-person focus groups because of the dynamics of an in-person focus group and the ability to have more control over the discussion.[33]

Microtargeting, Modeling, Big Data, and Campaigns

Beginning with the Republican Party following the 2000 presidential election, microtargeting has played an increasing role in elections. Microtargeting involves using consumer data, appended to voter files, to more precisely target individual voters. As the amount of information in these databases has increased, researchers have been able to use sophisticated algorithms to model the behavior of individuals. For example, there can be turnout models that allow everyone on a voter file to be given a specific likelihood of voting, between 1 and 100 percent. There are models of partisanship, issue preferences, and ideological preferences, to name just a few.

The Obama campaign in 2012 successfully used modeling and large data sets for fundraising, media buys, and voter registration and turnout. One of the senior advisers said:

> The new megafile didn't just tell the campaign how to find voters and get their attention; it also allowed the number crunchers to run tests predicting which types of people would be persuaded by certain kinds of appeals. Call lists in field offices, for instance, didn't just list names and numbers; they also ranked names in order of their persuadability, with the campaign's most important priorities first. About 75% of the determining factors were basics like age, sex, race, neighborhood and voting record. Consumer data about voters helped round out the picture. We could [predict] people who were going to give online. We could model people who were going to give through mail. We could model volunteers. . . . In the end, modeling became something way bigger for us in '12 than in '08 because it made our time more efficient.

The analytics team used four streams of polling data to build a detailed picture of voters in key states. In the past month, said one official, "the analytics team had polling data from about 29,000 people in Ohio alone—a whopping sample that composed nearly half of 1% of all voters there—allowing for deep dives into exactly where each demographic and regional group was trending at any given moment."[34]

The Democratic Party continued to develop its analytics program during the 2014 elections. Led by the Democratic Senatorial Campaign Committee (DSCC), the party developed the Bannock Street Project to incorporate the Obama campaign's 2012 get-out-the-vote techniques into the 2014 electorate.[35]

While the Republicans were outdone on data analytics in the 2012 presidential election, Republican operatives have begun to take steps to correct that for the 2016 elections. An organization called the Center for Strategic Initiatives (CSI) began meeting informally in late 2013 to discuss how data analytics could be used by Republicans. Blaise Hazelwood, the founder of CSI and a key player in the Republican Party's 72-Hour Project following the 2000 presidential election, explains the goal of CSI: "After 2004 the drive just left. It was no longer there—we no longer did the testing and we ended up where we ended up in 2012. We just kind of stopped. It was terribly frustrating after 2012 to see what happened, and know we needed to get back to testing, and having that housed in one place to help all conservatives."[36] Hazelwood explained the difference between the 72-Hour Project and the Republican Party's current initiative. "Back then we framed it completely differently. It was, 'We're getting back to grassroots and showing why grassroots works.' Now it's about tests, and getting to test return on investment and how you measure efficiency and effectiveness."[37]

As modeling has become more prevalent, the question has arisen as to how modeling fits with survey research. If models can predict turnout and partisanship, do these questions still need to be asked in surveys? Or, more generally, given the amount of data now available, is there still a role for traditional polling?

Campaign pollsters think modeling will play an increasingly important role in surveys in the future.[38] If models can predict a potential voter's likelihood of voting, participation questions will not need to be asked in surveys. If modeling can predict the likelihood of voting for a particular candidate, the "horse race question"— if the election were held today, would you vote for candidate A or candidate B?— no longer needs to be asked. Modeling also can address the problem with contacting voters in Election Day registration states. While the voters are not on the voter file, modeling allows campaigns to predict both likelihood of voting and likely partisan support. However, pollsters also believe that there will continue to be a need for survey research. Benchmark polls at the beginning of campaigns will still be important, as will surveys to test messages.

Social Media

The percentage of Americans using social media increases each year. A study by the Pew Research Center in September 2014 found that 52 percent of adult American Internet users use two or more social media sites.[39] While Facebook continues to be the most popular social media site—71 percent of Internet users use Facebook—that percentage did not increase between 2013 and 2014, except among Americans sixty-five years and older; in 2014, 56 percent of these older Internet users reported using Facebook.[40] Twitter, LinkedIn, Pinterest, and Instagram all saw increased use between 2013 and 2014.[41] With the continued growth in the use of social media, the question arises as to what role social media might play in survey research.

The AAPOR Task Force on Emerging Technologies in Public Opinion Research explored that question. One problem in using social media for public opinion data collection is its lack of randomness, the same problem that faces online data collection. The AAPOR task force concluded that "to date, there has been little progress in attempts to show how data collected through the use of social-media sites can represent the general population."[42] Because political campaigns are still reluctant to use nonprobability surveys, social media at present is not feasible for campaign surveys, apart from, as the AAPOR task force pointed out, "to derive qualitative insights for pretesting purposes [for example, for questionnaire design, to provide insights into potential survey topics], and for a recruiting resource for nonprobability surveys."[43] A study by the Pew Research Center reached a similar conclusion when looking at using Facebook for research. "The nature of Facebook as a mostly private network limits what can be learned from it."[44] Social media also present ethical concerns. The Pew study concluded that "even with just publicly available data, researchers face ethical and privacy concerns when deciding what to publish."[45]

The Future of Survey Research and Campaigns

The one thing campaign pollsters agree on is that there are serious questions about how survey research will be conducted in the future. One pollster interviewed for this project suggested that there may be one more cycle of traditional survey research, but by 2020, there will be a "completely different way we collect data."[46] But no one has really good answers or a vision of what survey research will look like in the next five or ten years. Cell phones will increasingly become an important part of survey research, and eventually they will probably be the only phones used in surveys. Internet research may eventually be the way surveys are conducted, but for the past ten years, Internet surveys have been seen as something in the future, and that is still the way they are seen. Some campaign pollsters expect there to be multimodal surveys, with a mixture of phones and Internet, yet others worry about the validity of such multimodal surveys, because some things that can be done online can't be replicated with phones, and vice versa. It seems likely that using data to model voter contact will be an integral part of campaigns going forward. In an interview with Dan Balz, a political reporter with *The Washington Post*, following the 2012 election, Mitt Romney described how his campaign's reliance on polls led the campaign to misunderstand what happened on Election Day. "We were looking at our own poll numbers, and there were two things we believed. . . . We believed that some of the polls that showed me not winning were just simply wrong, because they showed that there was going to be more turnout from African American voters, for instance, than had existed in 2008. We said no way, absolutely no way."[47] The Obama campaign used sophisticated algorithms to project voter choice and turnout, and came much closer to understanding the electorate in 2012.

In the final stretch of the 2014 Senate elections, most political operatives thought that control of the Senate was still up for grabs. Public polls showed close races in Kansas, Kentucky, Iowa, North Carolina, and Georgia. In two of those states, Kansas and Kentucky, it looked as though a Democrat might defeat long-term Republican incumbents Senator Pat Roberts and Senator Minority Leader Mitch McConnell. On Election Day, Republicans won in all five states, and in all but North Carolina, by comfortable margins. While there are many factors that affected the outcomes of those races, and others in 2014, uncertainties about how to conduct accurate polls likely played a role.

The accuracy of polls will also play a role in the 2016 presidential elections. With a crowded Republican field for the nomination, sponsors of the early Republican debates announced that the criteria for being invited to participate in the debates would include standing in public opinion polls. Both Fox News and CNN, sponsors of the first two debates, planned to limit participation to only the top ten candidates in an average of national public opinion polls. The irony is that with concerns about how to best survey Americans greater than they have been in decades, the first glimpses of the Republican field of candidates together will be determined by public opinion polls, some of which will use the techniques questioned in this chapter.

Cell phones, modeling, Internet, mobile, and social media are likely to play a role in how survey research is conducted over the next several election cycles. There are a lot of questions for a profession that asks questions, but very few answers. In the meantime, despite all the questions about the future of survey research—online, mobile, social media—the merging of traditional surveys, though now with cell phones and voter files, with modeling is likely the immediate future.

Notes

1. Stephen J. Blumberg and Julian V. Lake, "Wireless Substitution: Early Release of Estimates from the National Health Interview Survey, July–December, 2014" (U.S. Department of Health and Human Resources, Centers for Disease Control and Prevention, National Center for Health Statistics, Released June 2015).
2. Blumberg and Lake, "Wireless Substitution."
3. Blumberg and Lake, "Wireless Substitution."
4. The cell-only population increased from 34 percent in December 2011 to 45.4 percent in December 2014. Blumberg and Lake, "Wireless Substitution."

5. Blumberg and Lake, "Wireless Substitution."

6. Off-the-record conversation with someone familiar with polling in the 2012 election, April 2015.

7. Interviews with Glen Bolger, Founding Partner, Public Opinion Strategies, April 24, 2015, and Molly O'Rourke, Executive in Residence, School of Communication, American University, April 14, 2015.

8. Scott Keeter and Kyley McGeeney, "Pew Research Will Call More Cellphones in 2015" (Pew Research Center, January 7, 2015).

9. Keeter and McGeeney, "Pew Research Will Call More Cellphones in 2015."

10. Interview with Molly O'Rourke, April 2015. Scott Keeter, Comments on Keeter and McGeeney, January 2015.

11. Keeter and McGeeney, January 2015.

12. Randy Guthermuth, Chief Operating Officer, American Viewpoint, Presentation to the Campaign Management Institute, American University, May 12, 2015.

13. Some campaign pollsters suggest that while voter files in states with competitive partisan elections are quite accurate and updated often, voter files in solidly Democratic and Republican states are less accurate and not updated as frequently. Interview with Molly O'Rourke, April 2015.

14. Drew Desilver, "Facing Challenges, Pollsters Broaden Experiments with New Methodologies" (Pew Research Center, November 24, 2014).

15. Interview with Tom Bonier, CEO, Target Smart Communications, January 9, 2015.

16. Aaron Smith, "U.S. Smartphone Use in 2015" (Pew Research Center, April 1, 2015).

17. Smith, "U.S. Smartphone Use in 2015."

18. Smith, "U.S. Smartphone Use in 2015."

19. Michael W. Link, Joe Murphy, Michael F. Schober, Trent Buskirk, Jennifer Hunter Childs, and Casey Langer Tesfaye, "Mobile Devices for Conducting, Augmenting and Potentially Replacing Surveys: Executive Summary of the AAPOR Task Force on Emerging Technologies in Public Opinion Research" (*Public Opinion Quarterly*, Vol. 78, No. 4, Winter 2014), 782.

20. Link et al., "Mobile Devices for Conducting, Augmenting and Potentially Replacing Surveys," 782.

21. Link et al., "Mobile Devices for Conducting, Augmenting and Potentially Replacing Surveys," 785.

22. Link et al., "Mobile Devices for Conducting, Augmenting and Potentially Replacing Surveys," 781.

23. Ninety-nine percent of those living in households that earn $75,000 or more, 97 percent of eighteen- to twenty-nine-year-olds, and 97 percent of those with a college education use the Internet. Susannah Fox, "The Web at 25 in the U.S." (Pew Research Center, February 17, 2014).

24. Interview with Scott Keeter, April 20, 2015.

25. Robert Greszki, Marco Meyer, and Harald Schoen, "Exploring the Effects of 'Too Fast' Responses and Respondents in Web Surveys" (*Public Opinion Quarterly*, Vol. 79, No. 2), 472.

26. Interview with Molly O'Rourke, April 2015.

27. Email from Molly O'Rourke, July 19, 2015.

28. "From Telephone to the Web: The Challenge of Mode of Interview Effects in Public Opinion Polls" (Pew Research Center, May 13, 2015).

29. "From Telephone to the Web," May 2015.

30. "From Telephone to the Web," May 2015.

31. "From Telephone to the Web," May 2015.

32. Interview with Molly O'Rourke, April 2015.

33. Interview with Molly O'Rourke, April 2015.

34. Michael Scherer, "How Obama's Data Crunchers Helped Him Win" (CNN, November 8, 2012). Accessed on October 11, 2015, from http://www.cnn.com/2012/11/07/tech/web/obama-campaign-tech-team/index.html.

35. Ed Kilgore, *Election 2014: Why the Republicans Swept the Midterms* (University of Pennsylvania Press, 2015), 14–15.

36. Sasha Issenberg, "Inside the GOP's Effort to Close the Campaign-Science Gap with Democrats" (*Bloomberg Politics*, July 8, 2015). Accessed on October 11, 2015, from http://www.bloomberg.com/politics/features/2015-07-08/inside-the-gop-s-effort-to-close-the-campaign-science-gap-with-democrats.

37. Issenberg, "Insider the GOP's Effort to Close the Campaign-Science Gap with Democrats."

38. Interview with Tom Bonier, January 9, 2015; Interview with Bob Carpenter, President, Chesapeake Beach Consulting, January 9, 2015.

39. Maeve Duggan, Nicole Ellison, Cliff Lampe, Amanda Lenhart, and Mary Madden, "Social Media Update 2014" (Pew Research Center, January 9, 2015).

40. Duggan et al., "Social Media Update 2014."

41. Duggan et al., "Social Media Update 2014."

42. Joe Murphy, Michael Link, Jennifer Hunter Childs, Casey Langer Tesfaye, Elizabeth Dean, Michael Stern, Josh Pasek, Jon Cohen, Mario Callegaro, and Paul Harwood, "Social Media in Public Opinion Research: Executive Summary of the AAPOR Task Force on Emerging Technologies in Public Opinion Research" (*Public Opinion Quarterly*, Vol. 78, No. 4, Winter 2014), 791.

43. Murphy et al., "Social Media in Public Opinion Research," 792–793.

44. Kenneth Olmstead, "The Challenges of Using Facebook for Research" (Pew Research Center, March 16, 2015).

45. Olmstead, "The Challenges of Using Facebook for Research."

46. Interview with Bob Carpenter, January 2015.

47. Dan Balz, *Collision 2012: Obama vs. Romney and the Future of Elections in America* (Viking, 2013), 345.

CHAPTER 6

Voter Mobilization — The Future Is Now

Richard J. Semiatin

AN ORCA IS KNOWN AS A KILLER WHALE. The Romney presidential campaign of 2012 named its Election Day get-out-the-vote operation "ORCA" because it believed that it had neutralized the Obama campaign's technological advantage from 2008 with a powerful, integrated, and state-of-the-art system to identify key voting groups to help Mitt Romney win the election. Instead, the leviathan called ORCA crashed on Election Day. Romney spokesperson Andrea Saul related that "ORCA was . . . the game-changer that would blow even the Obama campaign's sophisticated GOTV (get-out-the-vote) system out of the water."[1] Instead, the app that was supposed to provide data lists for campaign workers in the field on Election Day was difficult to download and finally crashed at about 4 p.m. on Election Day.[2] By the 2014 midterm election, Republicans had solved their dilemma by out-distancing Democrats (who had a decade-long advantage) in getting-out-the-vote for Senate, House, and gubernatorial races.

ORCA reminds all campaigns that get-out-the-vote operations can easily be plagued with problems. Even in a well-planned GOTV operation, as first utilized by the Obama campaign in 2008, there were technical problems. Yet, "the Obama campaign built an unprecedented network of support, which included an e-mail list with 10 million names and cell phone numbers, [and] had . . . 1.5 million active volunteers."[3] With ever-increasingly sophisticated technology, humans still plan and operate such programs. The size and scope of such operations have become mammoth today and involve thousands of workers on the state level and millions on a national-level campaign for president.

Getting voters to the polls mean that campaigns are using new technology and traditional GOTV tactics to get voters to the polls. How this is being accomplished differs dramatically from the past.

Up until recent decades, political parties served as the engine to deliver votes for candidates from the presidency all the way down to the local level. Today, campaigns are much more on their own—campaign staff use smartphones and tablets to research individual voter information. While precincts were the level of analysis of campaigns for decades, that level of analysis is now down to neighborhoods and individual households. They know what voters eat, where they shop, and what they watch on television. Given all the personal information out in public and cyberspace, presidential, senatorial, congressional, and gubernatorial elections will become more individualized. The merging of all the personal information with the voting information is known as "big data." Big data can help predict the probability of an individual voting and for whom. What is fascinating is that this technology is not new but much more accurate in the twenty-first century. It is true that the electoral process has become less of a civic ritual, less communal, and more personalized. The future of campaigns is showing that presidential, senatorial, and gubernatorial candidate organizations, not national parties, are becoming the primary delivery vehicle of identifying, targeting, and getting-out-to-vote citizens.

Therefore, the chapter begins with a look at the background of GOTV operations, then proceeds to the current state of affairs of traditional and new methods of voter mobilization, and finally moves to where such efforts are headed in the future.

The Tradition of Parties Delivering Votes

The political science literature and history books of presidential campaigns have focused on the long, historical, and central role of parties that candidates could rely upon to bring out their voters on Election Day. Political scientists of the 1950s and 1960s discussed the symbiotic bond between candidates and parties—that candidates owed their allegiance to parties and supported the platform accordingly; parties would then provide the organizational muscle to bring enough of their voters to the polls to help win elections.[4] The long-standing model of party-driven politics was ended by the era of television, as candidates, beginning with John Kennedy, became their own electoral entrepreneurs. With television, candidates no longer needed ambassadors to introduce them to voters in presidential and later on other federal elections (Senate and House).

The model of candidate-driven politics emerged, but still parties played a role in delivering votes on Election Day. A hybrid system emerged where parties would provide a basic organization and delivery system for each campaign. Campaigns would then supplement that effort with their own campaign workers who would target key precincts and neighborhoods—identifying likely voters and marginal voters for their candidates. Parties under the Federal Election Campaign Act (FECA) Amendments of 1974 were given the power to provide coordinated expenditures to help candidates for Congress, Senate, and president get-out-the-vote. The expenditures were based on population and for general election purposes.[5] That expenditure could extend to advice, tactical planning, and organizational help to identify, contact, and get-out-to-vote key groups essential for victory.

Traditional Model of Targeting Voters

Campaigns have utilized voting data, voter registration lists, voter registration, turnout mail, radio, and ID calls as part of their voter contact operations for the last several decades. Such tactics are used as the basis for a voter identification and GOTV operation. Each party and its candidates (Democrats and Republicans) seek out their voters in precincts throughout the congressional district. They then prioritize those precincts depending on their partisanship and voter turnout rates.

Voting Data

The voting data from the past several elections are distilled, and the campaign identifies precincts on a zero- to ten-point scale. Ten is a maximum-performing district for the candidate, and zero is a district where there is no hope. Thus, for a Republican, a ten-point district would be classified as the strongest Republican, and a zero as the weakest Republican; Democrats classify their districts in a similar way. The precincts that are rated in the middle—four, five, and six—are dominated by neither party and are called "swing" precincts.[6] If the election has a high number of undecided voters, then swing precincts are the focus of both parties as they seek to persuade undecided or weakly identified voters of their own party. However, in base-driven elections (such as the 2012 presidential campaign between Obama and Romney), where there are few undecided voters, the emphasis for Democrats and Republicans is more firmly focused on squeezing every vote out of high-performing partisan precincts. Since the early 2000s, elections have become increasingly base-driven. Why? The explanation is simple: in swing precincts, you have to inform, convert, motivate, and turn out voters. In partisan districts, there is one less step: you do not have to convert potential loyalists. That saves both cost and time. Federal party organizations play a coordinated effort with campaigns to identify voters for a campaign, often assisting them (as an in-kind service) with voting lists and advice on how to develop a voter contact list.

All targeting operations begin by looking at the partisan vote for Democrats and Republicans. For example, if we were to average the presidential performance from 2000 to 2012 in the swing state of Ohio, the data would show Democrats with 50.2 percent and Republicans with 49.8 percent.[7] Since congressional races often traverse county lines, it is slightly more technical to obtain and compute average performance data in congressional districts, but not a barrier.

Voter Registration Lists

Supplementing voting data are voter registration lists. The voter registration lists are matched up with voting data for precincts to see where candidates perform as well as expected, underperform, or overperform. For example, in a precinct of 500 voters, the figures might show that Republican candidates in federal races are winning on average 60 percent of the vote, compared with 40 percent for Democrats. However, if the voter registration figures show that the precinct has 70 percent registered Republicans, then that district is underperforming for Republicans, meaning that Republican candidates are averaging 10 percent less than they should.

Underperforming precincts are of highest concern to a candidate because they are potentially the greatest source of votes. After identifying the problem, the party and candidate have to figure out why the district is underperforming. Is it because candidates are out of step with their own votes? Is it because of neglect from previous campaigns? Has the district started to change behaviorally (voting for the opposing party's candidate) even though party registration is still in the first party and candidate's favor? The campaign then has to decide what tactics it will employ to target that district (statewide or national federal races) or precinct (congressional races).

Voter Registration

Increasing party registration is key for any voter mobilization effort. Parties, partisan interest groups, and "527" organizations (i.e., independent political organizations including some Super PACs) work at increasing a partisan voter base. In particular, the Democratic Party has conducted extensive voter registration drives in the past focusing on the African American and Latino communities in urban areas, which tend to have lower voter registration rates, and thus lower voter turnout rates. Republicans will sometimes counter with voter registration efforts in rural areas to offset increased registration of Democrats in urban areas. The U.S. Census Bureau reported that in 2012, 153 million adults were registered to vote—or 71.2 percent of the adult population. The percentage of registered voters who voted on Election Day was 86.8 (a slight decline from 2008). There is no mistaking that voter registration is highly predictive of who turns out on Election Day.[8]

Turnout Mail

Turnout mail is critical to GOTV plans for candidates and parties because it plays two roles as Election Day approaches: it advertises candidates to citizens, and it reminds those citizens to vote on Election Day. Sometimes mail comes in the form of a literature drop at your doorstep by the candidate. Candidates and parties partake in these endeavors. Usually, campaigns will send out five to ten mailers to get the desired effect of maximizing their vote on Election Day. The Dover Group's award-winning direct mail piece titled "Eat Last" was released on November 4, 2014, for Democrat Seth Moulton running for election in Massachusetts' Sixth District. The ad illustrates the importance of voter mail before the election. Moulton, a Marine officer, served four tours in Iraq. The mailer shows a photo of Moulton, in full battle gear while on patrol in Iraq, pausing to talk to his platoon. On the left bar is a quote: "In Iraq, I always ate last, after my platoon. I believe Congress should have the same ethic. If they shut down the government, they shouldn't get paid. No excuses." The second page of the mailer discusses how Moulton shares values with his constituents. The third page has testimony from his mother how he will stand up for women's rights. The back page summarizes the campaign and takes us back to Moulton's military service—touting the theme of his campaign: "True. Blue. Democrat."[9]

The newest trend is digital direct mail, which is still in its nascent stage. According to direct mail consultants Kevin Mack and Shanon Henry: "The next frontier is embedding computer chips in direct mail pieces. . . . Just wave your mobile phone over the mail piece the way you wave your credit card over a high-tech key pad. The computer chip will then match tested messaging to the user's profile and online history, generating a personalized message for the user."[10] As the election approaches, the campaign provides more prominent reminders about Election Day voting (or even early voting).

Radio

Radio has served as a classic method for GOTV, especially for niche populations, which are hard to influence by turnout mail or phone banks. Lower-middle-class or poor voters and African American and Latino communities are often targeted for radio ads. Promos run on hip-hop, rap, R&B, soul, and gospel stations with messages urging people to vote. Other promotions have included hip-hop conventions urging people to vote. On November 2, 2010, President Barack Obama did interviews on hip-hop stations such as WGCI in Chicago, urging young voters and minorities to vote in the closely contested Senate and gubernatorial elections in Illinois to help elect Democrats to those posts.[11] (A Democrat won the governorship but not the Senate seat.) Obama is the first president to speak extensively to rap and hip-hop stations, demonstrating that reaching voters goes beyond the news station interviews of the last century.

ID Calls

ID or identification calls help to locate supporters, ascertain their voting plans, and finally ensure that they get-out-to-vote. ID calls are the surest and most direct method to reach voters personally, and voter registration lists plus available voter lists are used to help ensure that the population they reach can vote. The calls help to identify the candidate a citizen might vote for and assess the likelihood of his or her voting. The purpose of ID calls is to build a relationship between the voter and the caller (whether the latter is from a candidate or party organization). Wally Clinton, a consultant who specializes in phones and communications for Democrats, has said that building a relationship with a potential voter is "about listening, not yelling."[12]

ID calls normally begin several weeks before the election to determine the level of support, where it is located, and where the candidate has to go to increase support. As the election approaches, the campaign ascertains the likelihood of whether individuals on the list will vote. If a citizen is infirm or aged or lacks transportation, the campaign identifies that person, sets a time, and then provides transportation to take that individual to the polls. Young voters are more likely to use cell phones, but seniors are more reachable on landlines, particularly in the evening; however, that model is beginning to change as Baby Boomers become the newest generation of seniors. ID calls are one of the most effective techniques to boost GOTV. According to research by Green and Gerber, phone bank contacts by volunteers will add about one vote for every thirty-five calls made.[13]

Door-to-Door

Despite being labor intensive, the most effective form of traditional voter contact is through door-to-door canvassing. The fact that voters meet face-to-face with representatives of local parties and candidates can make a difference. According to Green and Gerber, this methodology yields one vote for every fourteen contacts, which is not insubstantial.[14]

A memo from the GOTV operation for the Obama campaign in 2012 showed that the ground game before election weekend had already conducted 126 million door knocks and phone contacts with voters.[15] This was unprecedented in voting history. The Romney campaign made about 50 million contacts.[16] The disparity may have made the difference in 2012; and if not the difference, it bolstered Obama's winning margin.

Each of the aforementioned tactics demonstrates the importance of candidate organization and field operations. In fact, the field division is the largest in any campaign because it involves dozens or hundreds or thousands of volunteers communicating candidate or party messages urging citizens to get-out-to-vote. Campaigns have continued to refine and adapt their strategies in the modern campaign era, as campaigns move away from television and as voters become more diverse consumers of new technologies.

Voter Mobilization in the
Twenty-First Century: Recent Developments

Campaigns are moving into a new era—customer-driven campaigns. Campaigns are now using a strategy developed from the corporate world called customer relationship management (CRM). CRM enables campaigns to blend traditional strategies of voter contact with new techniques. New techniques employ microtargeting (which will be discussed later on), multiple points of contact with voters (or customers), and multiple methods to get voters to the polls. In other words, the entire process focuses on the needs of each voter. The Obama campaign used this "bottoms up" approach in its GOTV effort in 2008. In this model, the individual volunteer contacts the voter through personal interaction. Patrick Ruffini, a Republican consultant, criticized his own party's GOTV efforts in 2008: "Obama volunteers are expected to do a lot more than volunteers on other campaigns, which is basically to park your butt in a headquarters and make lots of calls."[17]

Voters have increasing control of the media content that enables them to manipulate or alter information. Furthermore, as television viewing decreases and voters spend more time online, campaigns have to develop new techniques to entice voters to come to their websites. In terms of voter mobilization, this means creating a virtual community where voters participate in the online campaign. Blogs, email, web campaign events, and webinars represent some of the activities where individuals participate.

Campaigns have to develop more personalized and stylized messages to interest voters who are barraged with visual cues at the click of a mouse. Statistical methods have become more precise in predicting turnout. Merging traditional targeting methods, utilizing "big data," and employing the latest technology played an essential role in the 2012 Obama and 2014 Republican Party campaigns. In fact, the 2012 Obama campaign was so secret in guarding its data operation that "the team [analytics group] even worked at a remove from the rest of the campaign staff, setting up shop in a windowless room at the north end of the vast headquarters office."[18] Campaigns are so secretive about this information because they do not want a morsel of information to slither out to give their opponents any advantage.

"The analytics team used four streams of polling data . . . [it] had polling data from about 29,000 people in Ohio alone . . . allowing for a deep dives into where each demographic and regional group was trending at any given moment."[19]

Furthermore, the Obama campaign merged this with social media, such as Facebook, to do online get-out-the-vote. For example, Jane Q. Public's home was door knocked in Virginia, and she was asked how she planned to vote in 2012. The data file on the canvasser's iPhone showed Ms. Public had voted for Obama in the 2008 election. But she had voted for President Bush in 2000 and 2004. Ms. Public told the canvasser that she planned to vote for Romney. The data on the household showed that Ms. Public had two children including a male of voting age at College X. The canvasser then asked Ms. Public: "Do you know how your son plans to vote?" Ms. Public said, "No, I'm not sure." The canvasser said "Thank you" and left. Instantly, he sent a text back to the headquarters about the son. The campaign then located friends of the son on Facebook who were supporting Obama at College X. Within an hour or two, the son received multiple messages on his smartphone from friends at College X urging him: "We need you to vote for Obama!"[20] Social media can produce peer pressure regarding how to vote and making sure you get there.

As we can see, the new age of voter mobilization strategy is vested in merging consumer or lifestyle information with traditional targeting models. High-level campaigns and political parties now have the ability to target individual homes based on profile information available through public files or obtained through purchasing lists, and this is known as "microtargeting." Finally, new technology helps expedite the process of locating, contacting, and getting out voters. The amount of personal information becoming available to private industry and, thus, to campaigns and parties has raised fears about privacy issues because what are the parameters to determine what personal information should or should not be available for political campaigns?

Merging Traditional Models of Voter Mobilization with New Variables

The traditional models of GOTV operations have incorporated utilizing voting behavior histories and issue polling to mobilize interested citizens to vote. However, new elements have been utilized in the targeting process to make voter mobilization more precise and effective. Such techniques look at voters as customers and consumers to understand their lifestyles. A voter's lifestyle enables the campaign to engage that voter and get him or her out to vote on Election Day, as long as the voter is persuadable. Thus, today's world incorporates voting history + issue salience + consumer or lifestyle behavior.

According to TargetPoint, a Republican firm specializing in GOTV, "The control has switched from seller to buyer. Voters and consumers now have multiple sources for information and entertainment."[21] Thus, direct mail and personal contact alone will not suffice—the consumer (i.e., voter) must be reached by multiple sources of information, multiple times, in order for a campaign to get out his or her vote.

Pioneering efforts in this field were made by the 2004 Bush presidential campaign, which assembled profiles of nearly five thousand voters and "grouped (them) into thirty-four segments."[22] For example, in Michigan, segments included "Archie in the Bunker," "Religious Independents," and "Wageable Weak Democrats." Each potential Republican segment was valued in terms of its size and commitment to

George W. Bush. Moreover, the Bush team was able to accurately predict (80–90 percent) how likely that segment was to vote for President Bush.[23]

By 2008, Democrats had employed similar targeting, yielding a base vote of seven million more individuals—with large increases among young and African American voters.[24]

In 2010, however, it appeared that there was a resurgence in traditional GOTV activity. Tea Party supporters had either galvanized the Republican base as in Kentucky (for Senate candidate Rand Paul) or motivated the Democratic base as in Nevada (for incumbent senator Harry Reid). The back-to-basics GOTV program was best exemplified by the Tea Party in Kentucky. FreedomWorks, which is associated with the Tea Party, used hundreds of volunteers each weekend to conduct door-to-door canvassing for Senate candidate Rand Paul (R). The group was without the convenience of sophisticated microtargeting information on smartphones and tablets. Instead, FreedomWorks supporters were encouraged by group activities that built cohesion such as sign waves, placing yard signs, leaving door hangers, and so forth. The concept of "fun" was used to describe such activities for volunteers. Tea Partiers were more "Republican, white, male, married and older than 45."[25] It also characterized the activists. This contrasted with a much larger cohort of younger volunteers who worked for the Obama campaign—who were more technologically savvy.

The Emergence of Technology and
GOTV Programs in the Twenty-First Century

Modern technology has brought critical information into the hands of field organizations. Voting history, issue preferences, and lifestyle/consumer information are now available on smartphones and tablets for precinct workers. No one wants to be caught napping. In 1976, one of the leading Democratic candidates for president, Senator Birch Bayh (D-IN), asked his campaign for its GOTV plan on the weekend before the New Hampshire primary. No plan existed.[26] Today, that would be unheard of by a leading presidential campaign in a major primary.

Technology also must be tested well in advance of Election Day. The Bush reelection campaign planned its GOTV operation well in advance—and the president was not burdened by having a primary opponent. The Bush campaign tested its GOTV effort in a simulation in July 2004.[27] This enabled the campaign to determine what was working well and what needed fine-tuning. The Kerry campaign did not have such a luxury, given the campaign's early contentious primary season, which shortened its planning for its GOTV effort. That was not true in 2012 for Romney, who sewed up the Republican presidential nomination by early spring.

Finally, the technology and its input have to be tested often before an election for two reasons. One is early voting. Millions of voters today vote early. Second is that no one wants an ORCA-like failure again on Election Day. Get-out-the-vote campaigns used to be organized about three to four months prior to a presidential election. Today, that window is at least six months. For an incumbent president, it is one year or more. The 2012 Obama campaign spent the better part of two years operationalizing its voter contact and get-out-the-vote program. The scope of a GOTV effort is different on the state level, where the candidate and party capacity are not the same with the financial input that can produce massive get-out-the-vote drives.

Case Study: Cutting-Edge Methods to Get-Out-the-Vote by the Obama Campaign in 2012

With a polarized electorate, the Obama campaign planned early on for a base-driven election. A base-driven election is one where campaigns try to maximize their base turnout because there are few undecided voters. As mentioned earlier, the Obama campaign used advanced data analytics. The campaign also retained its massive volunteer and voter contact list from 2008. After the election, a group called Organizing for America (OFA, now known as Organizing for Action) was created by the Democratic National Committee. The purpose of OFA was to provide a field organization to support the president's policy initiatives (such as health care) but even more importantly to maintain and build the 2008 volunteer base in preparation for the 2012 presidential campaign. OFA was launched in January 2009 in all fifty states. According to *The New York Times*, the announcement was made via YouTube to the thirteen million people who were on the campaign's email list.[28] Under campaign finance laws, the Obama White House was precluded from using the list because it was for "political purposes."[29] Among OFA's principal advisers were Mitch Stewart and Jeremy Bird, who later ran the Obama campaign's field organization and GOTV effort. By April 2011, many of the OFA principals had moved over to the Obama reelection campaign.

The GOTV effort the Obama campaign built had military precision. Nothing on this scale had ever been attempted before. The cutting-edge change was more about the size and scope of the operation than the utilization of social media. For example, the campaign had 5,117 GOTV "staging locations in the battleground states."[30] It reported that 1.8 million potential voters in the battleground states were registered. The campaign reported that 28 percent of the new voters had voted early, before Election Day. (The process of early voting is discussed later in the chapter.) The campaign reported that volunteers had signed up for 700,000 shifts in the final four days of the campaign.[31]

While social media has become refined and better since 2008, technology has enabled campaigns to better do traditional GOTV efforts on an army-like scale.

Traditional, personal face-to-face or phone contacts were greater in 2012 than in any previous presidential election. The idea that campaigns have become more virtual and less personalized is countered by the evidence of individual personal contacts made by the Obama reelection campaign. As mentioned earlier, the campaign made 126 million personal contacts by door knocks and phone. The Obama campaign did a tremendous job mobilizing its base of women, African Americans, Latinos, and other minorities. In fact, the African American turnout exceeded the white turnout for the first time ever.[32]

Republicans Rebound in 2014

Republicans undone by operation ORCA took the lessons to heart and planned their own long-term strategy for the 2014 national midterm elections.

On August 28, 2014, the Republican National Committee (RNC) announced that it would spend $100 million for getting-out-the-vote on Election Day.[33] Over a year before, the RNC created a website called "Victory 365" for a year-round effort aimed at voter identification, contact, and GOTV. Victory 365 had three components: (1) Ground Game: Republicans identified "13,000 precinct captains and tens of thousands of volunteers"; (2) Voter Contact: "Equipped with the latest RNC-backed data and voter contact tools, our volunteers are responsible for identifying, recruiting and building relationships with voters in their communities"; and (3) Data and Technology: "We are becoming a data-driven and grassroots powered RNC. . . . The precinct captains and volunteers are talking to voters using our mobile phone and walk apps, and using and transferring data in real time."[34] What did the results show?

Republicans got out their vote on Election Day. Republicans used both technology and old-fashioned shoe leather. The digital side was particularly impressive. For example, the RNC increased real contact data points by 95 percent. They targeted 11.7 million low-turnout voters for their GOTV operation. Republicans increased social media contacts from 225 million in 2013 to 2.6 billion in 2014. The RNC also sent out 17 million GOTV emails.[35] This macro-level effort, combined with operations on the micro level—in states and congressional districts—demonstrated the impact of the combined effort by Republicans.

The Georgia Senate and gubernatorial races provide excellent examples of how traditional voter contact played a key role on the micro level. Polls showed near dead heats in contests for the Senate and governor. However, on Election Day, the races were not even close. Republicans created "14 Victory Offices" across the state that propelled Republican governor Nathan Deal and Senate candidate David Perdue to victory. The Democrats had multiple organizations working on voter registration and GOTV, particularly among the state's large African American population. While it is not the singular cause why Democrats did not turn out on

Election Day, the fact that the Republicans had one unified organization versus splintered efforts by Democrats certainly contributed to the Republican victories.[36] In all, Republicans gained nine Senate seats in 2014.

The Cutting Edge of Change: Into the Future with Voter Mobilization

The tactics of voter mobilization by campaigns and parties have become more diverse as we head into the second decade of the twenty-first century. The tactics discussed below demonstrate how voter mobilization changes involve many more moving parts than they did just twenty years ago.

Social Media and Virtual Community Building Igniting GOTV Efforts

The development and use of social media on the Internet (called Web 2.0) marked a profound change for campaigns between 2004 and 2008. The change between 2008 and 2012 was profound as well but not as unique because while the communication techniques have been refined in social media, they are not new. For example, Twitter was created in 2006, and Facebook was only four years old in 2008.

The holistic approach to GOTV was first embraced by the Obama campaign in 2008. It was ahead of the curve. Not only was the Internet used for volunteers, but it was also used to inform, persuade, motivate, and mobilize voters through social and other forms of communal digital media. Democratic strategist Joe Trippi noted that "the campaign's official stuff they created for YouTube was watched for 14.5 million hours," which was the equivalent of "$47 million" worth of television. The difference between social media and television media is that the recipient, as Trippi noted, actively "chooses" the information he or she wishes to receive.[37]

In 2012, social media, such as Facebook, was used as a tool to put peer pressure on voters. But Facebook is now a middle-aged social media tool used much more by Boomers and Gen-Xers than Millennials. Given that social media is becoming more visual—such as Instagram and Tumblr, for example—campaigns are now appealing to Millennials. One way is through photos of groups of young volunteers posing for fun, throwing their arms in the air, with open mouths and smiles, while wearing the same campaign T-shirts. Thus, social media is a growing and expanding motivating tool to get-out-the-vote, particularly for Millennials. However, the traditional and personal voter contact still remains the king of effective GOTV.

Building Relationships

Expanding on the previous point, one of the developments in GOTV efforts over the last four election cycles (2008, 2010, 2012, and 2014) has been to build stronger relationships between voters and campaigns. This means that campaigns are coordinating new technology (such as social media and mobile technology) with traditional GOTV tactics (such as phone contacts and door-to-door canvassing). Failure to utilize all the tools at one's disposal carries an inherent risk. Republican consultant Patrick Ruffini points out that the 2008 McCain campaign failed in its GOTV effort because it was overly reliant on phone calls and not on door-to-door canvassing. In fact, technology has enabled campaigns to become more community based and personal. The Obama campaign built its organization from the ground up in 2008 utilizing "Neighborhood Team Leaders" who "were in supervisory roles on the ground, not desk jockeys parceling out call sheets and walk lists," according to Ruffini.[38] Bottom-up strategies are not cheap—they require a lot of manpower, research, and monitoring. However, in large-scale campaigns such as both Obama campaigns and Victory 365 by Republicans, will be mimicked and refined over the next several election cycles.

Greater Citizen Diversity Makes GOTV More Complex

Over the next forty years, a majority of the U.S. population will become non-white and Latino according to demographer Leon Bouvier. That means that candidates will have to communicate not only bilingually but also multilingually to get-out-the-vote. The 2000 campaign was the first to feature both presidential candidates—Gore and Bush—"record[ing] messages in Spanish."[39] As Latino, Eastern European, Southeast Asian, and Central Asian populations increase, campaigns will need more field organizers who are bi- or multilingual to canvas potential voters whose second language is English. As the population continues to shift to the Southwest from the North and Midwest, this will become critical over the next decade. States such as Arizona and Florida are becoming electoral behemoths, where the largest-growing segment of the population is Latino. Texas gained four congressional districts and Florida two new districts based on the 2010 reapportionment. Texas, Florida, and Arizona are among the states that are likely to continue to gain more seats following the 2020 reapportionment. This reflects the nation's continued population shift from the Northeast and Midwest to the South and Southwest.

The New World: The Mobilization of Early, Absentee, and Mail Voting

Early and absentee voting is transforming elections because campaigns have to spend more up front in general election campaigns compared with the past. Florida allows early (i.e., "in-person absentee") voting. Oregon, Washington, and Colorado all allow voting by mail.

As of November 2, 2014, 17 million people had already voted, which ended up being approximately 20 percent of the total vote in the election.[40] Registered

Republicans turned out in larger numbers than expected in many states. For example, Republican Senate candidate Michael Gardner was leading Democratic incumbent senator Mark Udall in early voting by 8 percent. In Florida, Republican governor Rick Scott had a 4.1 percent lead in the early vote over the former governor, Democrat Charlie Crist.[41] While in 2010 Democrats made up the difference in turnout on Election Day, they did not do so in 2014, because minorities, particularly Latinos, turned out in low percentages. The Latino vote is key for Democrats in southwestern states and Florida to win statewide. The question is whether such efforts suppress voter turnout. (Chapter 11 discusses voter identification laws and their effects in detail.)

Cost

As national advertising becomes less appealing to presidential candidates, and as media convergence (television and the Internet) becomes a greater possibility, driving down cost, campaigns may delegate a higher portion of their resources to voter mobilization. Currently, about 50–80 percent of a senatorial, gubernatorial, or presidential campaign's budget is allocated to paid advertising. For example, winning a competitive Senate race in a large state in 2016 could cost in excess of $50 million. A 5 percent change in allocation of resources from paid advertising to voter mobilization would increase the GOTV budget by $2.5 million or yield approximately 300,000 new voters (at $8 per vote).

Voter registration activities are performed but by parties and independent organizations and not campaigns. In the future, presidential campaigns may subsume the GOTV effort by the parties in presidential election years, as previously noted; however, parties and other independent political groups still raise money for voter education activities under the auspices of the Federal Election Campaign Amendments of 1979. This enables parties to raise money in the states (what are called nonfederal funds).

Photo ID and GOTV Efforts

Voter identification laws require citizens to present an ID when voting on Election Day, ostensibly to prevent fraud. Republican state legislators have been pushing photo ID laws, saying that it would prevent fraudulent voting. Democrats oppose such laws, contending that many low-income and minority individuals (who are more likely to vote for Democrats) do not have photo identification such as driver's licenses. In 2014, seven states had photo ID laws (Georgia, Indiana, Kansas, Mississippi, Tennessee, Texas, and Virginia), up from two in 2010. Four additional states (Arizona, New Hampshire, North Dakota, and Ohio) require nonphoto IDs.[42] Campaigns and party organizations now have to find a way to assess which current voters and which potential voters have photo identification. Second, campaigns and parties may also seek to help individuals procure such identification. That issue is explored in greater detail later in the book.

The Future of Voter Mobilization—Marrying the New to the Old

The future of voter mobilization will enhance even more direct interface between candidate and voter, without the filter of television; the key is for campaigns to get access to more databases of information to communicate by mobile phone, tablet, email, and the newest entry—the mobile watch. Getting such lists will facilitate the different avenues and media for reaching each voter.

Just as importantly, the future of voter mobilization will coordinate technology with old-fashioned GOTV techniques. Campaigns strategizing how to use GOTV, even those running for congressional office, will have to plan more complex operations.

Since the first Obama campaign, iPhone technology has taken a major leap forward in aiding GOTV efforts. Republican Scott Brown's 2009 Senate campaign to replace the late Senator Ted Kennedy of Massachusetts was a perfect example. Brown's campaign provided walk lists for its canvassers, but "supplemented them with a clever web-based application" for iPhones. "By geo-locating users through native iphone features the app could show volunteers the nearest house to visit . . . and talking points to use in the conversation." Responses were then entered "into a Google Docs spreadsheet."[43] The micro level of analysis gave the Brown campaign an unparalleled level of precision for analysis. This new harbinger from 2009 is standard practice today.

Direct mail email can be tailored for each voter—the first stage is contact and introduction; the second stage is persuasion; and the third stage is mobilization to vote. For example, one possibility is that candidates will be able to send videos on email to potential supporters (targeted by the aforementioned methods); and that can be followed up by virtual zip code captains who can email their neighbors—all through a handheld device, like an iPhone or Droid. (Of course, this depends on whether campaigns can get actual addresses or zip codes that match email addresses.) Virtual zip code captains can dialogue with potential voters—for persuasion; for mobilization; and, perhaps, to volunteer. The campaign coordinates the activities among the virtual captains and the actual precinct captains in that zip code to ensure there is no overlap and overcommunication with any potential voter.

Campaigns will continue using an increasing number of tactics to reach voters through different media—moreover, the actual number of GOTV contacts per person is, thus, likely to increase. Campaigns will have to learn by trial and error how not to burden voters with too much pressure or information that could have the opposite effect—deterring voter turnout.

Conclusion

The conversion of big data, social media, and traditional get-out-the-vote efforts has reinvigorated the role of turnout operations by parties and campaigns to its most significant level in more than fifty years. Interestingly, while the focus has been on the sexier parts of big data and social media, the fact is that face-to-face or phone contact has been increased. While new digital technologies have been criticized as being impersonal in other modes of life, in campaigns they have actually been used to *increase personal contact*. As former baseball catcher Yogi Berra once said: "It's déjà vu, all over again."[44] A déjà vu that is helping to reinvigorate voter participation.

Notes

1. Grace Wyler, "Insiders Explain How Mitt Romney's Campaign Completely Fell Apart on Election Day" (*Business Insider*, November 12, 2012). Accessed on May 21, 2015, from http://www.businessinsider.com.

2. John Ekdahl, "Mitt Romney's Project ORCA Was a Disaster, and It May Have Cost Him the Election" (Reprinted in *Business Insider*, November 8, 2012). Accessed on May 22, 2015, from http://www.businessinsider.com.

3. John Berman, "Obama Supporters Without a Cause" (*ABC News*, November 8, 2008). Accessed on May 23, 2011, from http://abcnews.go.com.

4. See Samuel Eldersveld, *Political Parties in American Society* (New York: Basic Books 1982); Austin Ranney, *Political Parties: Democracy and the American Party System* (New York: Harcourt, Brace and Company, 1956); V. O. Key, *Southern Politics in State and Nation* (Knoxville: University of Tennessee Press, 1984).

5. Anthony Corrado, "Where Are We Now: The Current State of Campaign Finance Law," in *Campaign Finance Reform: A Sourcebook*, edited by Trevor Potter (Washington, DC: Brookings, 1997), 8–9.

6. Information confirmed by Tim Crawford, New Models Consulting. Interview on August 8, 2007.

7. The aggregate vote over four elections (2000, 2004, 2008, and 2012) was 20,835,000 votes in Ohio. Democrats won 10,462,000 and Republicans 10,373,000. The Democrats have a margin of 89,000 votes out of the nearly 21 million cast. All information calculated by the author.

8. Thom File, "Voting and Registration in the Election of November 2012" (Report P20-568, U.S. Census Bureau, May 2013). See Table 1: Reported Voting and Registration by Sex and Single Years of Age: November 2012.

9. "Eat Last." Direct Mail for Seth Moulton for Congress (The Dover Group, November 4, 2014). Accessed on May 21, 2015, from http://www.doverstrategygroup.com.

10. Kevin Mack and Shanon Henry, "The Future of Direct Mail Is Digital" (*Campaigns and Elections*, September 17, 2012). Accessed on May 22, 2015, from http://www.campaignsandelections.com.

11. "President Obama Talks to Chicago Radio Station, Asks Voters to Have His Back" (*The Huffington Post*, November 2, 2010). Accessed on July 25, 2011, from http://www.huffingtonpost.com.

12. Walter D. Clinton, "Building Relationships with Voters," in *Winning Elections*, edited by Ronald Faucheaux (New York: M. Evans and Co., 2003), 567.

13. Donald Phillip Green and Alan G. Gerber, *Get Out the Vote!* (Washington, DC: Brookings, 2004), 94.

14. Phillip and Gerber, *Get Out the Vote!*, 94.

15. Mitchell Stewart, Jeremy Bird, and Marion Marshall, "Brick-by-Brick: Building a Ground Game for 270" (Memo from Obama-Biden campaign 2012, undated).

16. Sam Stein, "Obama Campaign: We've Contacted One Out of Every 2.5 People in the Country" (*The Huffington Post*, November 3, 2012). Accessed on May 22, 2015, from http://www.huffingtonpost.com.

17. Patrick Ruffini, "Obama Opens the GOTV Firehose" (*The Next Right*, October 13, 2008). Accessed on May 26, 2011, from http://www.thenextright.com.

18. Michael Sherer, "Inside the Secret World of the Data Crunchers Who Helped Obama Win" (*Time*, November 7, 2012). Accessed on May 26, 2015, from http://www.time.com.

19. Ibid.

20. Ibid., and the hypothetical is based on a real example from another state where the identity of the individuals is not revealed.

21. TargetPoint Consulting. Accessed on June 12, 2007, from http://www.targetpointconsulting.com/.

22. Ibid., 36.

23. Ibid., 37.

24. Calculated by the author from turnout data in 2008 compared to turnout in 2004 in the presidential election.

25. Nan S., "GOTV in Northern Kentucky for Rand Paul Thursday and Friday," posted on September 28, 2010. Accessed on May 27, 2011, from http://teaparty.freedomworks.org; Kate Zernike and Megan Thee-Brenan, "Poll Finds Tea Party Backers Wealthier and More Educated" (*The New York Times*, April 14, 2010). Accessed on May 27, 2011, from http://www.nytimes.com.

26. Martin Schram, Running for President: A Journal of the Carter Campaign (New York: Pocket Books 1977), 23.

27. Terry Nelson, PowerPoint presentation on the Bush 2004 campaign (American University, February 15, 2006).

28. Jim Rutenberg and Adam Nagourney, "Melding Obama's Web to a YouTube Presidency" (*The New York Times,* January 26, 2009). Accessed on May 27, 2015, from http://www.nytimes.com.

29. Ibid.

30. Stewart et al., "Brick-by-Brick."

31. Ibid.

32. Hope Yen, "Black Voter Turnout Passes Whites in 2012 Election, A First in Census History" (*Associated Press,* reprinted in *The Huffington Post,* May 8, 2013). Accessed on June 5, 2015, from http://www.huffingtonpost.com.

33. David M. Drucker, "RNC to Spend $100m to Get Out the Vote" (*Washington Examiner,* August 28, 2014). Accessed on June 5, 2015, from http://www.washington examiner.com.

34. "Victory 365," website home page. Accessed on May 27, 2015, from http://www .gopvictory365.com.

35. "RNC Chairman Announces Key Data, Digital and Technology Changes" (Press release, Republican National Committee, January 28, 2015). Accessed on June 5, 2015, from http://www.rnc.org.

36. Daniel Malloy and Kristina Torres, "Georgia Uses Big Data to Get Out the Vote" (Tribune News Service, October 10, 2014). Accessed on May 22, 2015, from http:// www.governing.com.

37. Ibid.

38. Patrick Ruffini, "Obama Opens the GOTV Firehose."

39. Richard J. Semiatin, *Campaigns in the 21st Century: The Changing Mosaic of American Politics* (Boston: McGraw-Hill, 2005), 230; includes reference to Bouvier.

40. Michael McDonald, "Early Voting Pulling into the Station" (*The Huffington Post,* November 2, 2014). Accessed on May 28, 2015, from http://www.huffingtonpost.com.

41. Ibid.

42. Anita Earls, "New Strict Voter ID Laws Challenged in Court" (*Moyers and Company,* March 6, 2015). Accessed on May 28, 2015, from http://www.billmoyers.com.

43. Colin Delany, "How Candidates Can Use the Internet to Win in 2010," e-book, p. 10 for all quotes. Accessed on May 25, 2011, from http://www.epolitics.com. All references in the paragraph from this source.

44. "Yogisms," from the Yogi Berra Museum. Accessed on June 5, 2015, from http://www .yogiberramuseum.org.

Part II

The Evolving Campaign—Adaptation by Political Institutions and Groups

CHAPTER 7

Political Parties — Reinvigorated

Tari Renner

POLITICAL PARTIES IN THE UNITED STATES have been reinvigorated as seen in the last several elections. Both Democrats and Republicans have worked at building their party operations, which extends their power beyond Washington and into field operations across the country. The purpose is to energize their base supporters to communicate, volunteer, contribute, and ultimately get-out-the-vote (GOTV). Both Howard Dean (Democrat, 2008) and Reince Priebus (Republican, 2012 and 2014) served as strong chairs and modernized party operations.

The national parties have come a long way from their feeble position in the 1960s when the leading book on their role was titled *Politics without Power.*[1] Over the last generation, the national party organizations have dramatically increased their role in candidate recruitment, fundraising, targeting of campaigns, communication innovation, and GOTV operations. They have adapted to, and even thrived in, an era of changing campaign technologies. The latter set of activities is often referred to as the "Service Party Model."[2] The strategic role of party organizations has been broadened to provide a variety of services to candidates in the second decade of the twenty-first century. Those services include state-of-the-art television studios, mobile technology, and extensive online outreach programs.

Interest groups, political action committees (PACs), and independent expenditure movements may also contribute money, but parties confer nominations with legal authority. Indeed, the entire electoral process is organized around them. Practically speaking, with few exceptions, successful candidates for the highest offices in the country need to obtain a nomination from one of the two major political parties. In the general election, the party labels and communication processes clearly structure the campaign conflict. They are indeed unique entities in our nation's electoral process. This chapter discusses the evolving role of U.S. parties in political campaigns. The primary focus is elections at the federal level.

The chapter then goes on to examine political party organizational leadership, programs, fundraising, and campaign tactics. It concludes that the parties will continue to be critical and innovative actors, but they face a variety of serious challenges and coalitional realignments in the future.

Party Revitalization and Ideological Polarization

The primary cause of party resurgence has been organic—that is, the natural product of the coalitional shifts in the party bases and the increasing ideological polarization between the two major parties. Since the emergence of the New Deal coalition in the 1930s, Democrats have very gradually lost their most conservative wing (primarily white southerners) over civil rights and social/cultural issues. As this group left the Democrats and became behavioral Republicans, the Democrats moved left, and the GOP (Grand Old Party) was pulled even further to the right. The latter phenomenon caused liberal and moderate Republicans in the North to become either Democrats or Independents. In the process, the country went from having two ideologically diverse parties and a clear Democratic majority to having two ideologically distinctive parties whose strength is nearly equal.

The increase in ideological polarization between the two parties clearly helps the intraparty unity of elected officials (sometimes called the party in government) and party identifiers (sometimes called the party in the electorate). It also helps internal organizational unity and fundraising. Contemporary donors are likely to be highly motivated by ideology and more likely to open their pocketbooks when they know that their contributions are going to candidates with similar views of politics.

Ideological Purists and Pragmatists

The existence of a two-party system probably makes intraparty divisions inevitable between the most intense ideologues (sometimes called purists) and party pragmatists. The former are most likely to see politics in stark moral terms, and the latter are more likely to be practical and see things in shades of gray. The divisions between the two types of partisans emerged among the first U.S. parties and continue to the present. This is evidenced by the role of the Tea Party in the Republican Party since the 2010 elections, as we discuss later in this section. The differences appear in all three segments of parties—the formal party organization, the elected officeholders, and rank-and-file party voters.

The ideological realignment since the New Deal era has strengthened the purists in both major political parties. However, it is important to understand the differences between the internal positions of the most liberal wing within the Democratic Party and of the most conservative wing within the Republican Party.

The liberal Democratic purists have, of course, increased in size within their party, but they remain a very diverse coalition (on race, ethnicity, religion, and geography). They might include large numbers of African Americans; Latinos; white Christians, Jews, or unaffiliated urbanites and suburbanites; gays and lesbians; and other groups. In contrast, conservative Republican purists are likely to be a much more homogeneous coalition. They are overwhelmingly white and very likely to be born-again evangelical Christians whose conservatism is primarily grounded in social or cultural issues—especially abortion, immigration, and same-sex marriage. Consequently, the Republican purists are generally easier to communicate with and mobilize. This situation is often an advantage for Republicans but can also pose problems since internal disputes are liable to develop as stark bipolar contests between unified ideological purists and pragmatists.

The emergence of the so-called Tea Party from 2009 to the present, for example, has produced some serious intraparty splits in GOP primaries that probably prevented the Republicans from picking up three Senate seats in the 2010 midterms (Colorado, Delaware, and Nevada). The Tea Party backed candidates who won Senate primaries in "red states" such as Kentucky and Utah and did little to harm Republican general election prospects in 2010. However, in the 2012 presidential year, two Tea Party candidates won hotly contested GOP Senate primaries in Indiana and Missouri. Both of these states voted for Republican presidential nominee Mitt Romney by comfortable margins (approximately ten points). However, the Senate contests were won by the Democrats after the nominees, Todd Akin and Richard Mourdock, made controversial comments on rape and pregnancy that seemed at variance with scientific knowledge. In 2014, the Tea Party–backed purists were generally less successful in defeating Republican pragmatists within their party's primaries. Long-term incumbents held back strong purist right-wing challenges, for example, in two very conservative red states (Thad Cochran of Mississippi and Mitch McConnell of Kentucky).

Generally, purist ideologues within the parties tend to be the strongest after their party loses power and the opposition governing party begins to push its policy agenda. It's a type of political physics—force and counterforce. The "out" party has a negative figure in the White House pushing his agenda that motivates the out party's base (Reagan's economic and environmental policies, Clinton's health care reform and gays in the military, George W. Bush and the Iraq War, Obama's health care reform, etc.). The party pragmatists who may appear to compromise with the opposition party president, or don't describe him in evil terms, may be vulnerable in primary contests during the early phases of a new administration. The longer the out party stays out of power, however, the weaker the purists' appeal.

In the future, the power of the GOP's most conservative wing is likely to continue to be a serious obstacle to the pragmatist's attempts to appeal to an electorate experiencing increased diversity and generational change. Witness the events in the state of Indiana in the spring of 2015. The passage of a "religious freedom" law in the Hoosier State produced such a strong national backlash that the state's Republican governor Mike Pence and most of the Republican presidential candidates found themselves having to quickly backtrack on their initial support of the measure.[3]

National Party Organizations: Structure

The Republican National Committee (RNC) and the Democratic National Committee (DNC) are the primary national umbrella organizations for each major party. They are the centers of national campaign activity and are composed of the fifty state party organizations and those of U.S. territories such as the District of Columbia, Guam, and Puerto Rico. The national Republican Governors Association and the national Democratic Governors Association and the "Hill committees" are also member organizations.

The Hill committees represent the four congressional parties on Capitol Hill—House Democrats, House Republicans, Senate Democrats, and Senate Republicans. They include the Democratic Congressional Campaign Committee (DCCC), the National Republican Congressional Committee (NRCC), the Democratic Senatorial Campaign Committee (DSCC), and the National Republican Senatorial Committee (NRSC).

Political scientist Ronald Shaiko has effectively summarized how party organizations work: "Each organization has divisions that include finance (fundraising), administration (office operations and payroll), legal (interpreting campaign finance laws), political (candidate recruitment, training, advertising, tactical advice, and voter mobilization efforts), and communication (earned media, paid media, and new media), as well as an office of the chairman or chairwoman."[4] The older national party organizations performed few functions or services during the era of traditional campaigning. Contemporary parties, however, have adapted to the new style of elections and have become central players in U.S. campaigns. As a consequence, they have needed to form more complex national organizations to handle a wide variety of more specialized functions.

The Emergence and Institutionalization of the Service Party Model

The modern role of the national political party organizations as service providers has become institutionalized over the last generation. The national committees, the Hill committees, and, more recently, the national governors' associations provide services such as maintaining voter lists, raising increasing levels of campaign cash that they channel into the field in a variety of ways, organizing GOTV operations, and providing advice and training to candidates. However, they also do a lot more. They help recruit and legitimize candidates and continue to raise increasing levels of campaign cash that they channel into the field in a variety of ways. Further, the national parties' decisions to support candidates at the beginning of the process and the targeting choices they make in the "homestretch" serve as cues to the entire community of donors (PACs as well as wealthy individual contributors).

Table 7.1 presents the expenditures for each of the national party organizations (and their respective totals) from 2008 through 2014. This represents their campaign expenditures over the last two presidential and midterm elections. The expenditures of the organizations have generally increased over time (recognizing that there are natural spikes during presidential years). In fact, the combined Democratic and Republican Party totals reached around $1 billion each during the 2008 and 2012 presidential election cycles.

The emergence of the contemporary service provider function dates back to the 1970s for Republicans and to the 1980s for Democrats. For the GOP, the Watergate scandal, massive Democratic gains in the 1974 midterm elections, and the loss of the White House in 1976 were all catalysts for change. New party leaders emerged in this environment to rebuild and renew their national organization. They began aggressive programs for improving fundraising and professionalizing their staff. By 1980, the GOP even had a long-term strategy to recruit and groom candidates at the state legislative and local level to help build a Republican "farm team." The goal was to ensure there was a deep pool of party candidates for the

TABLE 7.1   Total Receipts: National Party Organizations, 2008–2014

Party Organization	2008	2010	2012	2014
Democratic Party:	$962,394,732	$817,478,013	$1,070,492,835	$854,975,876
DNC	277,847,035	229,592,109	316,329,766	168,332,831
DCCC	176,204,612	163,896,053	183,843,039	206,791,993
DSCC	162,791,453	129,543,443	145,906,977	168,323,308
Republican Party:	$920,525,787	$586,978,840	$1,023,187,790	$665,608,564
RNC	444,482,306	198,791,545	409,469,546	194,977,377
NRCC	118,324,756	133,779,119	155,724,615	153,448,112
NRSC	94,424,743	84,513,719	117,045,862	128,278,255

Source: Center for Responsive Politics. Accessed on May 31, 2015, from www.opensecrets.org.

Note: Total receipts include all reported donations to all party committees. DNC = Democratic National Committee; DCCC = Democratic Congressional Campaign Committee; DSCC = Democratic Senatorial Campaign Committee; RNC = Republican National Committee; NRCC = National Republican Congressional Committee; NRSC = National Republican Senatorial Committee.

future. The Democrats were, at first, comparatively slow to adapt to this modern service role. However, their catalyst for action was similar to the GOP's—devastating electoral defeat. After the Democrats' landslide loss to Ronald Reagan in 1980, the party began to supply the same kinds of services the GOP had been providing to its candidates. Today, both major parties have become the central players in strategic recruitment, training, and funding of congressional campaigns.

Party Leadership and Strategies

From 2000 to 2015, the DNC has had fairly consistent leadership while that of the RNC appears to be a revolving door. The DNC has had only four chairs (Terry McAuliffe, Howard Dean, Tim Kaine, and Debbie Wasserman Schultz) while the RNC has had eight chairs (Jim Gilmore, Marc Racicot, Ed Gillespie, Ken Mehlman, Mel Martinez, Mike Duncan, Michael Steele, and Reince Priebus).

Party Leaders, Styles, and Vision

These leaders brought a variety of different styles and strategic visions to their positions. Howard Dean, for example, attempted to change his party's mindset and target decisions with his fifty-state strategy. He believed the Democrats needed to broaden their battlefield in order to win back both houses of Congress in 2006 and the White House in 2008. This approach often led to strategic differences between Dean and DCCC chair Rahm Emanuel as the latter tended to favor a more traditional focused approach to targeting campaign resources.

In addition to strategic views, national party leaders differ in personal styles, and these differences can be very important in the performance of their public relations functions. Consider the brief tenure of RNC chair Michael Steele (2009–2011). Steele developed a reputation for being outspoken and unconventional. This style, however, turned out to be a double-edged sword. In the fall of 2010 midterm elections, Steele launched an unprecedented "Fire Pelosi Bus Tour" with the primary goal of publicizing his party campaign to win back the U.S. House. In a six-week trip from mid-September through late October, Steele held rallies in over one hundred cities across the forty-eight states in the continental United States. In these stops, Steele used his bombastic speaking style to fire up Republican activists across the country. While he was widely praised for such public efforts to rev up the base, Steele's blunt and off-the-cuff remarks to the media brought him much criticism and may have cost him his job. For example, he was forced to apologize after describing right-wing icon Rush Limbaugh's work as "incendiary" and "ugly."[5] These and other blunt public statements became an issue in Steele's unsuccessful bid to retain his post as RNC chair. One state party chair said he was opposing Steele's reelection because "I'm tired of all of the drama."[6]

In an interview after losing his job to Reince Priebus, Steele himself concluded that he lost because they (the RNC) wanted someone with a different style.[7] Priebus has been credited with revitalizing the Republican resurgence in turnout in 2014.

The Effectiveness of Party Leadership and Tactics on Outcomes

The effectiveness of party leadership and tactics in electoral outcomes is clearly affected, and often limited, by changes in the broader political environment. For example, while Rahm Emanuel (as head of the DCCC) received great praise for his party's winning control of the House in 2006 (with a gain of thirty-three seats), there is no doubt that he was operating within a very favorable national political climate for his party (the opposition president's popularity was at record low levels; the war in Iraq was increasingly unpopular; and the Republicans had been in power for six years). The same can be said of Chris Van Hollen, who chaired the DCCC in the 2008 elections as the Democrats' "Red to Blue" strategy continued. The president's popularity and the economy continued to decline, and the Democrats gained twenty-two additional House seats. However, the same cannot be said for Van Hollen in 2010, when his party faced devastating electoral losses as the GOP gained sixty-three House seats. The same leadership produced very different results because of a dramatic change in the national political environment. On the Republican side, NRCC chair Pete Sessions won little praise after the 2008 House elections but seemed to be able to do no wrong in 2010. So, in most cases, the leadership may be able to improve its party's success at the margins but can hardly do much to alter the intensity of an electoral tsunami. Put another way, it's easy to perform well (and look good) if you're dealt three or four aces as a party leader. It's quite another thing to succeed when you're dealt deuces.

The Importance of Strategy

Party leaders may realize when they've been dealt a bad hand and adjust their strategies accordingly. For example, Senator Patty Murray (D-WA) knew she was facing a tough job when she became DSCC chair for the 2012 election cycle. Regardless of whether the national partisan pendulum would swing back toward the Democrats in 2012, her party was going to be defending twenty-three of the thirty-three Senate seats at stake. Murray sought to maximize her party's chances by pushing on two distinctive fronts. First of all, in order to prevent Democrats from playing a totally defensive game, she aggressively attempted to expand the competitive playing field by targeting possible pickups in the traditionally red states of Arizona, Indiana, and Texas. Second, Murray pressured all Democrats in the caucus to take a greater and more direct role in maintaining their Senate majority.

This involved having "as many as 16 senators . . . dialing for dollars in what is known as 'power hour'—lunchtime at DSCC headquarters."[8] Murray's efforts likely contributed to her party's victory at the polls (actually gaining two additional seats). However, party leadership styles may vary, but their impact upon electoral outcomes is only liable to be realized at the margins.

The same point can be made for specific party strategies or programs. Consider the different effects of the Republicans' Young Guns program in two very different election cycles. It was proposed by Congressmen Eric Cantor (R-VA), Kevin McCarthy (R-CA), and Paul Ryan (R-WI) and was adopted for the 2007–2008 cycle and continued into the 2009–2010 cycle where it was much more successful. Young Guns recruited challengers to Democratic incumbents and open-seat candidates. It required those candidates enrolled to meet rigorous benchmark targets over time to improve their fundraising, campaign organization, and online communication strategies. Candidates could proceed through the three levels in the Young Guns program depending upon their success in meeting the targets: On the Radar, Contender, and Young Gun (the highest level). The latter group included those who met the most rigorous benchmarks, were considered the strongest candidates, and, therefore, were the most likely to receive the RNCC's financial support during the homestretch of the election (through the party's independent expenditure campaigns).[9]

In 2008, only a handful of Democratic incumbents or open seats fell into GOP hands. In 2010, however, the Republicans greatly broadened the battlefield. A total of ninety-two candidates were granted the Young Gun status. This program combined with effective targeting of financial contributions helped Republicans field viable candidates in an unprecedented number of congressional districts and enabled them to take full advantage of the national tsunami favoring their party. Ultimately, the NRCC waged independent expenditure campaigns in sixty-six districts. Of that group, it won fifty-two.[10]

The central point is that specific programs and strategic allocation of resources can permit parties to maximize their performance given the broader political environment. However, their impact is likely to be marginal since they can do little to alter that environment. In other words, as a party leader you can recruit great surfers and craft great surfboards, but you can't control the size or intensity of the partisan political waves of an election. Both parties have experienced their share of favorable and unfavorable tsunamis in the last several elections. Democrats had two very strong waves in a row (2006 and 2008), and Republicans have had the two strongest midterm waves in recent memory in 2010 and 2014. The overall political environment, however, includes more than just the changing partisan tides. The most important resource in U.S. elections is money, and the changing rules of the fundraising game have affected both of the major party organizations.

The World Today: Parties Compete with Outside Groups for Resources

In 2002, the Congress passed the Bipartisan Campaign Reform Act (BCRA), which prohibited national or state party organizations from raising "soft money" that had no formal contribution limits. However, the evidence shows that the national parties continued to increase their fundraising despite the BCRA. They were forced to adapt their strategies and use the independent expenditure loophole to influence their targeted races. Referring back to Table 7.1, it is clear that the BCRA did little to prevent the continuing increases in the receipts for all of the party committees. This is consistent with Ronald Shaiko's observation eight years ago: "Contrary to the conventional wisdom, not only have the parties adapted, but they are financially stronger than one might have anticipated following the law's enactment."[11] Supreme Court decisions in the 2000s affected individual rights to broadcast advocacy ads; however, the Court has left in place a ban for parties to collect unlimited sums for so-called issue advocacy. Despite the rise of independent organizations (called Super PACs as discussed in Chapter 8), the parties thus far have been able to survive. In fact, the total party expenditures rose from the 2010 to the 2014 midterm and from the 2008 to the 2012 presidential election. However, Michael Toner and Karen Trainer report that the national parties' spending as a percentage of all outside group spending decreased dramatically after the *Citizens United* decision, which allowed for independent expenditures directly advocating the election of candidates.[12] Since 2010, they report, independent expenditures have grown more dramatically than national party spending.

Independent expenditure efforts may not precisely choreograph a central message in the manner in which the parties and candidates might desire. Further, the rise of independent group expenditures might increase the negativity of campaigns in the future. There is empirical evidence that campaign ads geared toward express advocacy ("vote for or vote against") are significantly more negative than candidate advertisements.[13]

National Party Organizations: Traditional and New Technologies

Political parties use the same campaign techniques as individual candidates and independent expenditure groups. Beyond the core differences in the organizations discussed earlier, the operations of national party organizations are continuous whereas most individual campaigns have a discrete beginning and conclusion. The parties' activities obviously flare up during election season, but there is no clear beginning and end. Indeed, a devastating election may immediately spur the defeated party to begin a program of renewal for the next election. Cases in point include the above-mentioned Red to Blue and Young Guns programs by the Democrats and Republicans, respectively.

The biggest tactical challenge national parties currently face is to keep on top of changes in campaign communication. The Internet and associated new technologies, for example, have clearly emerged as critical "new" modes of communication since the first campaign website was set up in 1994 by California senator Dianne Feinstein's reelection campaign. However, just as we appear to get a handle on the likely impact of these technologies, new developments emerge to further complicate, and provide new opportunities to revolutionize, modern campaigning. These changes include the Howard Dean campaign's raising of unprecedented amounts of money online in the 2004 presidential race, the emergence of YouTube in 2006 (especially in the Virginia Senate race), Facebook and text messaging in the 2008 Obama campaign, and Sarah Palin's pioneering of Twitter in 2009. More recently, we've seen other new developments such as the use of political memes and the creation of campaign digital scrapbooks on Tumblr and Pinterest. In the section below, some of the most important methods of traditional and nontraditional communication are discussed.

Direct Mail and Microtargeting

The rise of new technologies doesn't mean that the old ones fade away. In fact, innovative new strategies are being used to improve many traditional means of communicating with voters and prospective supporters. Direct mail, for example, continues to thrive for both campaign fundraising and message communication and will likely remain critical in the immediate future. Why does direct mail still play such an important role? According to Karen Tucker, manager of transaction mail for the U.S. Postal Service, there are three core reasons. First of all, the vast majority of voters report that they read or at least review their mail. Second, direct mail is especially effective in influencing attitudes and providing knowledge because it "allows for the inclusion of longer messages than other mediums, which means mailers can clearly define a candidate's campaign platform or address a single issue head-on. And, since it's tangible, it can be a very handy reference tool for people who are voting by mail when they fill out their ballot at home. . . . Mail is a flexible form of communication that can support multiple goals."[14] Consequently, direct mail in campaigns may change but is unlikely to be replaced by newer technologies anytime soon. In fact, given the increase in digital communications via email and advertising, direct mail has become more of a novelty again. It is possible in the coming years that direct mail may have a more significant impact on voters as snail mail becomes rarer.

Future changes will continue to refine the efficiency and effectiveness of microtargeting techniques for direct mail and direct voter contact. The parties use political preference, voting history, lifestyle, and demographic information in their voter databases (previously called Voter Vault by the RNC and VoteBuilder by the

DNC) to tailor their fundraising or campaign messages to very specific groups of voters. This custom messaging is geared toward increasingly small segments of the electorate—micro audiences. The latest waves attempt to go well beyond voter history in an attempt to predict individual voter attitudes and behavior long before Election Day. This is accomplished through "voter modeling—a term that came into vogue with President Barack Obama's 2008 campaign and has dominated strategy discussions since."[15] More recently, John Phillips of Aristotle, one of the most prominent data collection firms, developed something called "Relationship Viewer" to probe more deeply into available data. It attempts to make more accurate predictions of individuals based upon the connections between them and other people they interact with—friends, neighbors, coworkers, and so on. The overall trajectory of this phenomenon was summarized by Laura Quinn, CEO of Catalist, a Democratic data firm: "Campaigns were generalizing the message for large swaths of people. Now campaigns are specializing the message for smaller swaths of people."[16]

GOTV—The Latest Voter Mobilization

Newer technologies such as microtargeting and Internet social networking have helped improve the effectiveness of another traditional campaign operation—GOTV. The voter modeling discussed above is also extremely useful in tailoring messages for GOTV. It can, for example, help in predicting what types of voters will be the most receptive to an absentee ballot or early voting program.[17] Further, David All, founder of TechRepublican.com, and Jerome Armstrong of WebstrongGroup.com maintain that organizing early on the Internet and social networking greatly improves the effectiveness of a campaign's GOTV.[18] They advocate "early engagement" that integrates GOTV with early social networking. "Things like forming a network of supporters, including groups, listserves and personal fundraising pages, will all serve to fully engage the supporters early on, instead of them sitting around for months waiting to get active." They conclude that in the future "the best run campaigns are going to be those that execute their traditional activities while fully integrating an online GOTV campaign."[19]

The Republicans have been playing "catch up" in recent years in linking new technologies with their GOTV operations. Democrats and the Obama campaigns of 2008 and 2012 seemed to be on the cutting edge of integrating a wide variety of social media communication with microtargeting and direct voter mobilization. The Republicans' traditional program, known as STOMP (Strategic Taskforce to Mobilize and Organize People, and also known as the 72-Hour Program back in 2004), morphed into an earlier operation by 2010 (in light of new turnout models accounting for early and absentee voting). As one observer concluded at the time: "It's 720 hours now."[20] By the 2014 midterm, however, the

GOP developed an even broader program called "Victory 365" that RNC Chair Reince Priebus called "a permanent year around field program."[21] However, the jury is still out on how effective the GOP's latest GOTV efforts have been. While the party obviously had a great year in 2014, the overall turnout in the country actually declined from the 2010 midterm (40.9 to 35.9 percent), and the Republican share of the national House vote was slightly lower in the latter year (51.4 percent in 2014 compared with 51.7 in 2010).[22]

Traditional Media and the New Media

No greater evidence of the blending of old and new campaign strategies exists than in the use of both traditional and new media. It is certainly the case that the sources of traditional media—television and radio—are losing their influence relative to other sources of information gathering on the Internet. It is also the case that the television itself as a medium has changed. Viewers have gone beyond watching the three major networks of thirty years ago to fifty or more today. So the contemporary television media environment has become more fragmented, and voters are harder to reach. This has put a premium on using the same type of microtargeting strategies discussed above in direct mail and GOTV.

Most modern campaigns, of course, use a variety of both traditional and nontraditional forms in an integrated strategy to communicate with voters. This pattern is certain to continue in the future. In fact, a campaign may use a controversial or unique television ad to leverage earned media coverage on its distinctiveness and encourage viewers to see it on YouTube or the campaign website (further reinforcing the message). Viral videos are now commonplace where a campaign spreads them through the Internet and earned media (such as the Mitt Romney 47 percent video that became popular after he made controversial remarks at a Republican fundraiser). If successful, they may keep an opponent "off his or her game," off message, and on the defensive.

A consultant who ran a concerted viral video effort for the Democrats in Missouri, Isaac Wright, points out that television ads are "meant to catch a viewer's eye for a 30-second window of advertising during the viewer's program of choice. The length of a viral video [however] is limited only by its ability to hold a viewer's attention."[23] Wright notes that the strategy "was to use the videos to drive earned media coverage, not only of the videos themselves, but also of selected issues in the campaign. Videos were posted repeatedly on newspaper websites and on political news blogs and even aired on the news. . . . The news in turn drove news consuming voters online to watch more of the videos, spreading the message even further."[24]

In 2012, the Obama campaign used political memes to accomplish some of the same goals—keeping an opponent on the defensive and off message. For example, it quickly developed a political meme to parody the bizarre performance of Clint Eastwood at the RNC. The actor's rambling came just minutes before Mitt Romney gave his acceptance speech. The rapid spread of the Eastwood incident on Twitter, Facebook, and cable news distracted from the substantive postconvention coverage of Romney's speech.

These examples help illustrate that there is no rigid dichotomy between traditional and nontraditional forms of communication. They are both evolving in modern campaigns that simultaneously use both to choreograph their messages to voters.

Party Organizations—Alive and Well

It is common for political observers to refer to the current era as one of party revitalization since the organizations have reemerged from their nadir in the 1960s and 1970s. U.S. parties have now moved beyond revitalization. They revitalized in the 1980s and 1990s by adapting to changing campaign technologies and increased ideological polarization. At this point, parties are firmly established as critical service providers and the central players in national elections. The two major national parties currently spend approximately $1 billion each per election cycle. They have elaborate organizational structures that perform a wide variety of campaign functions. In short, their service provider role in modern election campaigns has been firmly institutionalized. Therefore, any immediate future change in U.S. parties is likely to be incremental rather than radical.

Greater Integrated Roles and Functions of Parties

One likely change is that divergent campaign roles and functions will become increasingly integrated. The techniques of microtargeting, for example, are used in a variety of different forms of campaign communication—direct mail, fundraising, GOTV, and both traditional and new media. As discussed earlier, future campaigns must successfully integrate these seemingly divergent techniques.

A similar trend toward the merging of so-called traditional and new media is almost certain to continue. In the twenty-first century, no one or two means of communication are sufficient to get a campaign message out to voters. Today, campaigns must use direct mail, microtargeted television, and radio ads along with Internet ads, Facebook, YouTube, websites, emails, text messaging, Twitter, Tumblr, and Pinterest. The diversification of communication forms will certainly continue in the near future along with an increase in the importance of mobile technology. These various forms must be used in concert to choreograph a consistent message. The merging of campaign media is further indicated by the decreased distinctiveness of the instruments of communication. Cell phones, laptop computers, and televisions are beginning to perform many of the same core functions. Indeed, we may eventually get to the point where the distinction between traditional and new media itself becomes a relic of the past.

Future Challenges: Demographic Change and Realignment?

In the immediate future, both national parties will need to adapt to more than changing campaign technologies in order to thrive. The 2010 census clearly indicates that the electorate itself has changed in ways that will affect the future election campaigns of both major political parties. Overall, the minority population increased from 30.9 to 36.3 percent of the population from 2000 to 2010. There are now four majority-minority states in the Union—California, Hawaii, New Mexico, and Texas. Further, the minority populations in five states are rapidly approaching a majority—Arizona, Florida, Georgia, Maryland, and Nevada. The diversification has been most dramatic in the Southwest and was largely responsible for turning three 2004 Bush states in the region—Colorado, Nevada, and New Mexico—toward Obama in both 2008 and 2012 (all by margins exceeding the national average). These changes present new challenges to Republicans and potential opportunities to Democrats.

The demographic change in the electorate may complicate the Republicans' effort to take full advantage of the redistricting they dominated after the 2010 elections. Consider, for example, that all but one of the Bush/McCain/Romney states that gained congressional seats after 2010 have minority populations of 36 percent or more. The one exception is Utah, which had the second-highest percentage rate increase in racial minorities (64.8 percent) among the states.[25] In short, the "red states" are gaining population primarily because they are becoming more racially diverse.

To illustrate how changes in the composition of the electorate can dramatically affect election results, consider the state of New Mexico in 2004 compared with 2008. In the former year, George Bush managed to narrowly defeat John Kerry statewide (50–49 percent) by winning the white vote 56 to 43 percent. In the latter year, Barack Obama managed to win by a near landslide margin statewide (57–42 percent) solely by increasing his vote among non-whites (and their percentage of the electorate). The white vote was virtually identical between the two elections except that Obama was slightly weaker among whites than Kerry (56 percent for McCain to 42 percent for Obama).[26]

Republicans must increase their vote share among racial minorities, or they will need unrealistically high percentages among whites to prevail in future elections. Consider the critical case of Texas, which currently has a 55 percent minority population. The electoral arithmetic in contests for either the presidency or Congress would be very difficult for national Republicans if they lost their majority seats in the Lone Star State. Since exit polls were not conducted during the 2012 and 2014 elections in Texas, let's examine the top-of-the-ticket race for governor in 2010. Incumbent Rick Perry won the governor's race 55 percent to 42 percent. This 13 percent plurality might seem comfortable at the surface. However, in this election, the 45 percent white minority cast 67 percent of the state's votes. Further, Republican governor Perry won those white voters 69 percent to 29 percent. These are thresholds that the Texas GOP will not likely be able to maintain in the future. In order for the party to maintain competitiveness, much less its majority status, it will need to make substantial inroads among racial minorities.[27]

Clearly, the demographic changes in the electorate will affect the future election campaigns of both major political parties, but at this point, the Republicans appear to have the much greater challenge. They have to be able to appeal to racial minorities with greater success than in the past while not alienating their ideological base. The GOP already has the more intense ideological divide over critical issues that are unlikely to fade anytime soon. However, Republicans will have to diversify to remain competitive. As they do so, both parties will necessarily undergo a realignment of coalition groups. Indeed, the realignment has been progressing for many years. Democrats have become an increasingly diverse party demographically (while becoming more unified ideologically) as the Republicans have remained homogeneous demographically (but have maintained or increased their internal ideological divisions). A continuation of this trend in the future is unsustainable if we are to maintain a viable two-party system. The coalitional realignment will likely occur even if the balance of power between the parties remains the same—rough parity with a slight Democratic edge.[28]

Conclusion

We have seen that the parties continue to make strides in being effective service providers again. While it has not reached the level of effectiveness that existed before the era of candidate-centered politics (which emerged in the late 1960s), parties are once again key players who can affect the course of elections. They will likely continue to adapt to changes in the political environment, to demographic composition of the electorate, and to the ever-changing technological means of campaign communication and fundraising (although the *Citizens United* decision could continue to reduce their relative impact and control over message content). The new campaign technologies seem to revolutionize rather than replace the older, traditional means of communication. Successful campaigns of the future will continue to integrate the two. Indeed, the distinctions between old and new technologies may be becoming irrelevant.

The ideological polarization between the parties is likely to continue because both parties stand for something completely different. The consequences of increased interparty ideological polarization include increases in intraparty unity and discipline among elected officeholders, increased cohesion within the organizations, and the facilitation of campaign fundraising from ideological donors. However, while many observers claim that it also leads to overheated and exaggerated partisan rhetoric, campaign distortions are as American as apple pie.

Regular partisan pendulum swings are likely to continue to characterize our partisan electoral competition. Since the New Deal realignment when the Democrats won five successive presidential elections (1932–1948), for example, there have been fairly consistent eight-year swings in party control of the presidency (if Carter had won reelection in 1980, the swings would have been perfect). In the short term, however, the pendulum swings may continue within very narrow parameters. Consider the comparison of the post–New Deal realignment elections. From 1948 until 1988, a majority (seven out of eleven) presidential elections were won by comfortable margins or landslides (1952, 1956, 1964, 1972, 1980, 1984, 1988). Since the 1980s, all of our elections have been comparatively close (Obama's 52.9 percent in 2008 is the highest percentage received among candidates in the last six elections).

The balance of power between our ideologically polarized parties will remain very tight in the future since we really don't have a majority party in the United States today. In a sense, both the Democrats and the Republicans are minority parties. They are also nearly equal in their proportion of party identifiers in the electorate. In the current electoral environment, we consider winning 53 percent of the vote to be a decisive wave election (that was approximately the percentage won by the Republicans in 1994, 2010, and 2014; the Democrats in 2006; and Obama in 2008). The 53 percent figures (either Democratic or Republican) may come close to constituting the outer boundaries within which contemporary party competition is fought. This means a very small segment of the electorate will continue to hold the balance of power in the United States. Consequently, in the foreseeable future, political parties will continue to develop more sophisticated techniques to increase the precision and effectiveness of campaign communication in reaching these voters to win elections.

Notes

1. Cornelius P. Cotter and Bernard C. Hennessy, *Politics without Power: The National Party Committees* (New York: Atherton, 1964).
2. John Aldrich, *Why Parties? The Origin and Transformation of Party Politics in America* (Chicago: University of Chicago Press, 1995). One of the significant themes of the book.
3. Paul Waldman, "Indiana Controversy Shows What a Minefield 2016 GOP Primary Has Become" (*The Washington Post*, April 3, 2015). Accessed on October 11, 2015, from www.washingtonpost.com.

4. Ronald G. Shaiko, "Political Parties—On the Path to Revitalization," in *Campaigns on the Cutting Edge*, edited by Richard J. Semiatin (Washington, DC: CQ Press, 2008), 106.

5. Michael Saul, "GOP Chairman Michael Steele and Pundit Rush Limbaugh in War of Words" (*Daily News*, March 3, 2009).

6. Quoted in "Race for RNC Chairman Remains a Toss-Up as Steele Defends Tenure" (*The Hill*, December 26, 2010).

7. The Situation Room, "Interview with Former RNC Chairman Michael Steele" (*Real Clear Politics*, January 19, 2011).

8. Susan Davis, "Keeping Control of the Senate 2012 May Be a Hill Too Steep for Democrats. But Patty Murray Is Trying" (*National Journal*, June 9, 2011).

9. Aaron Blake, "NRCC Young Guns Run the Gamut as Party Eyes Possibility of Big Gains in '10" (*The Hill*, February 16, 2010).

10. Sean J. Miller, "Strategists Second-Guess Dem Spending Strategy after Losses in House" (*The Hill*, November 9, 2010).

11. Shaiko, "Political Parties," 110.

12. Michael E. Toner and Karen E. Trainer, "The Impact of the Federal Election Laws on the 2010 Midterm Election," in *Pendulum Swing*, edited by Larry J. Sabato (Boston, MA: Longman, 2011), 131–155.

13. See Sandy L. Maisel and Darrel West, "Running on Empty? Political Discourse," in *Congressional Elections* (Lanham, MD: Rowman and Littlefield, 2004); David B. Magleby and Marjorie Holt, *Outside Money, Soft Money and Issue Ads in Competitive 1998 Congressional Elections* (Provo, UT: Brigham Young University, 1999).

14. Karen Tucker, "Mail Power Is Your Power" (*Politics*, May 24, 2010). Accessed October 11, 2015 from http://www.campaignsandelections.com/magazine/2113/mail-power-is-your-power.

15. Jeremy P. Jacobs, "Buzzword: Modeling: Definition: Analysis of Voters Used to Win Elections" (*Politics*, October 2009), 16.

16. Jacobs, Buzzword," 18.

17. Ibid.

18. David All and Jerome Armstrong, "Why You Should Start Your Online GOTV Early" (*Politics*, October 2009), 19.

19. Ibid.

20. Rich Beeson quoted in Erin Pike, "72 Hours Is So Five Years Ago" (*Politics*, October 2009), 51.

21. Reince Priebus, "Two Years Later, GOP Shows Growth and Opportunity" (*Real Clear Politics*, March 18, 2015). Accessed October 11, 2015, from www.realclearpolitics.com.

22. See Larry J. Sabato, "A Midterm Course Correction," in *The Surge: 2014's Big GOP Win and What It Means for the Next Presidential Election* (Lanham, MD: Rowman and Littlefield, 2015),1–36.

23. Issac Wright, "It's More Than Just Putting Ads Online" (*Politics*, November/December 2009), 39.

24. Wright, "It's More Than Just Putting Ads Online," 40.

25. See Table 11, "Non-Hispanic White Alone Population and the Minority Population for the U.S. Region, for States and for Puerto Rico: 2000 and 2010," in *Overview of*

Race and Hispanic Origin: 2010, issued March 2011. Accessed October 11, 2015, from www.census.gov/prod/cen2010/briefs/c2010br-02.pdf.

26. These data come from the 2004 and 2008 National Exit Polls (NEP) conducted by Edison Media Research. See also the analysis of New Mexico in Chuck Todd and Sheldon Gawsier, *How Barack Obama Won: A State-by-State Guide to the Historic 2008 Presidential Election* (New York: Vintage Books, 2009), 124–128.

27. These data come from the 2010 NEP conducted by Edison Media Research. See also "The Latino Vote in the 2010 Elections" (www.pewhispanic.org, updated December 30, 2010) and Jim Henson and Joshua Blank, "The Polling Center: Playing the Right Anglos" (*The Texas Tribune*, February 11, 2014).

28. See Bill McInturff and Martin Shull, "A Long Horizon: Some Observation about Party Identification Over the Last 25 Years" (*Public Opinion Strategies*, April 1, 2015). Accessed on October 11, 2015, from www.pos.org.

CHAPTER 8

Interest Groups, Super PACs, and Independent Expenditures

Nina Therese Kasniunas, Mark J. Rozell, and Charles N. W. Keckler

POLITICIANS OF ALL PARTIES AGREE ON THIS ONE THING—they are ready to take on "the special interests," because interest groups are too powerful in U.S. democracy. At the same time, and to an increasing degree, most candidates for office have come to rely on outside expenditures to get elected or reelected. Interest groups have become the potent intervening force in political campaigns by influencing the choices of voters. In recent years, interest groups have often resembled political parties in their ability to inform, influence, and mobilize hundreds of thousands or even millions of voters to get to the polls.[1]

As we prepare for the 2016 elections, it is clear that outside groups are having a larger and more pervasive influence on campaigns than ever before. Formally independent entities organized to support a candidate, most notably one or more Super PACs, are now a de rigueur accompaniment for any serious federal campaign. But genuinely independent forces representing ideological interests rather than a particular candidate, and driven especially by a "donor class" of a few hundred politically active wealthy individuals, have also dramatically increased their election spending.

Two events laid the groundwork for these ongoing changes. At the level of process, the deregulation of campaign finance in 2010 greatly facilitated higher donation levels by the wealthy to both causes and candidates. Almost at the same time, a set of new interest groups supporting broad goals of limited government arose, commonly labeled collectively as the "Tea Party." These groups, a form of populist conservatism that can also be considered a proto-faction of the Republican Party, had a strong incentive to immediately use the new campaign mechanisms in both primary and general elections, which they could define around their core issues. This encouraged more establishment Republicans, Democrats, and traditional interest groups all to adopt the new forms of finance, partly in order to keep up. The consequent "arms race" with different interests and parties attempting to outspend one another in order to get a decisive advantage—but, in fact, usually canceling each other out—is the situation in which we find ourselves today, and for the near future.

What ensues is a discussion of the traditional role of interest groups in national elections. We then build off that with the major developments of Super PACs and a new type of electoral interest group known as a 501(c)(4).

Traditional Approaches by Interest Groups in Campaigns

Interest groups become involved in electoral politics in a variety of ways. For example, groups try to identify voters who are sympathetic to certain issue positions and then provide resources to ensure that those people vote. Many groups purchase campaign broadcast ads in areas of the country where there are competitive elections. The 2014 race for Colorado's Senate seat attracted much interest group spending. The conservative group Crossroads GPS, for example, spent $8.7 million in independent expenditures against the incumbent, Democrat Mark Udall, while the liberal NextGen Climate Action spent $7.4 million advocating against the challenger, Republican Cory Gardner, and for the Democratic incumbent. Some groups train activists in the techniques of campaigns, and other groups actively recruit and train candidates for public office. EMILY's List, a group that supports pro-choice Democratic women, does so with great success. These are among the many ways in which interest groups try to affect the outcomes of U.S. elections at all levels.

Groups' efforts to influence elections have become increasingly sophisticated. Groups with substantial resources make use of the latest technologies to communicate with large numbers of activists, supporters, and other potential voters. New technologies have made it possible for groups with fewer resources also to communicate with large numbers of people in campaigns.

Although new technologies are rapidly transforming the ways in which groups become involved in campaigns, most still rely on tried and tested techniques. If anything, technology is enabling more efficient use of those methods. Most every interest group and campaign has a presence on social networking sites like Facebook, Twitter, Instagram, and YouTube. This is particularly important for Millennials who are less brand and bond oriented than previous generations.

Recruiting and Training Candidates

Traditionally, by reaching out to potential candidates and offering encouragement and support, interest groups can also influence who decides to run for office.

By offering training, groups can potentially influence who wins elections. Many groups find that the most reliable and loyal candidates are drawn from the ranks of their own organizations. The American Federation of Labor and Congress of Industrial Organizations (AFL-CIO), for example, decided that it can best promote its policy goals by recruiting its own members, rather than by recruiting and training candidates from outside the labor movement, who may agree with some—but not all—of the labor agenda. The organization thus has pursued a program of actively recruiting and training labor union members to run for public offices.

The National Women's Political Caucus (NWPC) has mounted a large-scale effort to recruit women to run for public office. The caucus holds training events to teach state and local activists how to identify potentially strong candidates and campaign managers. Thousands of women have participated in NWPC candidate training seminars, including Rep. Linda Sánchez (D-CA), who says that she got her start in politics by attending one of these events.[2] Many other groups hold training seminars for potential candidates and provide various other resources such as training manuals, video and audio tapes, and access to pollsters and campaign consultants.

The decision to recruit and train candidates is based on two considerations: first, whether the person agrees with the policy goals of the organization, and second, whether the person has a realistic chance of winning. Groups want to expend their resources strategically and may turn away from an ambitious person who supports key policy stands but is not likely to win an election for whatever reason.

Endorsements and Hit Lists

Organizations issue formal endorsements to signal to their members which candidates best represent their viewpoints. Endorsements are primarily a means to convince group members to vote for the candidates who will be most friendly to the group's interests once elected. Not all groups issue endorsements. Some do not so as to maintain tax-exempt status. Others make a strategic decision not to alienate candidates who might win and become unfavorably inclined toward those who had endorsed their opponent.

The endorsement is not only a signal to group members as to which candidates win the "seal of approval," but it is also a means to persuade a larger public. Thus, an endorsement from the Sierra Club or the League of Conservation Voters (LCV) would be a strong signal to voters as to which candidate in a campaign is more environmentally friendly. A National Rifle Association (NRA) endorsement tells many voters which candidate is likely to uphold the interests of gun owners. Groups have to issue endorsements carefully and strategically, however, because they can backfire. In addition to issuing positive endorsements, interest groups may single out candidates for defeat via what is commonly known as a "hit list." Perhaps the best-known hit list is the "Dirty Dozen" named by the LCV. It is a list of those the league considers the twelve most environmentally unfriendly members of Congress. By using a catchy and memorable name for the list, the LCV succeeds in attracting media and public attention to the races where it has targeted candidates for defeat.

But groups can also target candidates for defeat without calling the roll of names a hit list. With the use of social networking media, interest groups are quickly and cheaply sending out newsfeeds requesting donations to support the opponents of candidates targeted for defeat. For example, EMILY's List will add to its Facebook newsfeed an item listing the members in Congress who are most hostile to the pro-choice agenda, requesting support for the challengers to these incumbents.

Modern Techniques Employed by Traditional Interest Groups in Campaigns

Although groups use a variety of techniques to try to influence campaigns, technology is changing at a rapid pace and redefining how races are conducted. Groups can offer resources to candidates in an environment that is demanding more and more exploitation of every possible source of support.

An Overview of Cutting-Edge Fundraising Techniques

Well before Super PACs were ever thought of, a fundamental but extremely important strategy of interest groups in campaigns was raising and contributing money. Since the Federal Election Campaign Act (FECA) was enacted in the early 1970s, interest groups that want to contribute to a candidate or party have had to do so through a political action committee (PAC). PACs are simply organizations that exist to raise and contribute money in federal elections. Although some PACs are unconnected—they are not affiliated with another organization—most are the fundraising entities of parent organizations. For example, BankPac is the PAC of the American Bankers Association. BluePac is affiliated with the Blue Cross and Blue Shield Association. An example of an unconnected PAC is the Prostate Cancer Research PAC, which was formed as an organization in its own right, without ties to any other.

Interest groups have various reasons for wanting to make campaign contributions. Some contribute to try to affect the membership of Congress. They want to elect members of Congress who support the ideas, ideologies, and policy positions of their organizations. This is the case with labor unions, which are among the most prolific fundraisers. Because labor unions follow this strategy, they strongly support Democratic candidates; few Republican candidates have platforms that are compatible with unionism. The round of state legislative action against collective bargaining rights witnessed in Wisconsin, Ohio, and Indiana in early 2011 underscores why the ideological composition of a legislative body is the primary goal of labor unions. Other interest groups make campaign contributions to the candidates they believe are most likely to win, to seek favor with them once they become elected officials. This explains why the National Association of Realtors contributed slightly more money to Democrats in the 2008 and 2010 elections, but more to Republicans in 2012 and 2014 and in the elections from 1996 to 2006; the group uses incumbency as the cue for whom it will support.

Even if an interest group chooses not to engage in elections by making campaign contributions, it has an interest in raising money. No organization can maintain itself without financial resources; rents, salaries, and other bills need to be paid. Interest groups that are businesses, corporations, or other for-profit entities use a portion of their profits to cover the costs of their lobbying efforts. Some support themselves financially through foundation or government grants or through the generosity of patrons. But other groups, especially membership groups, solicit contributions from individuals. Such solicitation has traditionally been done through massive direct mailings. AARP, the NRA, and the Sierra Club all have raised millions of dollars through direct mailings. Purchasing the mailing lists for these appeals can be costlier, as is creating a professional, attractive brochure or packet. While direct mailings were cutting-edge technology in the 1980s, many groups still find it an effective way to communicate a message.

New Trends in Interest Group Websites

Most interest groups now maintain their own websites, which characterize their personalities. Some, such as the NRA, have a lot of live-action video and movement, highlighting action and independence. Others, such as the Communications Workers of America's Committee on Political Education (CWA-COPE), display a blog-style menu that invites group participation. Technology now makes it possible for a group to collect contributions securely through its website. An interest group site may feature a page that enables the visitor to contribute using a credit card or check. At the very least, the webpage can provide the user with a downloadable contribution form, which can be printed and sent to the organization. In some sectors of membership groups, such as civil rights and human rights, environmental, and single-issue groups, almost every website allows the user to donate money. Having an interactive website allows the interest group to collect contact information that is then used to communicate information during a campaign or solicit a contribution for its PAC, 527 group, or Super PAC.

Pop-ups Advance the Interest Group Cause

The pop-up windows soliciting donations are used strategically. A candidate might reveal a policy position in a debate or campaign stop that might be opposed by an interest group's supporters. As soon as that controversial position is revealed, the interest group can create a pop-up window to educate the website visitor of the stance followed by a request for a campaign contribution. The publicized event may have prompted the individual to visit the website because he or she either wanted more information or wanted to do something about the issue at stake. Playing on the possible emotional state of visitors, the pop-up immediately was in the face of the user, asking for money. In this way, pop-ups are akin to direct mail sent to individual households, soliciting money by making an emotional appeal. Although direct mail is used on an ongoing basis by some groups, some appeals are timed to follow events that might raise concern about the issue the group represents, a strategy we also see being used with the pop-ups.

Email Alerts

Collecting email updates from a number of these interest groups over several months reveals how most groups use this feature. The League of United Latin American Citizens sends its email network policy updates a couple of times a week. Although the emails are primarily informational, a prompt that is part of the template says "Donate." Defenders of Wildlife uses its network similarly to the way that the NRA and the National Organization for Women (NOW) use theirs. All of these groups have similar templates and thus afford the same opportunity to their users. Greenpeace sends out an email alert that breaks the pattern. Prominently featured on the right side of its email, in an eye-catching green color, is the list "3 Ways to Help." The first is "Donate." The prominence and frequency with which one can find an option to donate or contribute give points to the utility of the website as a fundraising venue.

A few groups use email for the sole purpose of fundraising. For instance, the Wilderness Society distributed an email urging contributions on behalf of saving the Tongass National Forest. Defenders of Wildlife has also employed this technique.

Although it seems as if an email network would frequently be used to solicit contributions, most emails include only a passive prompt in the background, giving the option of making a donation online. Very few groups use the network solely to raise money, and even the ones that do more frequently send emails requesting some other type of political action. Emails asking for money are used sparingly. The Sierra Club, the American Civil Liberties Union (ACLU), Defenders of Wildlife, the National Wildlife Federation, People for the American Way, Greenpeace, and Beyond Pesticides are just a handful of senders of the almost-daily direct mailings. Not only have groups not yet abandoned the age-old practice of using direct mail, but they are fattening their lists with addresses that are provided when individuals subscribe to email alerts.[3]

Interest Groups, Elections, and Mobile Technology

Ninety-one percent of Americans in 2013 owned a cell phone, and more than half of Americans use their cell phones to go online for information, according to the Pew Research Center, with 17 percent doing most of their browsing on smartphones.[4] Not willing to neglect an opportunity to connect with supporters, interest groups are also harnessing mobile technology. Text messages to direct supporters to online links where they can make financial contributions, much like website pop-up messaging does. All the interest group needs is a user's cell phone number. Interest groups are also holding true to the saying "There's an app for that!" While this is an emerging avenue for interest groups, already the NRA and America Votes have free smartphone applications available. As the 2016 elections draw nearer, one can only imagine the number of applications to be developed by interest groups, for example displaying voter guides that individuals can use at the polls.

Informing via Webcasts, Podcasts, and Blogs

Another way in which groups attempt to shape the issue agenda of elections is by providing information directly to like-minded individuals. That way, the groups can frame the issue so as to emphasize their own policy positions. Technology has transformed this technique by enabling rapid transmission of news, campaign updates, and policy updates via webcasts, podcasts, blogs, and social media sites such as Facebook and Twitter.

A webcast is a live video feed or broadcast over the Internet. Webcasts are scheduled for live airing much as television shows are. A group's leadership can schedule a webcast, advertise it to its membership and other interested individuals, and then be able to enter the homes of the many supporters watching. An added benefit of webcasts is that usually they are then stored as a video file, accessible on the website for multiple viewings after the initial broadcast.

Podcasts are audio files that are fed over the Internet in a format that can be downloaded and listened to on an MP3 player. Podcasting enables a radio type of broadcast that is freely available to any subscriber. The advantage of podcasting is that the organization can feature news that is of interest to its members. The organization gets to pick the subject of the podcast and frame issues that serve its own interests.

Many groups feature blogs to try to engage activists regularly on core issues in campaigns. Human Rights Campaign, for example, features on its website its "HRC Blog" to update gay and lesbian activists on a variety of developing policy- and campaign-related issues. Interest groups even help to inspire and coordinate individual bloggers who may follow a campaign closely and write about it regularly. Almost all groups have Twitter feeds for activists to receive frequent updates and alerts on issues and campaigns.

Social Networking Sites for Interest Groups

Increasingly, however, the medium of choice is Facebook. Facebook allows the interest group to post news updates, which are then included in the newsfeeds of subscribers. When a subscriber logs onto his or her Facebook page, he or she will see the news item posted by the interest group.

Additionally, Facebook allows commentary to be posted by subscribers, which can build a sense of solidarity. Subscribers can receive the information passively, or they can engage with others who are also compelled to respond. When the comments affirm or reinforce one another, a sense of community develops. Lastly, Facebook can be used to build social networks, literally. Increasingly, groups are using Facebook to announce meet-ups and demonstrations. In 2011, the Tea Party Patriots used Facebook to announce and encourage attendance to the opening of *Atlas Shrugged* in movie theaters. Mass attendance of Tea Partiers could create a sense of solidarity, which would affirm and strengthen their ideology. Various locals of the American Federation of Teachers frequently post demonstration dates and times on their Facebook page. For instance, a New York local announced a rally in twelve different regions of the state for "Fair Contracts, No Layoffs." Demonstrations in state capitals involved in the debate over public bargaining were largely publicized and disseminated through Facebook.

Facebook also continues to introduce programming that is useful and relevant for interest groups. The conservative 527 committee RightChange, for instance, created a Facebook page that features the option to "Connect," which prompts the user to sign up for email updates similar to the requests found on group websites. Facebook pages now often supplement websites as the central information and solicitation portals for interest groups.

The Blogosphere

Interest groups have long cultivated relationships with the media not only to become trusted sources of information for reporters but also to gain favorable coverage in reporting. As bloggers now constitute an important sector of the media, they receive a lot of attention from the various groups involved in campaigns and elections. A number of groups will host events and conferences that feature candidates. For example, the American Conservative Union hosts a Conservative Political Action Conference (CPAC) each year to showcase the actual or potential

Republican presidential candidates. When the group announces such events, it specifically invites bloggers and allows them special access to candidates immediately following their speeches.

Issue Advocacy and Independent Expenditures

The law limits how much money PACs can contribute to campaigns. The current campaign finance law stipulates that no more than $5,000 per election may be contributed to any candidate. For those PACs and interest groups that raise tens of millions of dollars each election cycle, these are severe constraints. Even before Super PACs came on the scene, interest groups found ways to circumvent them, however, raising and spending money in ways that are influential in elections yet still legal.

The first way is by engaging in issue advocacy. *Issue advocacy* is the term used to identify any money that is spent advocating some specific issue or policy position. For example, in both 2010 and 2012, Citizens Against Government Waste ran a controversial one-minute campaign ad that depicts a Beijing, China, lecture hall in the year 2030. The visual presentation shows images of ancient Greece, the Roman Empire, the British Empire, and the United States, while the professor lectures how none of these nations embraced the lesson that made them great. Their one failure: they attempted to tax and spend their way out of recession. Health care spending and public takeover of private industry are noted, and the professor laughs, saying that because China owns most of the U.S. debt, Americans now work for the Chinese. The commercial ends with the message "Stop the spending that is bankrupting America."[5] The ad implies that the viewer should vote out of office those responsible for the runaway spending—the Democrats—without ever explicitly calling for the election or defeat of any one candidate or party.

Because they contain no explicit call for the election or defeat of a candidate, these types of ads technically are about issues, not the elections, and therefore are protected by a PAC's free speech rights. There is therefore no limit on the amount of money an interest group may spend on issue advocacy. However, the seemingly small but critical advantage of the Super PAC over the traditional PAC is that the Super PAC can *also* engage in express advocacy and urge the viewer to vote one way or another (i.e., "Vote free-spending Senator X out of office before he squanders our legacy"). If this is what the group actually desires, it will usually choose to operate via a Super PAC and approach its goal directly rather than indirectly, as discussed below.

The Emergence of Super PACs

One major recent development that will continue to have an impact in the 2016 elections is the Supreme Court ruling in *Citizens United v. FEC* (558 U.S. 310

[2010]) and the companion decision of the U.S. Court of Appeals in *SpeechNow .org v. FEC* (599 F.3d 686 [D.C. Cir. 2010]), which eliminated limits on individual contributions made to independent expenditure organizations. Together, as the Federal Election Commission (FEC) soon recognized in new rules, these decisions meant that corporations and unions could also make unlimited contributions to these entities; importantly, this includes nonprofit corporations (like the original plaintiff Citizens United, in fact). The term *Super PAC* has been created to identify those entities that engage solely in independent expenditures, which still must register with the FEC and disclose their donors but which otherwise have great flexibility and thus are the new vehicle of choice for much political fundraising and activity.

Super PACs emerged in the 2010 elections with quite a presence and grew quickly. According to the Center for Responsive Politics,[6] Super PACs spent $62.6 million in the 2010 midterm elections, with 60 percent of the money spent by conservative groups such as American Crossroads and 39 percent spent by liberal groups. In 2012, however, that increased nearly by an order of magnitude to $609.4 million. The conservative emphasis, driven by well-funded Super PACs supporting presidential candidate Mitt Romney, and heavy Republican primary expenditure, actually increased the difference to 67–32 percent. However, the most recent election cycle, the 2014 midterm, which lacked these factors, shows the left end of the spectrum has more than caught up when it comes to Super PACs: in 2014, liberal supporting groups spent 52 percent of the Super PAC dollars and conservatives only 44 percent.[7]

Super PACs were not completely unprecedented. Individual millionaires and billionaires always had the ability to sponsor independent ads at whatever level they chose so long as they reported what they did to the FEC and identified themselves as sponsors of the ads. However, few chose to go through the hassle and public exposure of personally organizing such efforts. Especially since 2004, unlimited contributions could also flow into what is called 527 groups (named after part of the tax code), which did facilitate big-dollar donations and provide an organizational structure for political activity but which were limited solely to *issue* advocacy. That is, they could promote a position like more support for oral health but could not urge the election of a dentist to Congress. Because Super PACs can do both types of advocacy, they have quickly supplanted 527s as an organizational form for interest groups to process large donations.

Today, there have evolved four kinds of Super PACs, which differ in function rather than legal status. First, there is the Super PAC operated on behalf of the traditional special interest, like the National Association of Realtors or the League of Conservation Voters (ninth and tenth on the Super PAC list for 2014 compiled by the Center for Responsive Politics). Second, there is the shadow party Super PAC, technically independent of the major parties but staffed by loyal operatives and directed at gaining partisan political power, such as the Senate Majority PAC (a Democratic Super PAC that led all groups in 2014 by spending $29.4 million in an attempt to hold the Senate). Third, there are Super PACs in between the first two categories, essentially representing Republican Party factions but that could alternatively, as we discuss above, be conceived of as ideological interest groups supporting or opposing the Tea Party agenda. This, on the libertarian conservative side, would include the Koch-led Freedom Partners and, on the mainstream conservative side, Karl Rove's American Crossroads (which could also be characterized as a shadow party Super PAC).[8]

The final important species of Super PAC is the single-candidate Super PAC, also known as an "alter-ego" Super PAC. This is a candidate-specific entity that, like party Super PACs but at the individual level, is technically "independent" of its sponsor but staffed by loyalists and directed at the same ends such as the Right to Rise USA Super PAC for 2016 Republican presidential candidate Jeb Bush. The candidate—once he or she declares himself or herself officially in the race—cannot ask for mega-donations for this "separate" entity but even then can ask for smaller donations and appear on its behalf. Nor can the official campaign (once it starts) and the alter-ego Super PAC coordinate their activities legally, but this provision has turned out to be difficult to enforce in practice, as the positions, activities, and advertisements of the candidate are usually easily available on the campaign websites.

Even though this is a way, as with the party Super PACs, for the political insiders to get back some control of the money flow, alter-ego Super PACs represent a new important conduit for outsiders. Despite having similar staff and goals, the reason for the Super PAC is its capacity to accept unlimited donations, which means that high-value donors can potentially come to exert outsize control over its activities. In the current cycle, Sen. Ted Cruz (R-TX) has not one but four alter-ego Super PACs to support his presidential ambitions (named Keep the Promise I through Keep the Promise IV), apparently in order to offer a menu of potential activities that might appeal to different mega-donors. For instance, some might want to fund attacks on Cruz's opponents, and some would prefer more positive activities—the multiple organizations allow multiple people to put their own stamp on a Super PAC, all while bolstering Cruz.

501(c)(4) Groups and "Dark Money"

In addition to Super PACs, the next-largest category of independent expenditures in the last two cycles were made by 501(c)(4) organizations, which in practice tend to be intertwined with Super PAC activities. These groups accounted for a quarter of nonparty outside spending in 2012 and a slightly smaller 21 percent in 2014.[9] 501(c)(4) entities refer to the relevant provision of the tax code and have long existed as a form of nonprofit tax-exempt organization, the generic designation of which by the Internal Revenue Service (IRS) is a "social welfare organization." Traditionally, this meant civic organizations and clubs pursuing (their own version) of the public interest. Unlike 501(c)(3) nonprofits, groups operating under 501(c)(4) can engage in political activity so long as it is not their principal activity. One aspect of the *Citizens United* decision allowed them (like other corporations) broader scope in making electioneering communications up to the date of the election, and so long as they spend other money on issue advocacy (of the sort 527s can engage in), grassroots lobbying, and voter education, interest groups using this form seem to be operating within the law as it currently exists.

Another aspect of campaign finance deregulation, stemming from the logic of the *SpeechNow* case, is that a 501(c)(4) may also make unlimited donations to an independent expenditure Super PAC. It is now common for both types of organizations to be created together and operate symbiotically. For instance, American Crossroads (Super PAC) is twinned with Crossroads GPS (501(c)(4)). Crossroads GPS can supply American Crossroads with money, but it makes its own expenditures and does other sorts of advocacy and policy development. The great advantage of the 501(c)(4) is that it is protected by the principles of both freedom of speech and freedom of association, and as a consequence, its "membership" or donor list can remain private, while the Super PAC donors must be disclosed. Funds of this sort that are difficult to trace back to their sources are often referred to as "dark money."

The Cutting Edge of Super PACs and 501(c)(4) Organizations

The cutting-edge system for candidates is to create at least one entity of each type, along with a traditional PAC (useful for small-dollar donations and with permissible campaign coordination) and the campaign proper. This produces a minimum of four affiliated but distinct entities each with different capabilities and, when well organized, with a suitable division of labor. Former governor Jeb Bush's Right to Rise USA Super PAC is expected to undertake certain traditional campaign functions such as opposition research with its unlimited funds, while Right to Rise Policy Solutions (the 501(c)(4)) will develop white papers and positions (as well as capture those donors seeking discretion). By posting whatever material they develop on their websites, they can effectively keep the Bush campaign informed of their progress without violating the FEC or IRS rules.[10] This in turn will allow the more regulated entity—the campaign—to marshal its resources for other things. Especially if Bush is successful, we can expect this sort of "horizontally integrated" conglomerate to characterize campaigns going forward, and with the absence of the campaign organization, this will apply to many interest groups as well.

While very few publicly held corporations are contributors to Super PACs—they still normally give to trade associations—these *nonprofits* may now donate freely, and wealthy individuals also may use either nonprofits or their privately held companies as vehicles; this disguises the source of funds while it increases the money flow. The regulatory concern turns out to be not principally with corporations "pretending" to be persons, but instead with natural persons pretending to be corporations.

New Technologies Enhance the Power of Interest Groups in Campaigns

What, then, is the future of interest groups in campaigns? It is likely that groups will be increasingly active and influential as they exploit new technologies and means of communication. As one group leader put it, "The speed, scale, and precision with which issue groups can target candidates for communications from their membership and supporter base" will continue to advance. Viral communication techniques can "geometrically multiply the power of the membership base."[11] Whereas in the past groups focused on communication to mobilize a finite membership base to political action, in the future they will look not only to mobilize their bases but to use it to create much broader and more diffuse political pressure in campaigns. The emphasis will be on pushing issue agendas out into the public, rather than on forming bonds with candidates and party organizations as in the past.

Groups are also experimenting with ways to connect to potential voters through popular social networking sites on the Internet. As the Sierra Club's Greg Haegele put it, the potential payoff for groups could be substantial, if they can find ways to tap into social networks without undermining the very thing that attracts people to the sites in the first place—social bonds. Influencing potential voters, especially young people, to think of political activism and group politics as part of a social bond is a special challenge but one with strong potential for groups to exploit. Young voters used to adopt the party affiliation of their parents and hold on to those political bonds for a lifetime. As voters have become increasingly independent of the parties, they have also sought out alternative sources of political identification and networking. Groups will need to look for ways to attract the attention of these potential voters and convince them that certain issues are more paramount than others.[12]

Internet fundraising and organizing have been increasingly successful in recent election cycles, as particular issues or even candidates have attracted voter enthusiasm. For groups, this means that it will be more difficult in the future to rely on traditional means of building a steady core of dues-paying members; they will have to exert more effort to attract the attention of issues-conscious citizens. Haegele, for example, may have found convincing many environmentally conscious people to join the Sierra Club and write a check every year a greater challenge than did his predecessors. But he had available to him many more technologies to promote environmental issues before the public and to influence voters and candidates to place those issues at the forefront of campaigns.

Interest groups can use websites as effectively as, if not better than, parties or candidates because they have an ideological constituency that will normally direct traffic to their sites. In the next decade, interest groups will likely become more adept at mobilizing their existing bases to participate in the elections process. Moreover, if interest groups can harness that advance to substantially increase their fundraising, then their potency and reach will increase as well.

Conclusion: Looking Ahead to Group-Centered Politics

Despite all of the work that groups do to advertise issues and promote the fortunes of sympathetic candidates, campaigns will continue to lambaste "the politics of special interests." Whether they are Democrats, Republicans, or Independents, candidates find that attacking interest groups has populist appeal. But interest groups are healthier than ever today because sophisticated techniques to reach constituents—such as email, blogs, podcasting, and online videos, as well as traditional snail mail—enable them to remain in continual contact with their members. This is critical not only for fundraising but for mobilization to get-out-the-vote. Although interest groups may never be a popular feature of the electoral environment, they will continue to be at the forefront of campaigns in U.S. politics.

Although parties have always been stronger than the candidate-centered-politics thesis suggests, there is no doubt that campaigns have evolved to allow for more independence from the parties on the part of political candidates. That trend is being fostered in part by the ever-increasing role of interest groups. Candidates today do not need to rely so heavily on party organizations as in the past because they can benefit from the electoral activities of supportive groups to advertise a message and mobilize voters. With the deregulation of campaign contributions and expenditures, and the new energy of broad ideological pressure groups like the Tea Party, interest groups have come to play a stronger independent role. Although interest groups may not supplant parties, it is likely that as we approach the 2016 elections the power of such groups will rival the power of political parties.

We write this before even the first primaries have begun for the 2016 election cycle. Nevertheless, the role of Super PACs is already accelerating, with Sen. Ted Cruz's four Super PACs taking in $31 million in their first week, much from hedge-fund billionaire Robert Mercer.[13] The growth of well-funded alter-ego Super PACs moves some political power at least in the "orbit" of the candidate, although the influence and personality of the donors (including other organizations) will still be felt in these Super PACs.

At the same time, the network of large donors led by David and Charles Koch, Freedom Partners, has indicated a substantial increase in more clearly independent expenditures. This independence allows them to incentivize Republican candidates (especially in primaries) to agree with their libertarian objectives, and thus to *shape* the political party rather than merely support it. The new expenditure target of the Koch group, which will fund not only the candidates themselves but a whole chain of nonprofits and other entities (including money nominally attributed to other "special interests" like the Chamber of Commerce or NRA), is $889 million, more than doubling the estimated $400 million raised for the 2012 cycle.[14] However, other Republicans are mobilizing to use tens of millions to sway candidates toward more moderate positions on climate change, which easily might clash with Freedom Partners' positions.[15]

While it would be dangerous to specify a number in the 2016 election to compare with the outside expenditures of over $1 billion in 2012, according to the Center for Responsive Politics, we feel ourselves on safe ground stating it will be much higher.[16] Outside money in federal elections went up by more than four times between 2006 and 2010, and almost doubled again between 2010 and 2014. It grew almost three times between 2008 and 2012. It is possible to expect that number to exceed the $2 billion mark on expenditures reported to the FEC for 2016. This would not be at all surprising as the presumptive Democratic nominee, Hillary Clinton, has unusually strong ties to the financial sector, while the myriad Republican candidates guarantee an extended (and expensive) primary on the conservative side. In addition to what will likely be a close and highly consequential presidential election, the U.S. Senate will also be in play in 2016.

At some point, this geometric rate of increase in expenditures will have to stop, but it will not be before 2017. And what will likely slow it down will not be a newly activist Supreme Court or even growing public disquiet with the role of money in politics. Instead, the brakes will more probably be applied if and when donors perceive fewer advantages in giving. This could in principle occur if the parties and their candidates came to converge more closely on the issues, a prospect that is not impossible but seems unlikely to us at the moment. Perhaps more probable is the emergence of a sophisticated data-driven approach by donors that would quantify and act upon the diminishing returns to campaign activity, and identify alternatives—lobbying, research, and public education, for instance— that can achieve desired impacts at lower cost. But as long as interest groups and their backers perceive that they must outspend their ideological opponents in order to achieve their goals, the amount of outside money will continue to escalate without obvious limit.

Notes

1. Mark J. Rozell, Clyde Wilcox, and Michael Franz, *Interest Groups in American Campaigns: The New Face of Electioneering*, 3rd ed. (New York: Oxford University Press, 2012); Richard J. Semiatin and Mark J. Rozell, "Interest Groups in Congressional Elections," in *The Interest Group Connection*, 2nd ed., edited by Paul Herrnson, Ronald Shaiko, and Clyde Wilcox (Washington, DC: CQ Press, 2005), 75–88.

2. National Women's Political Caucus, "National Women's Political Caucus Training Program." Accessed on July 16, 2007, from www.nwpc.org/ht/d/sp/i/47229/pid/47229.

3. Although the individual is signing up for an email alert, the interest group typically asks for a name and home address in addition to the email address. This technique not only helps the interest group add to its own mailing lists, but the lists are also sold to other groups for profit.

4. Lee Rainie, "Cell Phone Ownership Hits 91% of Adults" (Pew Research Center, June 6, 2013). Accessed on June 30, 2015, from http://www.pewresearch.org/fact-tank/2013/06/06/cell-phone-ownership-hits-91-of-adults/.

5. "Chinese Professor" ad. Citizens Against Government Waste (CAGW). Uploaded on October 20, 2010, by CAGW to YouTube. Accessed on June 13, 2015, from YouTube.com.

6. All data from Center for Responsive Politics. Accessed on June 30, 2015, from www.opensecrets.org/outsidespending.

7. Ibid. All data from the paragraph come from the same source.

8. Data from Center for Responsive Politics. Accessed on June 30, 2015, from https://www.opensecrets.org/pacs/superpacs.php (2014 cycle).

9. See Center for Responsive Politics. Accessed on June 30, 2015, from https://www.opensecrets.org/outsidespending/fes_summ.php (comparing 2012 and 2014 tabs).

10. "How a Bush-Allied Nonprofit Could Inject More Secret Money into '16 Race" (*The Washington Post*, March 31, 2015). Accessed on June 30, 2015, from http://www.washingtonpost.com/politics/how-secret-donors-could-play-a-big-role-boosting-jeb-bush/2015/03/31/05647310-d7cd-11e4-b3f2-607bd612aeac_story.html.

11. Greg Haegele, Sierra Club, personal interview by email, July 5, 2007.

12. Haegele interview.

13. Mark Halperin, "Exclusive: New Ted Cruz Super-PACs Take in Record Haul" (*Bloomberg Politics*, April 8, 2015). Accessed on June 30, 2015, from http://www.bloomberg.com/politics/articles/2015-04-08/exclusive-new-ted-cruz-super-pacs-take-in-record-haul.

14. Kenneth P. Vogel, "The Kochs Put a Price on 2016: $889 Million" (*Politico*, January 26, 2015). Accessed on June 30, 2015, from http://www.politico.com/story/2015/01/koch-2016-spending-goal-114604.html.

15. Darren Goode, "Republican Pledges $175 Million to Push Party on Climate" (*Politico*, June 8, 2015). Accessed on June 30, 2015, from http://www.politico.com/story/2015/06/republican-climate-change-jay-faison-118755.html?ml=po.

16. Center for Responsive Politics, "Outside Spending" (Data from 2012). Accessed on June 12, 2015, from opensecrets.org.

CHAPTER 9

Campaign Press Coverage—Changed Forever

Jeremy D. Mayer, Richard J. Semiatin, and Joseph Graf

"IN THE 21ST CENTURY, that news is transmitted in more ways than ever before—in print, on the air and on the Web, with words, images, graphics, sounds and video. But always and in all media, we insist on the highest standards of integrity and ethical behavior when we gather and deliver news."[1] These core news values shared by the Associated Press on its website in 2015 represent the gold standard of news coverage. However, in a world with increasing social media where blogs and tweets opine on daily issues at a moment's notice, the shape and scope of reportage can change instantly.

No one is immune from such coverage, especially those in political campaigns. At 9 a.m. local time, June 10, 2011, the state of Alaska released five boxes with 24,000 printed emails sent while Sarah Palin was governor from 2006 to 2009. The emails were released after requests from media outlets under Alaska's open records law, a typical and even mundane exercise undertaken by political journalists. They use such laws to pry loose documents from the government. There was also nothing unusual that these emails were released long after she was tapped by Senator John McCain as his presidential running mate in 2008, and nearly two years after Palin left office in Alaska.

This was fairly typical. What was extraordinary was the extent of the coverage, the speed at which it took place, the fascination with the *event* of the release, and the little attention paid to the documents themselves. The six boxes carted into a hallway before television cameras *were* the news. At least three networks broadcast live and counted down the hours to the release. More than thirty-five reporters were on the scene. On-air reporters worked their way through one live standup after another all afternoon, trying to project interest in a few emails about Palin's workout schedule, comments about the news, or notes to her family. Whatever was inside those boxes was almost beside the point. The news *was* the release. Once the boxes arrived, journalists seemed unsure what to do next. It was impossible to sift through 24,000 pages live, on the air, so once the lights dimmed, everyone flew home.

Jon Stewart lampooned the broadcast media mercilessly on his late-night *Daily Show*. Blogs and discussion boards lit up with commentary. The media's curious fascination with technology was on display. *The New York Times* took the unusual step of asking readers "to help us identify interesting and newsworthy e-mails, people and events that we may want to highlight."[2] Palin supporters organized to analyze the email themselves. Stewart's lampoon became the next day's news, and by the end of the week, he had appeared on *Fox News Sunday with Chris Wallace*. The story had come full circle. This story from 2011 is just as valid today.

U.S. campaigns are getting faster and paradoxically longer at the same time. Sound bites that played on the news for sixty seconds in 1968 have been reduced to seven seconds or less today, and the presidential campaign begins nearly two years before the election. A record twenty-two presidential candidates—seventeen Republicans and five Democrats—announced their candidacies nearly a year and a half before the 2016 election. The rhythm of media coverage determines the pace of the modern campaign at all levels of politics. The speed of coverage makes for more volatile campaigns where the dynamic of a race can be altered by a video on YouTube or a photo on Instagram. Political attacks, which used to take weeks or at least days to hit the airwaves and make an impact on the voters, now reach citizens at the click of a button. Given the declining ratings for national news networks and the even more rapid decline in newspaper circulation, campaign news has begun to go online all the time. That is why the emergence of online media is the focus of our attention in this chapter.

The Internet and social media will have even more decentralizing effects on campaigns and media power. This process has already begun, as campaigns put more emphasis on online media. The age of the digital communications also raises fundamental questions about the divisions between citizens, reporters, and political actors. The clear lines that separated those groups are fraying, and no longer are reporters the primary conduits between politicians and the public.

The following essay traces the role of the press in covering campaigns then discusses the plight of the traditional media and its implications. Finally, the essay discusses the trends in how the Internet is shaping press coverage and how the traditional journalistic standards of review are missing. We call this "filterlessness," and its cutting-edge change is irrevocably changing press coverage because separating facts from rumors becomes muddled. New media has increased the reactiveness of politics, as we shall see.

Origins and Development of U.S. Press Coverage

The major form of political discourse for most of U.S. history was newspapers. When the United States was deciding how to govern itself after the Revolution, men like James Madison and Alexander Hamilton wrote newspaper articles advocating the new Constitution (today we know these articles as *The Federalist Papers*). The national campaigns for and against ratifying the Constitution were fought in the pages of the nation's newspapers.

The First Century: Strong Linkages between Parties and Newspapers

But during the nation's first century, newspapers had a relationship to campaigns that would surprise most of today's readers. Most papers were openly supportive of one party or the other. A survey of 359 newspapers published in 1810 could find only 33 that had no party affiliation.[3] The modern idea of a separation between the "news" section and the opinion page was also unknown. It was easy to tell by simply looking at the headlines of the day which party a newspaper supported. Indeed, many newspapers put the name of the party into their titles. For this reason, larger cities during the nineteenth century would have a minimum of two newspapers, one for each party. So tight was the relationship between parties and newspapers that often the local party would meet at the offices of the local newspaper, since parties lacked infrastructure at that time. Reporters were expected to follow the party line in their coverage. The printing presses of supportive newspapers also were used to print party pamphlets, and even presidents picked one newspaper, called a "house organ," to publish their views and to benefit from government contracts.[4] Several times during the United States' early history, mobs of supporters of one party attacked the newspaper controlled by the other party.[5] This "partisan press" era persisted well into the twentieth century in many U.S. cities, where the newspaper was a key to political machines run by local parties.

Linkages Weaken between Parties and Newspapers

At the national level, however, the strong linkage between parties and newspapers in campaigns began to weaken in the late nineteenth century with the rise of the mass media. Newspaper empires like those created by William Randolph Hearst and Joseph Pulitzer were designed to appeal to readers across party lines; they could not be so directly tied to the interests of a single party. At the same time, standards of professional journalistic ethics began to emerge. More and more, journalists were expected to at least attempt to be objective as they covered political campaigns, and to avoid conflicts of interest.[6] During political campaigns, newspapers became more like referees in a boxing match, rather than the cheering supporters they had been in the partisan press era. There were notable exceptions, and certainly journalists, editors, and publishers were not perfect in their adherence to objectivity. Journalism also became a true profession during the early twentieth century, as the first schools of journalism were founded. In the past, those covering U.S. campaigns were often working-class writers without college degrees or family wealth. Journalism, previously not a prestigious occupation, was becoming desirable and even occasionally well paid.

Emerging Mass Media

During the early years of the twentieth century, radio networks emerged across the United States and the world. Radio's rapid rise signaled that newspapers were vulnerable to electronic media. Television emerged after World War II and eventually replaced the papers as the dominant means of political communication. The moment when U.S. presidential campaigns moved into the television age is commonly identified as the first televised debate in 1960 between John F. Kennedy and Richard Nixon. Those listening on the radio believed the debate to have been a tie. Those watching on television believed the far more charismatic Kennedy had won.[7] Historians have since come to question whether this was true, but politicians and journalists believed in the power of television, and U.S. political campaigns would never be the same. It had of course been an advantage in politics to be reasonably attractive. Yet prior to television, we had elected men who were widely acknowledged to be homely-looking, such as Abraham Lincoln, or morbidly obese, such as William Howard Taft. Television has forced politicians at all levels of U.S. campaigns to pay more attention to their looks than ever before; and that has become news. Whether it was Mitt Romney and John Edwards criticized for spending thousands of campaign dollars using hairstylists or Donald Trump's manicured hairstyle in 2016, both examples demonstrate that looking as good or as powerful as possible, on television, has been a vital part of every modern U.S. campaign since the Kennedy and Nixon campaigns of 1960.

The Power of Television

The impact of television on campaigns has been vast and goes beyond makeup and hairstylists. It focused attention on image and sound, and less on logic and thought. Television contributed directly to the decline of issues and the rise of personality and individual character as a decisive factor in U.S. elections.[8] And television may be more powerful in its campaign coverage than print media ever was because it can have a dramatic effect on voter choice in presidential primaries.[9] This is not only through directly making a candidate look competent or incompetent, corrupt or honest, charismatic or dull. The media also helps set expectations, which can make winners of losers and losers of winners. Early press attention could enhance a candidacy. Jeb Bush, Marco Rubio, and Scott Walker were all doing well in summer 2015 polls for the Republican presidential nomination, which boosted their media profiles and campaign war chests.

An Era of Transformation: The Decline of Mainstream Media

The emergence of a powerful broadcast media has often been correlated with the decline of the newspaper industry. The number of daily papers in the United States declined from over 1,700 in 1990 to slightly under 1,400 by 2009, according to the Project for Excellence in Journalism.[10] The rise of Internet and social media coincided with this decline, and it would be foolhardy to think there is not some correlation.

The Effect on Campaign News Coverage

Campaign coverage has been consolidated in fewer newspapers. Large corporations such as Hearst and News Corporation (which bought *The Wall Street Journal* in 2007) have been accused of homogenizing news coverage. According to Federal Communications Commission (FCC) Commissioner Jonathan Adelstein, "It raises a real question as whether or not there is independence between ownership and the journalists."[11] This is true not only for newspapers but for broadcast television. Corporations hire consultants to improve the image of local and national news. Former *ABC News* anchor Charles Gibson points out the problem: "News directors who rely on consultants wind up producing newscasts that look like every other newscast around, and if they read the minute-by-minutes and program merely what they think people want to watch . . . they're not directing anything, they're being directed."[12]

Traditional Media Focuses More on Personality to Hold Viewers

The focus becomes less on reporting the news than on personality. Some candidates such as New Jersey Republican governor Chris Christie encourage it. According to the Associated Press, Christie's 2016 bid for the Republican presidential nomination "is largely driven by his outsized personality, and his resume, while notable, contains scattered land mines that have given many Republicans pause."[13]

The Christie example illustrates politics as reality television. The trend of reality shows that started with *Survivor* has worked its way into mainstream news coverage. The personality-driven aspect of campaigns, which networks are only too eager to carry, helps them compete with other media for audience share. Competition from new media has also driven down the audiences for evening network newscasts. More citizens are turning away from the filter of television news as online audiences increase dramatically, where often the only filter is the viewer.

Downsized Newsrooms Change How Campaigns Are Covered

Newsrooms are also in the midst of enormous upheaval. Advertising revenues have dropped precipitously. Craigslist and eBay have eviscerated the classified ad sections of newspapers, which were historically the most profitable advertising. Media writer Eric Alterman calls the atmosphere at newspapers "a palpable sense of doom."[14] Billionaires such as Jeff Bezos of Amazon (*The Washington Post*) and Rupert Murdoch of News Corp. (*The Wall Street Journal*) bought two of the most prestigious newspapers in the United States. Mexican billionaire Carlos Slim Helú became the largest investor in *The New York Times*.[15] While some of the lost audience has moved online, online advertising rates make up only a fraction of the lost revenue. In response, many media properties, especially newspapers, have laid off thousands of journalists. Some organizations have been dramatically cut. ABC News laid off one-quarter of its staff in 2010; the BBC did the same in 2011. One estimate is that from 1990 to 2008 a quarter of all newspaper jobs were lost.[16] Fewer journalists working with smaller budgets are less able to fulfill their role as watchdogs on power. Not a single newspaper reporter works in the newsroom of the Department of Agriculture, one of the largest government employers.[17] Newspaper analyst John Morton argues that the cutbacks have diminished the journalism produced by newspapers. "What the industry partly sacrificed with its cost-cutting is the one attribute that has protected it against all previous competitive threats—the overall quality of its journalism," he wrote.[18]

These changes are particularly evident in Washington reporting and campaign coverage, but they are not all bad. The number of mainstream political journalists has declined in the past twenty-five years, but more importantly, the nature of the Washington press corps has changed. Whereas there are fewer mainstream journalists—who might have worked for outlets such as *Newsweek*, *The Washington Post*, or ABC News—there are many more journalists working for newsletters, blogs, and websites. But new outlets are emerging such as FiveThirtyEight.com, which was founded by political and sports statistician Nate Silver in 2008. (FiveThirtyEight represents the total number of electoral votes in the United States.) By 2012, Silver's FiveThirtyEight.com was in partnership with *The New York Times* to do election forecasts. Following the election, Silver parted with *The New York Times* and went independent again. His accurate predictions of the last two presidential elections using econometric and other statistical models have put him (and his team of statistical journalists) in high demand in the media.

The new model of working in a converged newsroom is called "individualization," where journalists are expected to be more flexible, more varied in their skill set, and more mobile.[19] Most political journalists are expected to blog, send Twitter messages, maintain a presence on social networks, and some post photographs (Instagram) or video (YouTube). In the past, those roles were more strictly prescribed to photographers or videographers. In broadcasting, this has led to increased use of "one-man bands" or "backpack journalism."[20] A single journalist with a video camera much lighter than those of just ten years ago can take high-quality footage, edit the footage on a portable computer, and produce a complete package alone, far from the office. The impact of these changes can be seen in some far-flung correspondents and in immediate self-produced coverage of political campaigns. This model of news coverage is expanding.

Politico: *A Successful Traditional Media Outlier*

One exception to the decline of traditional media is *Politico*. *Politico*, a newspaper about politics and campaigns, was founded by former *Washington Post* writers John Harris and Jim VandeHei in 2007 whose focus was on politics. The newspaper tripled its staff from 2008 to 2011 and has become an important source of political news, in some cases setting the national agenda.[21] The venture was financed by Robert Allbritton, a Washington, D.C., media mogul. Because *Politico* was created by journalists not pushing an ideological agenda, it has credibility in the Washington, D.C., political community.[22] *Politico* remains vibrant, covering campaign politics and policy making in Washington, D.C. The print version is more policy-wonkish, while the online version focuses more on personality and breaking news on campaigns such as retrospectives on the character of Donald Trump who questioned John McCain's status as hero because he served five-and-a-half years as a prisoner of war (POW) during the Vietnam conflict. The fact is that *Politico*'s coverage does not differ from that of many other news outlets that publish daily print and online editions.

Cutting-Edge Effects on Political Campaign Coverage

The era of unlimited or fat budgets for coverage of political campaigns is gone, as mentioned earlier. Television news used to generate enormous revenues for the networks. The major newspapers and news chains were highly profitable. However, with a more diverse marketplace and segmented audience, the revenue picture has turned from black to red.

The Advantage of Online News Production: Costs Driven Down

It is on the production side that the Internet is having a greater impact, particularly for the new wave of media bloggers. Reputable political bloggers such as Markos Moulitsas Zúniga (Daily Kos—liberal) or Erick Erickson (RedState—conservative) have remarkably low overheads. Printed newspapers are limited because every inch of space has a fixed cost. However, on the Internet, there is limitless space. Reporters face competition from anyone with a laptop and Internet access, and that can matter in a campaign. Many of these political bloggers in 2008 and 2012 fashioned themselves as outsiders, and indeed may not have the training or experience of mainstream political reporters. *The Huffington Post* generated a great deal of campaign coverage from bloggers who were not formally trained journalists and often were not paid. Finally, some of those independent bloggers have been "captured" in a way by the mainstream media. "The 2008 campaign made it clear that the old model, in which journalists interpret campaign events for the masses, is kaput," wrote journalist John McQuaid, "and that the new model is more chaotic and interactive."[23] The old model was gone by 2012. Opinion often leads news rather than follows it.

Part I — On the Edge of Change: Politics at the Speed of Light

Perhaps the greatest change the Internet has introduced into U.S. campaign coverage is the pace at which politics is conducted. The twenty-four-hour news cycle was much discussed when cable television first rose to prominence, since it suggested that campaigns and government institutions would no longer have a full day to plan reactions and make decisions. The Internet has sped this up even further.[24]

Lessons from the 2004–2012 Campaigns

If a reporter gets something that occurs at a public event wrong, an average citizen can challenge the media account directly. Some of the most famous mistakes in campaign coverage might have been caught earlier if they had happened in the age of digital dominance. Three examples below from the last three presidential elections illustrate how responsive journalism is so immediate and prone to greater error.

In 2004, CBS News ran a major story on documents that allegedly showed that President George W. Bush had refused a direct order to appear for duty during his service in the Texas Air National Guard during the Vietnam era. While the public had long known that Bush used family connections to get into the Guard during a time when it was a popular way for wealthy men to avoid the war, the documents revitalized the issue of Bush's wartime conduct, and his later failure to fulfill the terms of his enlistment. Very quickly, thanks to conservative bloggers, questions emerged about the documents' authenticity. Experts and amateurs pointed out factual and stylistic problems with the documents. In a massive humiliation for CBS News and the main reporter on the story, Dan Rather, the network was forced to admit that the documents were probably forgeries. Rather, long accused by conservatives of having a liberal bias, faced difficult questions about how he had accepted as legitimate anti-Bush documents rejected by other mainstream media outlets as highly questionable.

Without the Internet's amazing ability to link people rapidly, citizens would have lacked the ability to quickly challenge the CBS News story.

The story illustrates the synergistic power between traditional media and the Internet today. Stories are reported rapidly, often without fact-checking, as more media compete in the marketplace. Not only does it have implications for what the press does, but it forces campaigns to react. Damage control is now a 24/7 operation for major political national campaigns, and they have to rapidly respond to news events. Failure to do so can have profound implications. John Kerry (D-MA) discovered this in the summer of 2004 when he failed to respond to charges of the "Swift Boat Veterans for Truth," who questioned whether he truly was a Vietnam War hero. The Swift Boat Veterans advertisement was widely reported on the Internet, in major newspapers, and on national newscasts. Kerry was slow to respond, and that gave greater credibility to the charges. Eventually an ABC News *Nightline* investigation in Vietnam, with eyewitnesses, gave a more accurate story, but it was October, and the damage had already been done.[25]

Perhaps the richest example of what the Internet has wrought was the false, ongoing email campaign that President Obama is a follower of Islam. The Obama campaign carried on a long-running rearguard action against this email campaign that began at least as early as January 2007. The origination appears to be someone posting what he or she claims is an email he or she received detailing information about Obama's ties to Islam. The original source is never clear. True believers passed the email to others, never clear about where it began. "The labor of generating an email smear is divided and distributed amongst parties whose identities are secret even to each other," according to political scholar Danielle Allen. Someone makes a comment that is the original claim, then those claims are reposted and forwarded by another group of people. "No one coordinates the roles."[26] This was the Swift Boat campaign on steroids, and the rumors have never entirely ended. The truth about these claims does not penetrate the closed online communities where these ideas are fostered and flourish,[27] and in some cases, the myth has been helped by leaders who encouraged rumors about it.[28]

Prior to the 2012 election, the campaign "birthers" claimed that President Obama was born in Kenya, not the United States, and the group received prominent attention in the press ranging from blogs to *The New York Times*. Article II, Section 1 of the Constitution requires a citizen to be "naturally born" in the United States to serve as president. This "birther" movement was spearheaded by real estate mogul Donald Trump. The issue had first arisen during the 2008 campaign. On April 27, 2011, the White House published a PDF of the president's birth certificate from Hawaii (which it had also furnished in 2008). This put an end to most of the controversy, although Trump has never relented.[29]

Part II—On the Edge of Change: Citizen Groups as Campaign Reporters

Citizen groups have emerged as the new press in the twenty-first century. Unlike the mainstream media, citizen groups lack the reporting standards of *The New York Times* or ABC News. Their agenda is to promote and persuade, rather than report facts. As a result, they often lack standards to filter their stories and check them for veracity. This has profound consequences for campaigns because such groups serve as a third force in national politics and campaigns.

Citizen Groups: An Unfiltered Challenge to Mainstream Media Covering Campaigns

The Internet, in addition to speeding up campaigns and media coverage, makes it easy for a citizen activist to start up a webpage or blog, or to post a comment on an existing one. This poses serious problems for mainstream media outlets because they have competition for "news" and information. The grassroots fervor and involvement that voters experience on websites such as Daily Kos and Free Republic mean that major media companies are confounded in how to approach and compete with these groups for viewers. These viewers favor news from a distinct point of view, and this may encourage other websites and even mainstream news sources to cater to these audiences. At Daily Kos, one of the largest left-wing political websites in terms of number of unique daily visitors, anonymous posters can become famous quickly if they write well, post frequently, and battle the right with panache. The much smaller Free Republic plays a similar role for conservatives rallying against liberals.

The more recent emergence of the Tea Party provides another useful example because it is much more of a movement rather than a centralized political organization. While there is organized funding and expert political advice behind the Tea Party movement, much of its energy was fostered on independent political blogs, which represent much of its "news" coverage. A decentralized network of dozens, maybe hundreds, of these blogs organizes supporters and passes along information. The reason is that the Tea Party does not have a nucleus but rather is a loose confederation of hundreds of groups under the Tea Party banner.[30]

Over the Edge: When Online Groups Make Campaign News

MoveOn.org, the nation's largest political Internet grassroots organization, decided in 2004 to hold a national contest, called "Bush in 30 Seconds." MoveOn's Voter Fund invited submissions of thirty-second anti-Bush ads. The concept was brilliant—harness the diffused and wild creativity of Americans, and some ten or twenty unknown writers and directors will come up with ads that are better than those professional political consultants come up with. The judging process, in which MoveOn members would watch videos and vote for their favorites, boosted the visibility of the site. The contest was a huge success in terms of the number of submissions, the number of page views, the amount of money raised, and the stunning quality of the top thirty or so ads.

But 2 ads out of 1,500 on the site had images of Bush speaking juxtaposed with images of Adolf Hitler ranting. Although MoveOn.org eventually removed the offensive ads, the comparison attracted national media attention. The clips were prominently displayed on right-wing websites as examples of "MoveOn" ads. The fact that MoveOn merely provided a forum for these ads, and did not create or sponsor or in any way fund them, was irrelevant.[31]

The wave of the future may include Instagram and other forms of photo-journalism, as well. This new form of photojournalism and advertising has become part of U.S. culture. We are already seeing Instagram photo contests in the media from Starbucks (profit) and Habitat for Humanity (nonprofit). News coverage is becoming more visual as stories are being told through pictures. Presidential candidates such as Hillary Clinton and Ted Cruz are posting selfies, which become reported on by the press. In May 2015, Clinton showed a voter how to take a selfie with an iPhone. It became an instant news story. The implication was, isn't it cool the candidate is in touch with digital technology? What was amusing was that despite Clinton's giving the voter simple instructions such as "OK. Now press, press that white button. This right here," the voter was still unable to take the photo.[32]

Part III—On the Edge of Change: Campaigns as Reporters—Opponent Surveillance Expands in the Twenty-First Century

In the nineteenth century, many men ran for president while seldom leaving their homes. These "front porch" campaigns were possible in an era of print discourse. The level of media scrutiny of the daily lives of the candidates was minimal. In the twenty-first century, candidates find themselves trailed by opposition partisans, taping every moment of their campaigns and even their daily lives, hoping to find a gaffe; an unflattering or ridiculous image; or, best of all, some hint of scandal. These are known as trackers. The best-known tracker is S. R. Sidarth who captured Senator George Allen's (R-VA) "macaca" slur during the 2006 Virginia Senate election campaign. The slur aimed at Sidarth's ethnicity backfired and helped lead to Allen's defeat. Technology enables campaigns to do their own reporting cheaply, and they take advantage to get an edge over their opponents through surveillance.

Campaign Surveillance:
The Difference between the Present and the Past

The rise of the Internet combined with miniaturization of video technology has changed what is considered "fair game" for campaign coverage. Over thirty years ago, when Larry Sabato wrote *Feeding Frenzy*, about how the media have taken over the presidential campaign, he wrote of the media's endless appetite for scandal and negative information and images.[33] But the Internet has made the surveillance of candidates even more constant and damaging.

The contrast between today and 1968 is illustrative. On the campaign trail in 1968, film was shot of various candidates at most rallies, usually by the networks. Film cameras were large and bulky, and quite expensive. Typically, to get quality images required not only access to the equipment but training. And a news organization would have to rush the actual film to a studio for developing; and then processing; and, later in that day or the next day, broadcasting. Today, an amateur with a cell phone or a digital camera with video capability can capture images that can compete with the best professional footage of 1968. They do not need processing and can be posted on YouTube, Vimeo, or another free video distribution service within minutes. This change is not just the way of the Internet; it is also the miniaturization revolution in electronics, making video cameras and editing equipment smaller and affordable.

Campaigns have always sought ways to make their opponents look bad. The 1960 campaign of John F. Kennedy used myriad ways to get under the skin of Richard Nixon, the Republican opponent. Dick Tuck, the mischievous genius of the low blow in that race, came up with a tactic to make Nixon look like a loser in the presidential debate, regardless of how it turned out. The morning after Nixon's first presidential-campaign debate with Kennedy, Tuck asked an elderly woman to wear a Nixon button, hug the candidate, and say loudly, "Don't worry, son. He beat you last night, but you'll win next time."[34] The picture was captured nationally. The Internet changes the speed and impact of such dirty tricks. The Tuck trick was a minor moment in a long campaign. Today, a clip on YouTube can mean the end of a political career.

In the print media era, the nation elected leaders who were poor speakers (Jefferson), remarkably awkward in personal interactions (Nixon), extremely tight-lipped (Coolidge), close to dying (Roosevelt in 1944), prone to drunkenness (Grant), and recklessly promiscuous (Kennedy). Most of those men would not have been elected in the television era (Kennedy was at the turning point between print and television). Could any of them be elected in the social media age where privacy no longer exists for political figures? Perhaps, but the environment is far more challenging. The more access we have to the personalities and personal conduct of our leaders, the greater the likelihood we might vote on such ephemera as appearance and personality. Donald Trump's 2016 campaign was focused on his controversial persona of being a politically incorrect doer.

Part IV—On the Edge of Change: Campaign News Coverage in the Hands of Citizens

Social media, the Internet, and other forms of digital communication are interactive media, and unlike television, a passive medium, the Internet requires that the user be involved. Thus, the expanding digital world may also weaken the media's control over what citizens learn about politics. If they wish to be, citizens can become more independent of the power of media than at any time in human history. Compare a daily newspaper to a thirty-minute evening news broadcast to a CNN website available on a smartphone or tablet. The 40,000 words of text available in the newspaper represent the editors' view of current events that day. A reader has some degree of independence; a committed Republican could choose not to read any upbeat reports about President Obama, while a committed Democrat might choose not to read any positive stories about Republican presidential candidates. This "selective perception" by the viewer is reinforced by digital communications because that person interacts and manipulates the medium to their own satisfaction, which is the opposite of mainstream mass media.

Political Campaigns and Social Network News

The political campaigns of 2016 and beyond will focus enormous efforts with social networks. In a world of "selective perception" and limitless information, users need trusted sources of information. The information and recommendations people send to their friends and family on social networks fills this need, and campaigns know it. The Obama campaigns of 2008 and 2012 had an enormous presence on Facebook and even created its own social network on the campaign websites. These networks are fostered by the campaigns. In some respects, this gives local activists the power to start their own discussions and, in effect, wage their own mini-campaigns for the candidates of their choice, sending messages, persuading others, and raising money. Ordinary citizens become agents of political change and may play a larger role in the campaign and in a sense become "news reporters" to converted constituents by reporting for candidates with stylish videos and photos, preempting any desire for the recipient to seek out news from traditional sources whether they be *The New York Times*, *The Wall Street Journal*, or CNN.

Anonymous Campaign Reports: Narrowcasting News without a Gatekeeper

Another possibility that the Internet and social media raise is a new type of anonymous campaign messaging that masquerades as news. Narrowcasting enables the producer to send information to an end user who has logged on or registered at a website. In the past, the media could receive an anonymous or confidential tip on the campaign trail that one side hoped to put a rumor or negative story into the coverage. However, that changed by late 1900s.

Today, a campaign can put wild anonymous rumors into circulation with much greater ease and get attention. In 2007, an activist associated with the Mitt Romney campaign posted a website called PhoneyFred.org saying Republican rival Fred Thompson was "Once a Pro-Choice Skirt Chaser, (and) Now Standard Bearer of the Religious Right?" This was presented as fact. Moreover, it noted that Thompson had once lobbied for Planned Parenthood.[35] The inference was that Thompson dated attractive women and was pro-choice, and therefore no friend of the religious right. The distinction between news and rumor gets blurred even further because campaigns have to react immediately. The result is that narrowcasting messages often end up being broadcast to large audiences as news, and that can throw a campaign off message for days. The danger is that the more that appears online or in social media unfiltered, the longer it takes and the harder it is to refute even the most absurd claims that have the ring of truth and are reported as news.

Mobile News Technology and Campaigns

As mainstream media adapt to new technologies, mobile users will be able to access CNN, Fox News, and MSNBC, for example, to get their news. That will put more pressure on news organizations to produce news headlines at a faster rate because handheld devices facilitate frequent access by users. Campaign coverage, as well as all news, may become more focused on headline news coverage because the shorthand fits easily on the screen. Already on mainstream media, we see tickers on the bottom of the screen (such as CNN and Fox News) to make all news accessible in shorthand to viewers. The danger is that news coverage will become even more superficial and the seven-second sound bite from candidates even more important. Today, cable news stations are losing viewership as Millennials, in particular, seek other sources of news.

Comedy as an Interpretive News Source

Today, comedy plays a much more important role in *interpreting* and *opining* the news. Cable's Comedy Central has played that role to some extent for Millennials through *The Daily Show* and *The Colbert Report* (now defunct). However, that opinion may be overstated. According to Alex Weprin writing for *Adweek* in 2012, a survey by Comedy Central found that "a majority of millennials surveyed say they still get their election news from network TV newscasts and cable news, and while it is fun to say that 'The Daily Show' is a source of election news, the reality is they get their news elsewhere, and turn to the comedy shows for fun."[36]

The traditional talking-head media on the left-leaning MSBNC and right-leaning Fox News are losing younger-generation viewers who prefer the softer edge of comedy to the harder debate-driven opining that Baby Boomers and, to a lesser extent, Gen X prefer. Now that Millennials outnumber Baby Boomers as the nation's largest living generation, will the more ideological-leaning cable news networks continue to lose audience share and become less relevant? Will candidates seek out more time to appear with new *Daily Show* host Trevor Noah and avoid the harsher light of traditional news interviews?

Future Challenges

As we move further from the traditional media that dominated the second half of the twentieth century and further into our new century, the world of press campaign coverage has changed dramatically. With independent arbiters of news and opinion that sometimes lacks veracity, our new age reminds us in some ways of one in the past. In those days, newspapers were often surrogate campaigns for candidates. In the presidential election of 1800, the *Connecticut Current*, a Federalist newspaper allied with John Adams, warned that a Jeffersonian presidency would entail "murder, rape, adultery and incest" because he was deemed immoral.[37] In 1884, the *Indianapolis Sentinel* stated that Republican presidential candidate James G. Blaine married his wife, "betrayed the girl he had married, and then only married here . . . at the muzzle of a shotgun."[38] Today, much like the 1800s, the new campaign journalism of the social media era is opinion driven. This newest incarnation of the press threatens existing hard news journalism, which is in decline.

In the future, the Internet and social media will produce greater changes in campaign coverage than the rise of television. In the digital era, mainstream media elites will lose some power over political communication, but *The New York Times* will not disappear anytime soon. Yet those empowered by the rise of the Internet are unlikely to be politicians and party leaders, but rather will be a mix of new media figures and citizen activists. Bloggers and leaders of nonparty organizations like MoveOn.org and Free Republic are the ones who will thrive in this new media environment. In this sense, the Internet has opened up U.S. politics to a new set of players without discarding the old power structure. It means that candidates and media have to traverse this landscape, which continues to change and lacks the stability and predictability of the past.

There is value to having many independent media outlets with reporters who strive for objectivity and produce in-depth stories on important issues such as Social Security and military preparedness. Despite their lack of professional training or adequate resources, many bloggers and independent websites produce important campaign news coverage. At the same time, 10,000 bloggers mostly repeating the talking points of their respective parties cannot adequately replace one top national journalist investigating a vital national question in a rigorous and unbiased fashion.

Digital communications through the Internet and social media make traditional media outlets less profitable by stealing viewers and readers, thus forcing many newspapers and broadcast outlets to fire just the reporters we need. The new political journalism that has arisen online in the last ten years is extraordinarily valuable, but at the same time, we have lost a great deal.

The second challenge for media coverage is what Neil Postman called "infotainment." As political commentator H. L. Mencken said in the early twentieth century: "For every complex problem, there is a solution that is simple, neat and wrong."[39] But the voices arguing for nuanced and difficult solutions to complex problems may be softer now than at any time in the past, thanks in part to the vitriolic and biased way in which Internet media often treat political campaigns.

Conclusion

The mainstream media is not disappearing, but the Internet is having a profound effect on the superficiality of campaign news coverage, promoting a greater emphasis on personality, rumor, and infotainment. We may long for the days when the television news at least gave the voters seven-second sound bites by the presidential candidates. This old world where politicians and reporters engaged one another is disappearing, and it means the lack of trust between politicians and the press is likely to grow stronger in the future. More "journalists" in the social media age blend fact and rumor. In turn, campaigns are trying to filter more news themselves to control the flow of information so that reporters, bloggers, and opinion makers have less to work with.

The good part is that the press remains free and unfettered and can still report good news stories. The bad part is that the current trend probably increases the cynicism and distrust that citizens have for both politicians and press.

Notes

1. "AP News Values and Principles" (Associated Press, 2015). Accessed on June 26, 2015, from http://www.ap.org/company/News-Values.
2. Mike Baker, "Palin Emails Let Old Media Test New Media Methods" (Associated Press, June 13, 2011); Derek Willis, "Help Us Review the Sarah Palin E-Mail Records" (*The New York Times*, June 14, 2011).
3. Jeffrey L. Pasley, *The Tyranny of Printers: Newspaper Politics in the Early American Republic* (Charlottesville, VA: University Press of Virginia 2001), 201.
4. John Tebbel, *The Compact History of the American Newspaper* (New York: Hawthorne 1963), 87.

5. Tebbel, *The Compact History of the American Newspaper*, 67–68.

6. Michael Schudson, *Discovering the News: A Social History of American Newspapers* (New York: Basic Books, 1981).

7. Jeremy D. Mayer, *American Media Politics in Transition* (New York: McGraw Hill, 2007).

8. Scott Keeter, "The Illusion of Intimacy: Television and the Role of Candidate Personal Qualities in Voter Choice" (*Public Opinion Quarterly*, Vol. 51, No. 3, 1987), 344–358.

9. Thomas E. Patterson, *Out of Order* (New York: Vintage Press, 1994).

10. "Number of Newspapers Continues to Decline" (Pew Research Center's Project for Excellence in Journalism, State of the News Media, 2013). Accessed on June 26, 2015, from http://www.stateofthemedia.org/2013/newspapers-stabilizing-but-still-threatened/11-number-of-newspapers-continues-to-decline/.

11. Rick Karr, interview with FCC Commissioner Jonathan Adelstein (*NOW with Bill Moyers,* PBS, April 3, 2003). Accessed on September 14, 2007, from http://pbs.org/now/politics/bigmedia.html.

12. Charles Gibson, Paul White Award Speech (RTNDA convention, Las Vegas, NV, April 24, 2006). Accessed on September 14, 2007, from http://www.journalism.org.

13. Ann Colvin and Steve Peoples, "Chris Christie Warns of Blunt 2016 Campaign Even If It Makes People 'Cringe'" (Associated Press, June 30, 2015).

14. Eric Alterman, "Out of Print: The Death and Life of the American Newspaper" (*The New Yorker*, 2008). Accessed on June 18, 2011, from http://www.newyorker.com/reporting/2008/03/31/080331fa_fact_alterman.

15. "Carlos Slim Becomes Top *New York Times* Shareholder" (Reuters, January 14, 2015).

16. Sarah Lyall, "BBC, Facing Budget Cuts, Will Trim World Service and Lay Off 650" (*The New York Times,* January 27, 2011); Brian Stelter, "Job Cuts at ABC Leave Workers Stunned and Downcast" (*The New York Times,* May 1, 2010).

17. Jodi Enda, "Capital Flight" (*American Journalism Review*, 2010). Accessed on August 6, 2011, from http://www.ajr.org/article.asp?id=4877.

18. John Morton, "Costly Mistakes" (*American Journalism Review*, 2011). Accessed on June 12, 2011, from http://www.ajr.org/Article.asp?id=4994.

19. Mark Deuze, "Understanding Journalism as Newswork: How It Changes, and How It Remains the Same" (*Westminster Papers in Communication and Culture* Vol. 5, No. 2, 2008).

20. See, for example, the Backpack Journalism Project at American University. Accessed on August 4, 2011, from http://www.american.edu/soc/backpack/.

21. Jeremy W. Peters, "Political Blogs Are Ready to Flood Campaign Trail" (*The New York Times*, 2011). Accessed on August 4, 2011, from http://www.nytimes.com/2011/01/30/business/media/30blogs.html.

22. Michael Wolff, "*Politico*'s Washington Coup" (*Vanity Fair*, August 2009). Accessed on August 8, 2011, from http://www.vanityfair.com/.

23. John McQuaid, "The Netroots: Bloggers and the 2008 Presidential Campaign" (*Nieman Reports*, 2009). Accessed on August 2, 2011, from http://www.nieman.harvard.edu/reports/article/101910/The-Netroots-Bloggers-and-the-2008-Presidential-Campaign.aspx.

24. Bob Davis and Jeanne Cummings, "Hot Buttons: A Barrage of E-Mail Helps Candidates Hit Media Fast and Often" (*The Wall Street Journal*, September 21, 2000).

25. Andrew Morse, "What Happened in Kerry's Vietnam Battles?" (ABC News, October 14, 2004). Accessed on September 13, 2007, from abcnews.go.com.

26. Matthew Mosk, "An Attack That Came Out of the Ether; Scholar Looks for First Link in E-Mail Chain about Obama" (*The Washington Post,* June 28 2008).

27. Cass R. Sunstein, *Republic.com* (Princeton, NJ: Princeton University Press, 2001).

28. John Dickerson, "Why Won't Any Republicans Condemn the 'Obama Is a Muslim' Myth?" (*CBS News Political Hotsheet*, 2010). Accessed on August 9, 2011, from http://www.cbsnews.com/8301-503544_162-20014532-503544.html.

29. President Obama's Long Form Birth Certificate" (White House, April 27, 2011). Accessed on June 27, 2015, from https://www.whitehouse.gov/sites/default/files/rss_viewer/birth-certificate.pdf.

30. Hans Noel, "Ten Things Political Scientists Know That You Don't" (*The Forum*, Vol. 8, No. 3, 2010). Accessed on August 2, 2011, from http://www.bepress.com/forum/vol8/iss3/art12.

31. See Ari Shapiro, "Using Hitler to Make a Point" (NPR, July 4, 2004). Accessed on September 13, 2007, from npr.org.

32. Lisa Kreutz, "Hillary Clinton Teaches Voter How to Take a Selfie" (ABC News, May 23, 2015). Accessed on July 2, 2015, from http://abcnews.go.com/Politics/hillary-clinton-teaches-voter-selfie/story?id=31250402.

33. Larry J. Sabato, *Feeding Frenzy: Attack Journalism and American Politics* (Baltimore, MD: Lanahan Publishing, 2000).

34. Tom Miller, "Tricky Dick" (*The New Yorker*, August 30, 2004).

35. Glen Johnson, "Romney Denies OKing Anti-Thompson Website" (Associated Press, September 11, 2007).

36. Alex Weprin, "Comedy Central Study: A Majority of Millennials Still Get News from TV" (*Adweek*, October 18, 2012). Accessed on June 27, 2015, from http://www.adweek.com/tvnewser/comedy-central-study-a-majority-of-millennials-still-get-news-from-tv/151887.

37. Paul F. Boller Jr., *Presidential Campaigns* (New York: Oxford University Press, 1984), 12.

38. Boller, *Presidential Campaigns,* 152.

39. The quote is Mencken, but the original source of the quote, newspaper article, book, or other medium is not known.

CHAPTER 10

Campaign Finance—New Realities Beyond *Citizens United*

Peter L. Francia, Wesley Joe, and Clyde Wilcox

THE 2012 PRESIDENTIAL ELECTION was the most expensive in history, and it is likely that campaign spending by candidates, political parties, and outside groups will again reach new heights in 2016. Early speculation has Democratic front-runner Hillary Clinton raising as much as $2 billion for her nomination and general election campaigns.[1] Numerous Republican candidates have also begun to raise large sums of money for their presidential campaigns and will receive considerable financial backing and support from outside groups.[2] Many of the independent organizations that will be active in 2016 are well-established groups, such as the National Rifle Association (NRA), the Sierra Club, the Chamber of Commerce, and the American Federation of Labor and Congress of Industrial Organizations (AFL-CIO). Other groups will be relatively new players, such as NextGen Climate Action. For many of these new and old outside groups, it will be difficult and, in some cases, impossible to know who is funding them despite a complex set of existing campaign finance laws and rules that developed nearly four decades ago.

These statutes and regulations restrict how much individuals can give to candidates, parties, and certain types of interest groups, and regulate how individuals can spend various types of funds. Tax rules also govern the types of money that different kinds of groups can raise, as well as how each group can use that money to assist campaigns. Often the laws and regulations make subtle, sometimes murky, distinctions between different types of contributions and spending.

One example of this complexity is the law that limits what individual citizens can do with their money in an election. On grounds that individuals cannot corrupt themselves, the Supreme Court has prohibited any limits on the amounts of money that candidates can give to their own campaigns for office, although there are limits on the amounts that individuals can contribute to others, including family members who run for office. An individual can give larger, but limited, sums to political parties and to political action committees (PACs) sponsored by interest groups. However, an individual can give unlimited amounts to some committees and nonprofit organizations,[3] which can run ads that attack a candidate, pass out voter guides, and register voters. These distinctions are the result not of carefully planned regulations, but rather of episodic rulemaking and judicial action.

To elucidate the complexities of the campaign finance system and the factors that will shape its future, this chapter covers several important issues. First, we review the Federal Election Campaign Act and the Bipartisan Campaign Reform Act. Second, we discuss the major campaign finance decisions of the Roberts Court. Third, we examine how the unraveling of federal campaign finance law has altered the dynamics of campaigning for office, especially concerning fundraising. Fourth, we look at some new and prominent proposals for campaign finance reform and speculate about their prospects of ever becoming law.

The Evolution and Framework of Campaign Finance Reform

The 1974 comprehensive amendments to the Federal Election Campaign Act (FECA) of 1971 established the fundamental framework for the modern campaign finance system. The law set out four main elements: (1) to set limits on contributions and expenditures from individuals, parties, and interest groups; (2) to establish disclosure requirements for contributions and spending; (3) to complete a public financing system for presidential candidates; and (4) to create an enforcement agency, the Federal Election Commission (FEC), to regulate the new campaign finance system. It also required all significant actors in national campaigns to form committees, which would raise and spend money according to FECA rules and file regular reports. Interest groups were to set up PACs, which the law allowed to raise money in limited amounts from members and use it in election campaigns. Candidates were to form campaign committees, which would report all contributions and spending.

Although initially successful, the FECA regulatory system encountered significant problems in the late 1990s. Campaign professionals discovered ways to channel unregulated donations, termed "soft money" (contributions not subject to federal limits), to party committees. This practice was immensely attractive to party leaders because they could raise as much from a few interest groups in an evening as they could from tens of thousands of individuals over several months. In 1992, the national political party committees together collected $86 million in soft money. By 2000, that total had swelled to $495 million—a sixfold increase in just eight years.[4]

Reformers, including members of Congress, criticized the growth of soft money on several grounds. First, because these contributions were often very large, they had the capacity to influence the actions of Congress. If a PAC gave a candidate $5,000 before an election, it was unlikely that the PAC could expect any favors from that candidate if the candidate won. But interest groups could channel hundreds of thousands of dollars through political parties into the same election, and that amount was substantial enough that many members believed that it affected legislation.

Second, the process of raising soft money became increasingly unseemly. Both political parties sometimes held soft money fundraising events the day before major markups of legislation. Interest groups complained that they had no choice but to contribute if they wanted a voice in the negotiations. A number of prominent business leaders criticized soft money fundraisers as a form of extortion, but only a few were willing to make a public pledge not to contribute.[5]

Finally, some argued that soft money distorted the equality of the political process. Those who can afford to give hundreds of thousands are an elite group that already enjoys numerous advantages in politics. These large soft money contributions, which average citizens could not afford to give, amplified the voices of the wealthiest Americans.[6] Large sums of money spent on "issue advocacy" advertisements, which avoid the restrictions specified in FECA because they do not explicitly endorse a candidate, also caught the eye of reformers. Critics charged that issue ads were not transparent because it was difficult, and often impossible, to trace who was funding them.

The Bipartisan Campaign Reform Act

Nearly thirty years after the passage of FECA, Congress enacted the Bipartisan Campaign Reform Act (BCRA) in 2002. Unlike FECA, the new law did not try to create a comprehensive campaign finance regulatory system but instead sought to patch the biggest problems that had developed over time. BCRA banned large soft money contributions to political parties and barred politicians from soliciting soft money for interest groups. The law also required state and local parties to fund any federal activities with "hard money" (contributions subject to federal limits) as opposed to "soft money", although there are limited exceptions for voter registration and get-out-the-vote (GOTV) activities. State and local parties may pay for voter registration and GOTV efforts with soft money (known as "Levin Amendment" funds) up to $10,000 per source (if allowed under state law). Money raised for Levin Amendment funds must also meet a number of requirements.[7]

The law still allowed large contributions to various interest groups, which could run issue ads. There were, however, limits on the ads, as well as new standards for identifying campaign ads. Under the new law, "campaign ads" included those that mentioned a candidate by name or appeared on television or radio during the period of intense campaigning before the election. PACs could still fund these ads as independent expenditures, but they could do so only with funds raised through regulated contributions. Other political advocacy committees could run issue ads, but not during the final days of an election. BCRA contained one other important set of provisions. It doubled the amount that individuals could give to candidates for federal office, increased the amount that they could give to political parties, and left in place the limits on how much they could give to PACs. These provisions were intended to make it easier for candidates, and to a lesser extent parties, to raise hard money once the ban on soft money took effect.

An eclectic coalition of interest groups immediately challenged BCRA before the U.S. Supreme Court. The plaintiffs ranged from progressive groups such as the AFL-CIO to conservative groups such as the NRA. Despite the challenge, the Court upheld the core elements of the law in *McConnell v. FEC*, 540 U.S. 93 (2003). With the constitutionality of the law now seemingly settled, reformers hoped to strengthen regulations further and address some of the perceived short-comings in BCRA. The push for reform gained momentum after a highly publicized scandal sent "superlobbyist" Jack Abramoff to federal prison for fraud, tax evasion, and conspiracy to bribe public officials. Yet the prospects for reform became more complicated when two new conservative members, John Roberts (whom Congress also confirmed as chief justice) and Samuel Alito, joined the Court in 2005 and 2006 respectively. The new Roberts Court would dramatically alter campaign finance law and affect how candidates and organizations raised money for campaigns.

Rulings from the Roberts Court on BCRA

The first major campaign finance case brought before the new Roberts Court came in 2007 with *FEC v. Wisconsin Right to Life Inc.*, 551 U.S. 449. The Court significantly altered BCRA by striking down the law's electioneering communications restrictions (which banned the use of corporate and union treasury funds for advertising that featured the name or likeness of a clearly identified candidate for federal office in the final thirty days of the primary election and the final sixty days of the general election). The effect of this ruling according to one scholar was that the Court "essentially eviscerated the McCain-Feingold provisions and green-lit the efforts of nearly any group to fund pro-candidate ads close to elections."[8]

A year later, the Roberts Court again took aim at BCRA in *Davis v. FEC*, 554 U.S. 724 (2008). In this ruling, the Court struck down a provision in the law that increased the contribution limits for opponents of wealthy self-financed candidates. The Court ruled that the provision was "discriminatory" in singling out wealthy candidates and added that there was no "legitimate government objective" to level the playing field for candidates facing a wealthy self-financed opponent.[9] Yet the most significant ruling of all came in 2010 when the Court reached a decision in *Citizens United v. FEC*, 558 U.S. 08-205. The case involved nonprofit corporation Citizens United, which produced a critical film about presidential candidate Hillary Clinton and sought to use its general treasury funds to finance the film's distribution. In its decision, the U.S. Supreme Court overturned *Austin v. Michigan Chamber of Commerce*, 494 U.S. 652 (1990), and part of *McConnell v. FEC*. The majority ruled that the prohibition on corporations from using their general treasury funds to finance communications that expressly advocate for the election or defeat of a candidate, and that were made without the candidate's or candidate's campaign committee's cooperation or consultation (i.e., independent expenditures), violated the First Amendment of the Constitution.

Similar to the Court's rationale in an earlier 1976 case, *Buckley v. Valeo*, which considered the constitutionality of FECA, the majority in *Citizens United v. FEC* ruled that money spent independent of a candidate's campaign was not necessarily corruptive. According to Justice Anthony Kennedy, "Independent expenditures, including those made by corporations, do not give rise to corruption or the appearance of corruption."[10] Absent the establishment of corruption, the majority reasoned that the law's restrictions on free speech sufficiently burdened the First Amendment. As Kennedy explained, "If the First Amendment has any force, it prohibits Congress from fining or jailing citizens, or associations of citizens, for simply engaging in political speech."[11]

Put in plainer terms, *Citizens United* had the effect of allowing corporations to spend money that independently (i.e., when groups do not coordinate their activities with a candidate's campaign) and expressly advocated for the election or defeat of a candidate (i.e., language such as "vote for" or "vote against") beyond their PACs. For the first time in the modern campaign finance era, corporations would be able to use general treasury funds for independent expenditures in federal elections.[12] The decision would have far-reaching significance for elections and political campaigns in 2010 and beyond.

Since *Citizens United*, the Court has continued on its deregulatory spree. In *McComish v. Bennett*, 564 U.S. 664 (2011), the Court overturned a public financing provision in Arizona law that allowed candidates facing well-funded opponents to receive additional public funds to counter that spending. The Court ruled that this provision interfered with the freedom of speech of well-heeled candidates and groups, who might then voluntarily limit their spending rather than trigger additional public funds to the other candidate. The ruling made it clear how far the Court was willing to push the free speech argument. In this case, the mere fact that well-heeled candidates and groups might voluntarily limit their spending for strategic considerations, but were still free to spend as much as they wanted without legal limits, proved again to be more than the Court was willing to accept.

More recently, the Court ruled that aggregate hard money contribution limits violated the free speech rights of wealthy donors who wished to give to many candidates and committees. In another 5–4 ruling, the Court in *McCutcheon v. FEC*, 572 U.S. (2014), left in place contribution limits to individual candidates, although *Citizens United* allows unlimited contributions to candidate Super PACs. In 2015, the Court heard oral arguments about the constitutionality of bans on judicial candidates in state elections soliciting contributions. A ruling is expected soon.

Taken together, recent decisions show that five justices have elevated the value of free speech of big donors far above the values of equality and control of corruption. These rulings make the path to meaningful campaign finance more complicated. Furthermore, they narrow the range of acceptable options.

The Impact of the Roberts Court's Decisions on Federal Elections

The various rulings of the Roberts Court had some broad effects on federal elections. In the aftermath of the *Wisconsin Right to Life* decision, electioneering communications from outside independent groups increased to $131.1 million in 2008 from $98.9 million in the previous presidential election of 2004.[13] (As such, outside groups have an even stronger impact on campaigns, as mentioned in the interest groups chapter by Kasniunas, Rozell, and Keckler). Likewise, following the *Citizens United* ruling, outside money poured into federal elections. Independent groups not affiliated or connected with a candidate or party spent more than $300 million in the 2010 election and reached a high of more than $1 billion in 2012.[14]

Independent expenditures, in particular, increased significantly in the post–*Citizens United* period. Interest groups spent totals of $205.5 million on independent expenditures in 2010, $1 billion in 2012, and $550 million in 2014 compared with $143.6 million in 2008 and $37.8 million in 2006.[15] With more money available to use for independent expenditures in the aftermath of *Citizens United*, the post-ruling figures confirm that corporations and labor unions (which could also draw money from their treasury funds) took eager advantage of the ruling.

The increases in independent expenditures are also the product of another decision, *SpeechNow.org v. FEC*, 599 F.3d 686, 694-95 (D.C. Cir. 2010), although the case received considerably less attention than *Citizens United*. In *SpeechNow.org v. FEC*, the District of Columbia Circuit Court of Appeals ruled that federal PACs that made independent expenditures and did not contribute to any candidates or political parties could raise unlimited sums of money. The result of this ruling was a new group of "independent expenditure committees" that became known as Super

PACs. These Super PACs contributed to the rise in independent expenditures in the federal elections, accounting for $609 million in 2012 and $345 million in 2014.[16]

The Growth of Super PACs

Super PACs not only have contributed to the rise in independent expenditures but also have increased the influence of wealthy donors. Heading into the 2012 presidential election, reports surfaced that American Crossroads, formed by former George W. Bush adviser Karl Rove, received more than 90 percent of its money from just three billionaires.[17] Democrats, likewise, moved to create what one operative called their own "soft money Death Star."[18]

Similar developments followed in the 2016 presidential election, with Super PACs and their wealthy financial backers taking on an even more prominent role. Political observers have reported that the 2016 election could cost upwards of $5 billion, more than double the cost of the 2012 election.[19] With such high demands to raise money, Super PACs have become active players in the so-called money primary of the 2016 presidential election.

Democratic front-runner Hillary Clinton has two major Super PACs supporting her, Correct the Record and Priorities USA Action (which backed Barack Obama in 2012). On the Republican side, Jeb Bush's supporters have put considerable financial resources into the Super PAC Right to Rise USA—a group dubbed in one account as Bush's "exoskeleton."[20] Right to Rise has a tier structure in place for its donors and fundraisers of $50,000, $100,000, $250,000, and $500,000.[21] Some accounts have surfaced claiming that Right to Rise has helped Bush set an opening 100-day fundraising record in Republican presidential politics.[22] Right to Rise plans not only an aggressive television advertising strategy, but reports indicate that it will be involved in GOTV efforts as well.[23]

Super PACs, of course, are not exclusive to the front-runners in a presidential election. Former U.S. senator Rick Santorum, who lost the Republican nomination in 2012 and is a long shot to win the White House in 2016, has the financial backing of Foster Friess—a wealthy billionaire who has pledged to donate a considerable amount of money to Santorum's Super PAC. Yet the increased money that outside groups and their big-money patrons have funneled into elections that followed the rulings of the Roberts Court tells only part of the story. Deregulation of the campaign finance system also has had effects on campaigns themselves.

The Effects of Campaign Finance Deregulation on Campaign Activities

With more outside money allowed into the electoral process, the Court's various rulings have increased the ability of interest groups—including those with no connection at all to the candidate—to set the political agenda through advertising blitzes. Candidates and their campaigns, as a result, are under increased pressure to raise money to prevent ceding control of the issue agenda to outside groups. As one campaign finance expert explained, "[As the candidate,] you want to have control of your message, you want to call the shots and be able to spend the money where you want to spend it."[24] While outside groups have the potential to undercut a candidate's message,[25] they also provide cover for candidates who may need to attack an opponent to gain traction with voters. Instead of the campaign attacking the opponent directly, outside groups can do this, allowing the candidate to deny "going negative" while still reaping the advantage that the attack might generate. As one expert noted, "They [outside groups] can say things the campaign wants to keep a distance from."[26] This strategy can appeal to independent and swing voters who may turn against a candidate who makes what appears to be an unfair or overtly partisan attack against an opponent.

Fundraising Practices Have Changed

The deregulated campaign finance system also has altered campaign fundraising practices. Although the *Citizens United* ruling upheld the constitutionality of disclosure requirements, an FEC ruling in 2007 played a significant role in weakening disclosure. Nonprofit groups, according to the FEC, only have to disclose donations that are specifically earmarked and designated for use on election ads. This ruling in combination with the *Citizens United* ruling helped make nonprofit groups an especially attractive vehicle for wealthy donors who fear the possibility of political reprisals. One lobbyist remarked that nonprofit groups now hold "the keys to the political kingdom because they allow [wealthy donors] anonymity."[27] Political observers commonly refer to such untracked and undisclosed funds as "dark money."

Perhaps the most notorious example of dark money and the breakdown of the campaign finance system's disclosure requirements came in 2011. W Spann LLC, a mystery company with no corporate records about the owner of the firm, its address, or type of business, funneled $1 million into the Super PAC Restore Our Future. Only months after it formed, W Spann dissolved, creating what one campaign finance expert called a "roadmap for how [donors] can hide their identities."[28]

National Party Committees Adapt to Change

Party committees, similar to candidates' campaign organizations, have found ways to sidestep coordination prohibitions as well. During the 2010 election, for example, the National Republican Congressional Committee (NRCC) took the novel approach of publicly disclosing its ad buy strategy. This gave cues to conservative and pro-Republican outside groups about where to direct their spending.[29] These strategies have been repeated in the 2016 election. Numerous outside groups also have coordinated among themselves, sharing target lists and television-time ad buy data—a practice borrowed from Democratic-group efforts in 2006 and 2008. The political director of the Chamber of Commerce, Bill Miller, explained that the NRCC's information and coordination with other outside groups allowed the chamber to "see where the holes are and figure out who is filling what holes."[30]

In summary, the effects of recent rulings from the Roberts Court have been to turn the clock back to the pre-Watergate era or even much earlier for campaigns. As former FEC chairman Trevor Potter explained, "Well, it would be overstating it, but it would still be in the right ballpark to say it's going to look a lot like the 1904 campaign, which was the last one before there were federal laws regulating money in politics. You're going to find a lot of money being spent. I think you're going to find people who don't want to disclose donors being able to hide the money. So you'll find secret money."[31] Taken together, the primary goals of the modern campaign finance system under FECA and the BCRA reforms—to limit money in federal elections and to improve disclosure—now appear to have been largely undone by the rulings of the Roberts Court.

Prospects for Legislative Reform: An Overview

The earlier discussion of the Roberts Court decisions clarifies that in the twenty-first century, reform of federal campaign finance law and jurisprudence consists mostly of an activist U.S. Supreme Court dismantling the FECA framework and related law. Today, the most immediate open campaign finance policy-making question is whether the federal courts' deregulatory initiatives will eat away at what remains of the framework, mostly the disclosure requirements.

Whether the federal government's elected branches counter the judicial branch will turn largely on whether Democrats control them. As discussed later, campaign finance reform is now an almost completely partisan issue. Democrats have pledged to continue reform efforts. Democratic presidential prenomination front-runner Hillary Clinton has declared campaign finance one of her top priorities and advanced positions that will draw criticism (thereby promoting the issue's visibility) throughout the campaign. For example, Clinton said more than once that support for overturning the U.S. Supreme Court's decision in *Citizens United v. FEC* would serve as her litmus test for nominees to serve as justices of the U.S. Supreme Court.[32] Clinton also announced that, if necessary, she would support a constitutional amendment to "fix our dysfunctional political system and get unaccountable money out of it once and for all."[33] Sen. Bernie Sanders (I-VT), Clinton's most successful competitor as of this writing, has been a vocal critic of the *Citizens United* ruling and promised to continue to push aggressively for campaign finance reform. Additionally, with total campaign expenditures expected to reach about

$10 billion for the cycle, the news media will almost assuredly devote considerable attention to money in politics and efforts to curb the influence of large donors.

Yet even if the presidential election campaign draws public attention to campaign finance reform, it is unlikely that comprehensive reform will find its way onto the congressional agenda, let alone pass, in the near term. At the federal level, reform is now an almost completely partisan issue. No major proposal in the 113th or in the 114th Congress, as of this writing, has attracted even the nominal bipartisan support that BCRA enjoyed. Hence, any federal reform policies that might emerge in the near term will probably fall short of the scale of even BCRA, perhaps taking the form of measures that address relatively narrow targeted areas, such as elements of the disclosure regime.

In the longer term, the current five-justice conservative majority of the U.S. Supreme Court continues to narrow the range of options that it will accept as constitutional, pushing reformers toward policy responses that (1) do not conflict with that majority's claims about the First Amendment to the U.S. Constitution and (2), as a practical matter, fit within the Roberts Court's push toward a laissez-faire, market-oriented vision of campaign finance policy instead of an approach that emphasizes regulation. The initial Roberts Court era–reform efforts indicate that future large-scale proposals may need to look more market oriented, stressing the use of incentives (e.g., matching funds and tax credits) to increase small donor participation, and less like "Great Society" approaches that attempt to "level the playing field" by relying heavily on flat grants and regulating the activity of affluent political actors.

Nearer-Term Prospects: Repairing the Disclosure Regime's Widening "Coverage Error"

U.S. Supreme Court Justice Louis Brandeis wrote, "Publicity is justly commended as a remedy for social and industrial diseases. Sunlight is said to be the best of disinfectants; electric light the most efficient policeman."[34] Voters can only hold policy makers responsible for any special policies or favors they provide for donors if they have access to information about who has given to whom. Thus, disclosure is a necessary condition for accountability in campaign financing.[35]

As noted earlier, however, recent developments in campaign finance leave the disclosure system incomplete. While there is full disclosure to the FEC of contributions to candidates, political parties, and PACs, the Internal Revenue Service (IRS) is responsible for tracking contributions to some 527 committees, which results in less complete and timely disclosure. Moreover, no disclosure requirements govern contributions to some nonprofit organizations, such as those created under section 501(c)(4) (social welfare organizations) and 501(c)(6) (trade associations) of the Internal Revenue Code. The code thus leaves a major gap in the ability to trace money in elections. This allows independent groups allied with both major political parties to raise vast sums of money using legal entities that enable them to circumvent campaign finance disclosure requirements.

Shortly after the Court issued the *Citizens United* decision, congressional Democrats pressed to strengthen disclosure requirements. In 2010, Sen. Charles Schumer (D-NY) and Rep. Chris Van Hollen (D-MD) introduced legislation (S. 3628; H.R. 5175) that would have required corporations, labor unions, and other nonparty groups to disclose the identities of individuals who financed their spending on advertising. The Democracy Is Strengthened by Casting Light On Spending in Elections ("DISCLOSE") Act passed the U.S. House of Representatives by a largely party-line vote (all but thirty-six Democrats and only two Republicans supported the measure) but was stopped in the Senate by a Republican filibuster.[36] After the 111th Congress, Republicans took control of the House of Representatives. Democrats have introduced a version of the DISCLOSE Act in every session. Nonetheless, the measure has yet to attract more than one Republican cosponsor in either chamber of Congress and routinely dies in committee.

At the White House, the Obama administration's willingness to work through executive orders has not extended to requiring disclosure of campaign contributions. In April 2011, news surfaced that the White House had drafted an executive order that would have required federal contractors to disclose their contributions to political groups that claim exemption from campaign finance disclosure requirements. House Majority Whip Kevin McCarthy (R-CA) led his party's opposition to the order on the grounds that disclosure would have a chilling effect on the political speech of contractors who feared for "their livelihoods." In April 2012, the Obama administration gave up the effort.[37]

Nevertheless, some Republicans have historically supported, or at least tolerated, disclosure requirements, and there are scenarios in which a more narrowly tailored disclosure bill could conceivably pass. Legislators could agree, for example, on a requirement to inform a publicly traded corporation's shareholders of large political contributions made by the corporation. Alternatively, a coalition of incumbents could become more concerned about losing control over their own campaigns to large "dark money" donors than some other considerations that weigh against more comprehensive disclosure laws. Additionally, some Republican opposition to the DISCLOSE Act may depend on the party's advantage in undisclosed funds since the 2010 election cycle.[38] If that were to change, some opposition might yield.

Long-Term Prospects: The Changing Shape of Public Financing Proposals

Despite the collapse of the presidential public finance system, some members of Congress and public interest group allies continue to push for public financing of federal elections. Public financing remains a primary feature of the broadest proposals for campaign finance reform. Advocates of public funding of congressional elections cite a variety of reasons for promoting such programs. Many justifications arise from the broad goal of increasing the competitiveness of congressional elections.[39]

In the 2014 November general election, for example, seventy-seven candidates for the U.S. House of Representatives ran without opposition from a major political party, presenting voters with no effective choice.[40] Proponents claim that a system of public funding could reduce the need to raise a large sum of money as a barrier to running for office. Those who do not easily have access to money, but are otherwise candidate material, might be able to establish their credibility as candidates and attract the support needed to wage a campaign. Such programs could also increase the diversity of the pool of potential candidates by enabling women, members of some minority groups, and others who often lack access to networks of wealthy prospective donors to run for office more easily.[41]

Until very recently, public financing proposals ran the gamut. They included full public funding of major-party candidates in general elections, more limited proposals to provide some subsidies to candidates at the start of their campaigns or after they meet a certain threshold, and plans that give incentives to individuals to contribute to candidates (e.g., through tax credits). Confronted with the last decade of recent federal court rulings, proponents of public financing have begun to turn away from proposals that rely on large flat grants of money to qualifying candidates. Today, and for the foreseeable future, public financing policy designs will emphasize more heavily the role of small donors (however defined). The recent pivot toward a greater emphasis on small donors is evident in the trajectories of both the Fair Elections Now Act (FENA) and newer proposals.

The Evolution of the Fair Elections Now Act

This turn to small donors began in earnest with changes that sponsors in the 111th Congress (2009–2011) introduced in FENA, the most prominent legislative proposal for large-scale reform in the post-BCRA era. In the 110th Congress, Senate Assistant Majority Leader Dick Durbin (D-IL) (and fellow Illinois senator Barack Obama, among others) introduced a version of the bill (S. 1285) that drew heavily from the "clean elections" systems adopted in various forms in Arizona, Maine, and Connecticut. As in Arizona, FENA would have created a voluntary system that supported the campaigns of qualifying candidates with, among other things, a combination of flat grants, media broadcast vouchers, and supplemental "fair fight funds" that would be made available if a participating candidate confronted unusually high spending in support of a nonparticipating opponent. Congressional candidates could choose to finance their campaigns with public money if they could demonstrate sufficient public support for their candidacy. Candidates could raise some private funds at the earliest stage of the campaign. These contributions, however, could not exceed $100 from a particular individual. Ultimately, to qualify for public funding, a candidate would have to raise a specified number of "qualifying contributions" from residents of the candidate's state.

Similar to Arizona's state election public financing system, which served as a model for FENA, the FENA-qualifying contributions would be limited to $5. By raising many of these small contributions, a candidate would demonstrate his or her campaign's viability, thereby reducing the possibility that public funds would go to marginal candidates. Candidates receiving public funds would then have to agree to refuse private contributions to the campaign and to abide by voluntary limits on campaign expenditures. Rep. John Tierney (D-MA), who had annually introduced similar legislation for nearly the entire preceding decade, sponsored a companion measure, the Clean Money, Clean Elections Act of 2007 (H.R. 1614), in the U.S. House.

Proponents of FENA's new emphasis on small donors argued that the potential of small donor fundraising could be dramatic, particularly when coupled with matching funds. Consider the example of President Obama, whose presidential campaign spent more than any in history. In 2008, Barack Obama received nearly 69.5 million votes in the November general election. If half of the people who voted for Obama in November 2008 donated $20 to his general election campaign, or if 20 percent of his voters gave $50, he would have raised nearly $700 million from small donors. If one-third of those who voted for Obama in November 2008 gave $10 to his campaign and received a $2-to-$1 match, the campaign would have raised $695 million from extremely small donations under a matching fund program far more modest than the $4-to-$1 or $6-to-$1 matches proposed in the later versions of FENA.

A Sharper Turn to Small Donor Financing

FENA continues to enjoy support in Congress. Beginning in the 113th Congress, however, Rep. John Sarbanes (D-MD) introduced legislation that garnered far more cosponsors (148 in the 114th Congress by June 2015) for an even more aggressive small donor blueprint. Sarbanes's "Government by the People Act" (H.R. 20 in the 114th Congress) abandons FENA's flat-grant/small donor hybrid approach in favor of a system centered on small donors. The Sarbanes bill establishes a 50 percent "My Voice" federal income tax credit for the first $50 that a citizen contributes to a campaign; a donor who gives $50 would receive a $25 tax credit. The act also provides a 6-to-1 match for contributions of up to $150 from an individual resident of a candidate's home state; contributions in excess of $150 would not be matched. Hence, a candidate could receive $1,050 from a small donor's contribution of $150. Candidates could receive the matching funds only by voluntarily refusing contributions that (1) exceeded $1,000 and (2) came from a PAC that accepted contributions larger than $150.

A broader proposal from Reps. David Price (D-NC) and Chris Van Hollen (D-MD) would apply the high-leverage $6-to-$1 match to small donations to candidates for both president and Congress. The chief sponsors introduced two versions of the bill in the 114th Congress, the latest as of this writing. The "Empowering Citizens Act" (H.R. 424) would create a matching fund system for both congressional and presidential election campaigns. A later version (H.R. 2143 and its companion bill in the Senate, S. 1176) focuses exclusively on the presidential public financing system. The Price–Van Hollen bills define "small dollar" donors more broadly than does the Sarbanes bill. For Price and Van Hollen, such donors include those who give up to an aggregate of $1,000. Their bills would also match up to the first $250 that a donor gives. The Price–Van Hollen bills also attempt to enable political party committees that rely on small donors to compete with independent groups. Such committees could coordinate with candidates the spending of unlimited funds raised only from small donors.

In the near term, partisan polarization creates virtually insurmountable obstacles to the enactment of a public funding proposal. Moreover, even if citizens generally favor such a proposal in principle, will they spur Congress to put it on the active legislative agenda? If the Abramoff-era scandals have failed to engender sufficient public pressure for this reform, one wonders what it would take to mobilize sufficient public demand.

State-Level Initiatives

Although, as a practical matter, the federal government currently has no effective public financing program, states have experimented with such programs in Maine (1996), Vermont (1997), Arizona (1998), Connecticut (2005), as have some major U.S. cities. The U.S. Supreme Court, however, struck down a key provision of Arizona's program in 2011, complicating the future of many extant programs. Under the program, a publicly funded candidate could receive a large amount of additional funding if spending in support of his or her privately financed opponent exceeded a specified "trigger" threshold. The decision in *McComish v. Bennett* ruled that the prospect of triggering a large influx of funds to a publicly funded candidate unconstitutionally burdened the speech of the candidate's privately financed opponents.

Certainly, one can imagine a long-term scenario in which more states ultimately embrace public financing and that state legislators who embrace such systems eventually will move on to Congress and bolster support for a comparable federal-level system. If, at the same time, the systems garner favorable reviews from citizens, public support for comparable federal legislation could harden. Still, that is a long way off at best, and even the current systems must survive and/or adapt to further opposition in the courts.

Beyond public financing systems, state governments are also considering a variety of measures to address the rapidly escalating importance of undisclosed campaign funds. The Sunlight Foundation recently reported that in recent sessions state legislators have introduced 125 bills to strengthen disclosure requirements.[42] Some have already become law with bipartisan leadership support. In 2014, California senate Republican leader Bob Huff joined Democrats and other Republicans to pass the nation's first law to require some nonprofits that make large campaign expenditures to disclose their spending and the names of their donors.[43] The following year, a bipartisan coalition in Montana enacted a state-level DISCLOSE bill. The measure received support from moderate Republicans including Rep. Frank Garner, a Republican target of Americans for Prosperity–Montana. Fellow Republican Sen. Duane Ankney posed the choice to Garner this way: "You want a flier against you that says 'he voted for dark money' or do you want to send a flier that says, 'I voted to send those damn carpetbaggers out of the state?'"[44]

Conclusion

In the 1970s, Congress established a regulatory framework that built on earlier rules and designed a system so that different elements worked together. Contribution limits reduced the supply of campaign money somewhat and decreased the voice of the wealthiest donors, while spending limits, tied to the aceeptance of public funding, decreased the demand for private campaign funds. Public financing was available to help candidates reach voters, and all campaign activity became transparent through reporting to a national agency.

Today little of this framework remains operational. Contribution limits still regulate the size of contributions directly to candidates, but wealthy individuals and corporations can channel unlimited amounts into committees that openly support the same candidates. For all practical purposes, spending limits are gone; public financing is irrelevant to national campaigns; and a sizable (but unknowable) portion of activity is not transparent to voters.

The future of campaigns thus seems headed backward in time to the pre-Watergate era, or perhaps even as far back as the late nineteenth and early twentieth centuries, in which there were no meaningful restrictions on a donor giving unlimited amounts to candidates. Today, much like these earlier periods that were absent regulation, a few exceptionally wealthy donors wield significant power in elections. What is different, however, is that today's system has some remnants of the past regulatory regime, giving the illusion of regulation and transparency when none really exists. As a consequence of the rulings of the Roberts Court, campaigns now focus on a very small number of mega-donors, particularly in the so-called money primary. These donors can stay in the "dark" by avoiding disclosure requirements. The prospect of Congress enacting reforms to reverse these developments seems highly unlikely. Even if Congress did respond by passing new campaign finance reform legislation, it is not clear whether the Court would uphold a legislative response. In this environment, the current "Wild West" of campaign finance seems likely to remain in the years to come.

Notes

1. Gabriel Debenedetti and Annie Karni, "Hillary's Dash for Cash" (*Politico*, May 21, 2015). Accessed on June 20, 2015, from http://www.politico.com/story/2015/05/hillary-clinton-fundraising-goal-2-billion-118183.html.

2. Associated Press, "Presidential Candidates Defy Campaign Finance Limits through Well-Funded Outside Groups" (*U.S. News & World Report*, June 17, 2015). Accessed on June 20, 2015, from http://www.usnews.com/news/politics/articles/2015/06/17/presidential-candidates-lean-on-well-funded-outside-groups.

3. These organizations are known as "527" and "501(c)" organizations, which are labels that refer to the internal revenue codes that govern their tax status. Unlike a traditional PAC, some 527 groups do not contribute to candidates for federal office, but rather are established for the specific purpose of engaging in political advocacy. 501(c)s are tax-exempt organizations that, like some 527s, cannot contribute to campaigns but can engage in some political activities, such as voter mobilization and education, provided that political activity is nonpartisan for 501(c)(3) organizations or does not become the primary purpose for 501(c)(4) organizations. There are "Super" PACs as well that can raise funds without restrictions provided that these groups also do not make campaign contributions and that they spend their money in federal elections independent of candidates and political parties.

4. "Campaign Finance eGuide" (Campaign Finance Institute). Accessed July 15, 2011, from www.cfinst.org/legacy/eguide/basics.html.

5. Bradley A. Smith, "Faulty Assumptions and Undemocratic Consequences of Campaign Finance Reform" (*Yale Law Journal,* Vol. 105, No. 4, 1996), 1049–1091.

6. Clyde Wilcox, "Contributing as Political Participation," in *A User's Guide to Campaign Finance Reform*, edited by Gerald C. Lubenow (Lanham, MD: Rowman & Littlefield, 2001).

7. Levin Amendment funds must meet the following conditions: (1) Federal officeholders and national parties may not receive Levin Amendment funds; (2) all receipts and disbursements of Levin Amendment funds must be disclosed; (3) party committees in two or more states, or two or more party committees in the same state, are prohibited from jointly raising Levin Amendment funds; (4) a state party committee cannot raise the money for use in other states; (5) Levin Amendment funds cannot be used for federal candidate-specific or generic advertising; (6) Levin Amendment activities must be funded consistent with FEC hard money or soft money allocation rules; (7) the state or local party must raise its own matching hard money; and (8) Levin Amendment funds cannot be transferred between party committees.

8. Michael M. Franz, "The *Citizens United* Election? Or Same as It Ever Was?" (*The Forum*, Vol. 8, 2010), Article 7.

9. *Davis v. FEC*, 554 U.S. 724 (2008).

10. *Citizens United v. FEC*, 558 U.S. 08-205 (2010). Justice Kennedy's quotation in *Citizens United v. FEC* was accessed from http://www.law.cornell.edu/supct/html/08-205.ZO.html.

11. Ibid.

12. The *Citizens United v. FEC* decision did not directly rule on whether unions can use their general treasury funds on election-related independent expenditures in federal elections; however, there is near-unanimous legal agreement that the court's logic would apply to labor.

13. Center for Responsive Politics, "Outside Money." Accessed June 30, 2015, from http://www.opensecrets.org/outsidespending/index.php.

14. Tom Curry, "Big-Bucks Presidential Fundraising Still Vital in Citizens United Era" (*MSNBC*, August 3, 2011). Accessed on November 17, 2011, from http://firstread.msnbc.msn.com/_news/2011/08/03/7242125-big-bucks-presidential-fundraisers-still-vital-in-citizens-united-era; Center for Responsive Politics, "Outside Spending." Accessed on June 20, 2015, from https://www.opensecrets.org/outsidespending/fes_summ.php?cycle=2012. See also Phil Hirschkorn, "Outside Spending on 2012 Elections Reaches $1 Billion" (*CBS News*, October 28, 2012). Accessed on June 20, 2015, from http://www.cbsnews.com/news/outside-spending-on-2012-elections-reaches-1-billion.

15. Center for Responsive Politics, "Total Outside Spending by Election Cycle, Excluding Party Committees." Accessed on June 20, 2015, from https://www.opensecrets.org/outsidespending/cycle_tots.php.

16. Center for Responsive Politics, "2012 Outside Spending, by Super PAC." Accessed on June 20, 2015, from https://www.opensecrets.org/outsidespending/summ.php?cycle=2012&chrt=V&disp=O&type=S; Center for Responsive Politics, "2014 Outside Spending, by Super PAC." Accessed on June 20, 2015, from https://www.opensecrets.org/outsidespending/summ.php?cycle=2014&chrt=V&disp=O&type=S.

17. Michael Isikoff, "Billionaires Give Big to New 'Super PACs'" (*MSNBC*, June 26, 2011). Accessed on November 17, 2011, from http://www.nbcnews.com/id/43541131/ns/politics-decision_2012/t/billionaires-give-big-new-super-pacs/?ns=politics-decision_2012&t=billionaires-give-big-new-super-pacs.

18. Matt Bai, "This Donation Cycle Catches G.O.P. in the Upswing" (*The New York Times*, October 20, 2010). Accessed November 17, 2011, from http://www.nytimes.com/2010/10/21/us/politics/21bai.html.

19. Amie Parnes and Kevin Cirilli, "The $5 Billion Presidential Campaign" (*The Hill*, January 21, 2015). Accessed June 20, 2015, from http://thehill.com/blogs/ballot-box/presidential-races/230318-the-5-billion-campaign.

20. Philip Bump, "The Robots Are Here: Jeb Bush and the First Super PAC-Run Campaign" (*The Washington Post*, April 21, 2015). Accessed June 19, 2015, from http://www.washingtonpost.com/blogs/the-fix/wp/2015/04/21/the-robots-are-here-jeb-bush-and-the-first-super-pac-run-campaign.

21. Matea Gold, "Bush Blows Away GOP Rivals with 2016 War Chest" (*The Washington Post*, February 13, 2015). Accessed June 20, 2015, from http://www.washingtonpost.com/politics/jeb-bushs-war-chest-far-outpacing-field-of-gop-contenders/2015/02/13/1fd3c076-b2f1-11e4-886b-c22184f27c35_story.html.

22. Beth Reinhard and Rebecca Ballhaus, "Still Undeclared, Jeb Bush Touts Record Fundraising Haul" (*The Wall Street Journal*, April 27, 2015). Accessed June 19, 2015, from http://www.wsj.com/articles/still-undeclared-jeb-bush-touts-record-fundraising-haul-1430140658.

23. Ibid.

24. Curry, "Big-Bucks Presidential Fundraising Still Vital in Citizens United Era."

25. David B. Magleby, "Conclusions and Implications," in *Outside Money: Soft Money and Issue Advocacy in the 1998 Congressional Elections*, edited by David B. Magleby (Lanham, MD: Rowman and Littlefield, 2000).

26. Curry, "Big-Bucks Presidential Fundraising Still Vital in Citizens United Era."

27. Peter H. Stone, "Center for Public Integrity: Campaign Cash: The Independent Fundraising Gold Rush Since 'Citizens United' Ruling" (*Democracy 21*, October 4, 2010). Accessed June 30, 2011, from www.democracy21.org/index.asp?Type=B_PR&SEC=%7BAC81D4FF-0476-4E28-B9B1-7619D271A334%7D&DE=%7B037D17B6-F488-4FF6-A849-D519900C50A0%7D.

28. Isikoff, "Firm Gives $1 Million to Pro-Romney Group, Then Dissolves."

29. Jeanne Cummings, "Republican Groups Coordinated Firepower" (*Politico*, November 3, 2010). Accessed on November 17, 2011, from http://www.politico.com/news/stories/1110/44651.html.

30. Ibid.

31. Kathy Kiely, "Rules Be Damned" (*National Journal*, July 14, 2011). Accessed on August 10, 2011, from http://www.nationaljournal.com/magazine/former-fec-chairman-trevor-potter-on-campaign-finance-20110714.

32. Matea Gold and Anne Gearan, "Hillary Clinton's Litmus Test for Supreme Court Nominees: A Pledge to Overturn Citizens United" (*The Washington Post*, May 14, 2015). Accessed on June 16, 2015 from http://www.washingtonpost.com/blogs/post-politics/wp/2015/05/14/hillary-clintons-litmus-test-for-supreme-court-nominees-a-pledge-to-overturn-citizens-united.

33. Nicholas Confessore, "Another Clinton Promises to Fix Political Financing" (*The New York Times,* April 17, 2015), A22.

34. Louis D. Brandeis Legacy Fund for Social Justice. Accessed on June 30, 2015 at http://www.brandeis.edu/legacyfund/bio.html.

35. Herbert E. Alexander, Janet M. Box-Steffensmeier, Anthony J. Corrado, Ruth S. Jones, Jonathan S. Krasno, Michael J. Malbin, Gary Moncrief, Frank J. Sorauf, and John R. Wright, *New Realities, New Thinking* (Los Angeles: Citizen's Research Foundation, 1997), 9.

36. Ben Pershing, "House Passes Campaign Finance Bill: Disclose Act Would Curb Corporate Political Spending on Elections" (*The Washington Post*, June 25, 2010), A2. See also Dan Eggen, "Bill on Political Ad Disclosure Falls Short in Senate" (*The Washington Post*, July 28, 2010), A3.

37. Mike Lillis, "White House Abandons Push for Federal Contractors to Disclose Political Giving" (*The Hill*, April 8, 2012). Accessed October 15, 2015, from thehill.com/homenews/administration/220453-white-house-abandons-push-for-disclosure-of-political-giving-by-contractors.

38. See, for example, Paul Blumenthal, "The Citizens United Effect: 40 Percent of Outside Money Made Possible by Supreme Court Ruling" (*Sunlight Foundation*, November 4, 2010). Accessed on November 17, 2011, from http://sunlightfoundation .com/blog/2010/11/04/the-citizens-united-effect-40-percent-of-outside-money-made-possible-by-supreme-court-ruling. See also Peter Olsen-Phillips, "Dark Money Is Still a Republican Game" (*Sunlight Foundation*, October 28, 2014). Accessed on June 19, 2015, from http://sunlightfoundation.com/blog/2014/10/28/dark-money-still-a-republican-game.

39. Kenneth R. Mayer, Timothy Werner, and Amanda Williams, "Do Public Funding Programs Enhance Electoral Competition?" (Paper presented at the Fourth Annual Conference on State Politics and Policy Laboratories of Democracy: Public Policy in the American States, Kent State University, April 30–May 1, 2004).

40. Associated Press, "House Election Results" (*The New York Times*). Accessed on June 17, 2015, from atelections.nytimes.com/2014/results/house.

41. Timothy Werner and Kenneth R. Mayer, "The Impact of Public Election Funding on Women Candidates: Comparative Evidence from State Elections" (Paper presented at the 2005 Annual Meeting of the Midwest Political Science Association, Chicago, April 7–10, 2005).

42. Peter Olsen-Phillips, "State Legislatures Taking Aim at Dark Money, Disclosure" (*Sunlight Foundation*, March 17, 2015). Accessed on June 30, 2015, from http://sunlight foundation.com/blog/2015/03/17/state-legislatures-taking-aim-at-dark-money-disclosure.

43. Patrick McGreevy, "Bill to Boost Campaign Finance Disclosure Clears California Legislature" (*Los Angeles Times*, May 8, 2014). Accessed on June 30, 2015, from http:// www.latimes.com/local/political/la-me-pc-campaign-money-disclosure-bill-clears-calif-legislature-20140508-story.html.

44. Kristen Inbody, "Dark Money Ban Becomes Law" (*Great Falls Tribune*, April 22, 2015). Accessed on June 30, 2015, from http://www.greatfallstribune.com/story/news/local/2015/04/22/dark-money-ban-becomes-law/26197249.

CHAPTER 11

Voter Identification Laws — Necessary, Nefarious, or Neither?

Jeffrey Crouch

VOTER IDENTIFICATION LAWS HAVE EMERGED nationwide in the past decade and a half. Within that time span, they have become a new front in the war between polarized U.S. political parties. They may even play an important—if indirect—role in the 2016 presidential campaign.

States began to pass voter identification laws in earnest through the 2000s, and several key moments helped to spark their emergence. Those moments include the 2000 presidential election result, requirements established by the Help America Vote Act (HAVA), and the Carter-Baker Commission Report. Proponents (usually Republicans) have cited the need to prevent voter fraud as their motive for pursuing new or revised laws regarding identity verification at the polls.[1] At the same time, opponents have raised questions about whether voter identification laws are, at their core, just a partisan attempt to make it more difficult for certain groups of voters to cast their ballots.[2]

Perhaps the most famous example to date of a controversial voter identification law was enacted by the Indiana State Legislature in 2005. The law, which required voters to produce a government-issued photo ID, survived a Supreme Court challenge in *Crawford v. Marion County Election Board* (2008) and suggested that states may exercise wide latitude to determine their qualifications for voter eligibility.[3] Indiana and Georgia were the first two states to mandate a photo ID for voting.[4] Several other states followed suit in the ensuing years.[5]

However, recent developments suggest that voter identification law debates may soon become obsolete. As we gear up for the 2016 presidential campaign, several state legislatures have already begun to talk about the possibility of universal automatic voter registration,[6] and presidential candidates such as Hillary Clinton are discussing it as well.[7] Because the voter identification issue is evolving so quickly, now is a good time to assess its impact to date. Accordingly, in this chapter, I will consider the evolution of voter identification laws and will also connect them to the partisan polarization that has characterized U.S. elections in the twenty-first century.

This chapter addresses the following key questions about voter identification laws: What is the bigger picture? What are voter identification laws, and which states have them? How did they come about? Why are they controversial? What are the most important current issues, what impact have the laws had, and what is likely to happen in the future?

What Is the Bigger Picture?

The United States features two major political parties that are nationalized and demographically distinct. As Hicks et al. point out, we have a "decidedly white, male, older, evangelical Protestant, conservative, and southern-based Grand Old Party (GOP) now fac[ing] off against a racially and ethnically diverse, younger, secular, liberal, and northern-based Democratic Party."[8] Elections can be won or lost depending on how many members of these specific groups show up at the polls (or do not).

Voter ID laws may influence which members of these particular groups are eligible to vote. These laws are a consequence of contemporary elections held in a polarized political environment, and they help bring to light three important features of modern campaigns. First, members of the two major political parties will take advantage of any legal way to obtain an edge, including encouraging or discouraging voter participation; second, partisans will use close election results as a way to emphasize to their supporters that their votes really matter; third, both parties recognize the importance of getting their rank-and-file to the polls, so they look for any advantage that will help edge up their own turnout and/or drive down that of their opponents.[9] In a closely divided nation, every vote matters a lot. It is possible that these laws are being used as a political tool by partisans to potentially impact election results. Thus, it is important to closely consider the recent popularity of voter ID laws and their resulting implications.

What Are They?

Voter identification laws are rules established by a particular state laying out the specific type of identification required by that state from a citizen who wishes to vote on Election Day. The United States does not offer a "universal voting" card.[10] Instead, states basically establish their own rules for the type of identification required,[11] as well as where a voter may need to go to obtain that identification. Some states have revised their laws to make voting a more complicated process than others. For example, a voter in Indiana needs to produce a government-issued photo ID, but a voter in neighboring Illinois does not have to produce any paper-work to be able to vote.[12] There is not yet much scholarly research on why some states have toughened their voting requirements while others have not.[13] There is also not a consensus among academics as to whether it makes much of a difference who votes, as will be discussed later.

Which States Have Them?

Voter identification laws can vary widely from state to state. As a result, it is dif-ficult to make broad generalizations about them or place them into neat categories. One classification approach, established by the National Conference of State Legislatures (NCSL), contains detailed information demonstrating how the requirements may differ from state to state, ranging from fairly informal to quite rigid. According to the NCSL, voter identification laws nationwide can be classi-fied as either "strict" or "non-strict," depending on whether a voter who does not produce adequate identification will be allowed to have his or her vote count without having to follow up after the election. The laws can also be categorized according to whether or not the state requires the identification produced by the voter to contain a photograph of that voter.[14]

For 2014—the last time the NCSL comprehensively updated its table—the states that were "strict" and required photo identification to vote were Georgia, Indiana, Kansas, Mississippi, Tennessee, Texas, Virginia, and Wisconsin.[15] The states that were "strict" but did not require photo identification to vote were Arizona, North Dakota, and Ohio.[16] The "non-strict" states that nevertheless mandated a photo ID were Alabama, Florida, Hawaii, Idaho, Louisiana, Michigan, Rhode Island, and South Dakota.[17] Finally, the "non-strict" states that did not require photo identification from voters were Alaska, Arkansas, Colorado, Connecticut, Delaware, Kentucky, Missouri, Montana, New Hampshire, Oklahoma, South Carolina, Utah, and Washington.[18] The NCSL website also maintains a state-by-state breakdown of both the types of identification allowed and what the state will do if a voter shows up at the polls without one of these forms of identification.[19]

How Did the Laws Emerge?

Disputes over voter identification laws are a fairly recent phenomenon. Although today they are another issue that Republican and Democratic partisans fight over, they were less politically charged in the past.[20] Before 2000, there was no discern-ible mass movement to update voter identification requirements.

The first two states to enact voter identification laws were South Carolina (1950), Hawaii (1970), followed by Texas (1971), Florida (1977), and Alaska (1980).[21]

The total number of states with a voter ID requirement by 2000 was fourteen.[22] However, things picked up after the closely contested presidential election of 2000, which finally ended after the Supreme Court's ruling in *Bush v. Gore* (2000) that awarded Florida (and, thus, the presidency) to George W. Bush by a margin of just 537 votes in that state. Another contributing factor was HAVA, which was passed in 2002 to address some of the shortcomings in U.S. electoral procedures and also helped popularize voter fraud as an issue, with voter identification legislation as a means to end it.[23] Lastly, in 2005, former president Jimmy Carter and ex–cabinet secretary James A. Baker III, the bipartisan co-chairs of the Commission on Federal Election Reform, issued a report titled "Building Confidence in U.S. Elections."[24] In the report, nestled among a group of recommendations for electoral reforms, was a proposal for a REAL ID card to be used for voting.[25]

In order to comply with HAVA mandates,[26] states have either passed or revised their rules governing what a potential voter needs to produce in order to receive a regular ballot in an election. Although too nuanced to discuss in detail here,[27] in many cases, the new rules on voter identification have made it more difficult for a voter to provide the necessary identification to a poll worker to obtain a ballot.

From 2010 to the present, nearly two dozen states have passed laws that make voting more difficult, and over half of those states will have them ready to go for 2016 presidential election voters.[28] Still, as of 2015, the pace of states implementing strict voter ID laws has slowed dramatically.[29] Perhaps more importantly, Oregon recently enacted a law that would allow for automatic registration, and over a dozen other states decided to debate the same route, apparently signaling that the wave of the future is "to reduce the burden on individual voters and instead require the government to ensure eligible citizens are registered."[30]

Why Are They Controversial?

Voter identification laws have largely been sponsored—and advocated for—by Republican state legislators while Democrats have often opposed them. At least one study argues that this is a part of the GOP's electoral strategy: helping its candidates' chances by preventing likely Democratic voters from being able to easily participate in an election.[31]

Following the argument that there is political intent behind the Republican push for voter identification laws, critics say that voter identification laws are subtler than other tactics to manipulate election laws and keep likely Democratic voters from the polls. In contrast with other contemporary GOP moves to "to cut back on early voting days, Election Day registration, or reducing the amount of time for completing voter registration drives," this issue has a superficial neutrality, as "restrictive voter ID legislation at least holds the appearance of ensuring the integrity of the voting process" and looks less like a power move than the other techniques.[32] However, at least one prominent scholar disagrees that voter ID actually belongs in this "civil and voting rights movement" context and also finds that "voter ID appears to present no real barrier to access [to the ballot box]."[33]

While trying to decide whether voter ID laws are merely a tool of partisans or whether they legitimately serve larger goals, observers and scholars of the voter identification trend identify two main—and often competing—values at stake: (1) preserving the integrity of the election process by preventing voter fraud and (2) avoiding the disenfranchisement of otherwise eligible voters. The concern for avoiding voter fraud is often expressed by Republicans, while keeping the polls accessible to as many voters as possible is a position often held by Democrats. I will discuss each of these values and their major supporting arguments in turn.

Voter Fraud

Proponents of voter identification laws argue that they are necessary because they help protect the integrity of elections by ensuring that only qualified voters are able to cast their ballots, and no one is allowed to present himself as someone else in order to vote. They point to the decision in *Crawford v. Marion County Election Board* (2008) (discussed in detail later in the chapter) that suggests that a state can require even a photo ID, and argue that the Supreme Court has recognized that the costs to obtaining that ID are minimal. Given that a photo ID is often needed for airplane travel, access to some government buildings, and similar encounters with security checkpoints in the year 2015, they contend that it is not asking too much to require a voter to produce such identification before voting.[34]

However, modern examples of voter fraud are not widespread, a fact that complicates the efforts of voter identification law supporters who cite voter fraud concerns as their motivation. There is nothing today like elections in the 1800s that featured "widespread and readily admitted fraud."[35] According to election law expert Richard Hasen, "What we see is isolated, small-scale activities that often have not shown any kind of criminal intent."[36] Still, as noted by *The Washington Post*, Professor Justin Levitt of Loyola University Law School has found thirty-one examples of "documented, in-person voter fraud that would have been prevented by stricter rules around identification at the polling place."[37]

If clear and/or numerous examples of voter fraud exist, then one must weigh the potential damage that this illegal activity inflicts upon the integrity of elections on one hand and, on the other hand, the likelihood of depriving some otherwise eligible voters of their right to do so. A Public Religion Research Institute poll found that 68 percent of Republicans believed preventing voter fraud, not preserving ballot access, was the more important priority of the two.[38]

Voter Disenfranchisement

In a review of scholarly studies on voter identification laws, Marjorie Randon Hershey touches upon many of the arguments used by opponents of the laws. For example, they contend that the laws are simply the latest in a long line of procedural hurdles enacted to prevent certain groups of people from exercising their right to vote.[39] However, unlike poll taxes, literacy tests, and so on, voter identification laws are particularly nefarious because on their surface, they seem to apply to everyone equally: no matter who you are, you must produce the necessary identification, or you don't get to vote. According to Lorraine C. Minnite, voter ID opponents contend that the laws are "likely to have a suppressive effect on voting among eligible voters who are disproportionately racial minorities, youth, the elderly, and the poor."[40] Those same groups tend to support Democrats for public office. In a poll by the Public Religion Research Institute, 64 percent of Democrats found avoiding disenfranchisement to be a more important value than preventing voter fraud.[41]

Those who would challenge voter identification laws also argue that even if a state makes free IDs available, there is another whole layer of underlying costs of time, effort, and sometimes money required to obtain whatever information or follow whatever steps a state requires in order to secure that free ID.[42] These costs are especially difficult to bear for those who are most likely to face obstacles when obtaining identification: those with lower incomes, those who are young or old, and those who are members of minority groups. In fact, a study by the Brennan Center for Justice finds that "many rural, urban, poor, and minority voters must overcome substantial obstacles in order to retain their right to vote."[43] Those obstacles include getting to a government office that may not be open regular hours and/or may be located far away, finding time to do so, and being able to afford whatever documents they might need to provide in order to qualify for the voter ID.[44]

Current Issues

In a couple of particularly important cases, challenges to a state's voter identification law have ended up in court, even in front of the U.S. Supreme Court. Perhaps the most important voter identification case to date is *Crawford v. Marion County Election Board*, decided in 2008. In *Crawford*, what *The New York Times* called "one of the most awaited election-law cases in years," the Supreme Court ruled 6-3 in favor of Indiana's voter identification law that required government-issued photo ID from voters.[45] This particular law hints at the partisan divide on voter identification laws—as noted by Hicks et al., it came from "a completely party-line vote [and] made Indiana the first state to pass a law requiring voters to show a government-issued photo ID to vote at the polls."[46] In siding with Indiana, the Court disagreed that the law imposed an unacceptable hardship upon, as noted by a journalist, "people who are old, poor or members of a minority group and less likely to have driver's licenses or other acceptable forms of identification."[47] The state's interest in preventing voter fraud carried the day with the Court despite the fact that, as a commentator later noted, "there has not been a single prosecution for in-person vote fraud in the history of the state[.]"[48]

A potential reexamination of the issues raised in *Crawford* may be brewing in Texas, where "the strictest voter ID law in the country" was passed in 2011.[49] A federal court barred it, but it went back into effect after *Shelby County v. Holder* (2013), an Alabama case in which the Supreme Court removed the impediment by ruling unconstitutional the section of the Voting Rights Act that required preclearance for making changes to voting laws in Texas and several other states.[50] Opponents to the law sued again, under Section 2 of the Voting Rights Act, and in October 2014, a federal district court judge ruled in *Veasey v. Perry* that the law was intentionally discriminatory against minorities, finding that about 600,000 Texas voters (largely members of a minority group) would be harmed by the law.[51] The Supreme Court divided 6–3 in October 2014 in deciding to allow the law to temporarily take effect before the midterm elections.[52] Still, one observer called the federal district court ruling "the most sweeping court victory the challengers have won against [a photo ID law]."[53] Texas appealed, and the case is now set to go before the Fifth Circuit Court of Appeals.[54] It may even make it to the Supreme Court, possibly even before the 2016 elections.[55]

The larger import of *Crawford* was clear: according to Richard Hasen, "[The *Crawford* decision] was essentially a green light for ever more restrictive voter ID laws."[56] Other states have followed Indiana's lead by enacting restrictive voter identification laws (or revisions) of their own. The *Crawford* case is not set in stone, however, as the Court seemed willing to revisit these issues as studies came out showing the impact of the laws.[57] It is possible that the recent Texas case may ultimately be used by the Court to back away from its *Crawford* decision.

What Impact Have Voter ID Laws Had?

One of the biggest questions about voter identification laws is what impact passing a voter ID law has had on a state's voters and their likelihood of showing up at the polls with the necessary documents to vote a regular ballot. A number of studies have tackled this key question and related ones, but there is—as yet—no consensus on the results.

A 2014 study by Christensen and Schultz summarizes the state of the literature on voter ID laws by noting a number of findings by other scholars:

- Groups who are less likely to meet the laws' requirements for acceptable ID include the less affluent, the old, youth, those who have less schooling, and non-white voters.

- At the polls, non-white voters are more apt to be asked to provide their identification than white voters.
- Studies have produced "mixed evidence or no evidence" on voter ID laws' impact on voter turnout, whether they stop voters from showing up at the polls, or whether they make people feel more certain that the election was conducted according to the rules.
- The majority of legal scholars oppose voter ID laws for various reasons: they ask voters to do too much to be able to vote, their requirements are in effect a poll tax, they increase the likelihood of "voter suppression," and they may "disenfranchise political minorities."
- Regarding whether voter fraud is actually a major problem, scholars have found "little evidence to support claims that voter fraud is a widespread problem."[58]

In their study, Christensen and Schultz contribute their own findings on voter fraud, concluding that "electoral fraud, if it occurs, is an isolated and rare occurrence in modern U.S. elections."[59] These scholarly studies provide mixed results: on one hand, voter fraud may not be quite the worry that voter identification law proponents suggest it may be; at the same time, voter identification laws may not actually prevent significant numbers of voters from participating after all. The true impact (if any) of voter identification laws seems to lie somewhere between the conflicting positions of their proponents and opponents.

What Is Likely to Happen in the Future?

Predicting the future when it comes to voter ID laws is no simple task. An October 2014 article posted on FiveThirtyEight.com noted a "a longer trend toward more restrictive [voter ID] laws" in an article with the headline "Voter ID Laws Are Now in 17 More States Than They Were in 2000."[60] In that same article, the author also noted a "slight upward tick" in "[t]he number of states with proposals to loosen voter ID requirements." Only time will tell if more states follow Indiana post-*Crawford* and tighten identification requirements, or if a backlash will develop as people reassess the need for making voting requirements so difficult to satisfy.

Recently, a third possibility has presented itself: universal, automatic voter registration. The 2016 presidential campaign is under way, and Democratic contender Hillary Clinton has already started a conversation on this alternative to piecemeal voter identification laws.[61] She is not the only 2016 hopeful with opinions on the matter: As a Wisconsin state assemblyman, Walker proposed a photo ID bill; ten years later, the state passed a new photo ID law.[62] Walker, currently serving as governor of Wisconsin, is expected to be a Republican presidential candidate.

Conclusion

Voter identification laws proliferated in the 2000s, apparently spurred by Republican state legislatures intent on preventing voter fraud, or, more cynically, interested in keeping down the number of likely Democratic voters eligible at the polls. Scholars have devoted considerable attention to the topic in recent years, with little that is conclusive to show for their efforts. Still, voter identification laws have already become a topic worth mentioning by 2016 presidential candidates, including Hillary Clinton and Scott Walker. Even if automatic universal registration is the wave of the future, it is important to remember how we arrived at this point. Voter identification laws and the issues they raised have laid the groundwork for a conversation about our election laws that will inform—and perhaps caution—the debate about what comes next.

Notes

1. M. V. Hood III and Charles S. Bullock III, "Much Ado about Nothing? An Empirical Assessment of the Georgia Voter Identification Statute" (*State Politics & Policy Quarterly*, Vol. 12, No. 4, 2012), 395.

2. Ibid.

3. Crawford v. Marion County Election Board, 553 U.S. 181 (2008).

4. Wendy R. Weiser and Lawrence Norden, "Voting Law Changes in 2012" (Brennan Center for Justice at New York University School of Law, 2011), 4. Accessed June 18, 2015, from http://www.brennancenter.org/sites/default/files/legacy/Democracy/VRE/Brennan_Voting_Law_V10.pdf.

5. National Conference of State Legislatures, "Voter ID History" (October 16, 2014). Accessed June 18, 2015, from http://www.ncsl.org/research/elections-and-campaigns/voter-id-history.aspx.

6. Brennan Center for Justice, "Voting Laws Roundup 2015" (New York University School of Law, June 3, 2015). Accessed June 18, 2015, from http://www.brennancenter.org/analysis/voting-laws-roundup-2015.

7. Dan Merica and Eric Bradner, "Clinton Calls Out GOP Opponents by Name on Voting Rights" (*CNN*, June 5, 2015). Accessed June 18, 2015, from http://www.cnn.com/2015/06/04/politics/hillary-clinton-voting-rights-texas/.

8. William D. Hicks, Seth C. McKee, Mitchell D. Sellers, and Daniel A. Smith, "A Principle or a Strategy? Voter Identification Laws and Partisan Competition in the American States" (*Political Research Quarterly*, Vol. 68, No. 1, 2015), 20.

9. Hicks et al., "A Principle or a Strategy?" 18–19.

10. Merica and Bradner, "Clinton Calls Out GOP Opponents by Name on Voting Rights."

11. Hood and Bullock, "Much Ado about Nothing." 344.

12. Wendy Underhill, "Voter Identification Requirements: Voter ID Laws" (National Conference of State Legislatures, March 24, 2015). Accessed June 11, 2015, from http://www.ncsl.org/research/elections-and-campaigns/voter-id.aspx.

13. For an analysis of "why legislatures in some states are more likely to *introduce* restrictive voter ID bills relative to legislatures in other states" and "why some state governments are more likely to *adopt* restrictive voter ID policies relative to other states," see Hicks et al., "A Principle or a Strategy?" generally, and page 19.

14. Underhill, "Voter Identification Requirements."

15. Ibid.

16. Ibid.

17. Ibid.

18. Ibid.

19. Ibid.

20. Hicks et al., "A Principle or a Strategy?" 21.

21. National Conference of State Legislatures, "Voter ID History."

22. Ibid.

23. Charles Stewart III, "Voter ID: Who Has Them? Who Shows Them?" (*Oklahoma Law Review*, Vol. 66, 2013–2014), 50–51.

24. Jimmy Carter and James A. Baker III, "Building Confidence in U.S. Elections" (Commission on Federal Election Reform, September 2005). Accessed June 18, 2015, from http://www.eac.gov/assets/1/AssetManager/Exhibit%20M.PDF.

25. Carter and Baker, "Building Confidence in U.S. Elections," 19.

26. As noted in Hale and McNeal, HAVA (P.L. 107-252), Section 303, requires each state to "verify the identity of first-time voters who register by mail and do not provide verification with their registration application." What is more, "HAVA requires that individuals who register by mail provide an acceptable form of identification (broadly defined under HAVA) either with the registration application or at the time that they first vote in the state, whether in person or by absentee ballot." See Kathleen Hale and Ramona McNeal, "Election Administration Reform and State Choice: Voter Identification Requirements and HAVA" (*The Policy Studies Journal*, Vol. 38, No. 2, May 2010), 281.

27. For details, see National Conference of State Legislatures, "Voter ID History."

28. Brennan Center for Justice, "Voting Laws Roundup 2015."

29. Ibid.

30. Ibid.

31. Hicks et al., "A Principle or a Strategy?" 20.

32. Hicks et al., "A Principle or a Strategy?" 29.

33. Stephen Ansolabehere, "Effects of Identification Requirements on Voting: Evidence from the Experiences of Voters on Election Day" (*PS: Political Science & Politics*, Vol. 42, No. 1, January 2009), 129.

34. Weiser and Norden, "Voting Law Changes in 2012," 4.

35. Chandler Davidson, "The Historical Context of Voter Photo-ID Laws" (*PS: Political Science & Politics*, Vol. 42, No. 1, January 2009), 93.

36. Eric Lipton and Ian Urbina, "In 5-Year Effort, Scant Evidence of Voter Fraud" (*The New York Times*, April 12, 2007). Accessed June 18, 2015, from http://www.nytimes.com/2007/04/12/washington/12fraud.html?pagewanted=all&_r=0. Richard Hasen quote cited by Davidson, "The Historical Context," 95.

37. Philip Bump, "The Disconnect between Voter ID Laws and Voter Fraud" (*The Washington Post*, October 13, 2014). Accessed June 13, 2015, from http://www.wash ingtonpost.com/blogs/the-fix/wp/2014/10/13/the-disconnect-between-voter-id-laws-and-voter-fraud/.

38. Aaron Blake, "Voter ID Laws: A Microcosm of a Divided America" (*The Washington Post*, November 17, 2014). Accessed June 13, 2015, from http://www.washingtonpost .com/blogs/the-fix/wp/2014/11/17/voter-id-laws-a-microcosm-of-a-divided-america/.

39. Marjorie Randon Hershey, "What We Know about Voter-ID Laws, Registration, and Turnout" (*PS: Political Science & Politics*, Vol. 42, No. 1, January 2009), 88.

40. Lorraine C. Minnite, "Voter Identification Laws: The Controversy over Voter Fraud," in Matthew J. Streb (Ed.), *Law and Election Politics: The Rules of the Game*, 2nd ed. (New York: Routledge, 2013), 107.

41. Blake, "Voter ID Laws."

42. Hershey, "What We Know about Voter-ID Laws, Registration, and Turnout," 88.

43. Keesha Gaskins and Sundeep Iyer, "The Challenge of Obtaining Voter Identification" (Brennan Center for Justice at New York University School of Law, 2012), 2. Accessed June 15, 2015, from http://www.brennancenter.org/publication/challenge-obtaining-voter-identification.

44. Ibid.

45. David Stout, "Supreme Court Upholds Voter Identification Law in Indiana" (*The New York Times*, April 29, 2008). Accessed June 15, 2015, from http://www.nytimes .com/2008/04/29/washington/28cnd-scotus.html?_r=0.

46. Hicks et al., "A Principle or a Strategy?" 21.

47. Stout, "Supreme Court Upholds Voter Identification Law in Indiana."

48. Davidson, "The Historical Context," 94.

49. Brennan Center for Justice, "Fifth Circuit Should Uphold Ruling Striking Down Texas's Discriminatory Photo ID Law" (New York University School of Law, March 3, 2015). Accessed June 18, 2105, from https://www.brennancenter.org/press-release/fifth-circuit-should-uphold-ruling-striking-down-texas-discriminatory-photo-id-law.

50. Dahlia Lithwick, "Voter ID Laws May Worsen Voter Fraud: And Is Texas' Law Intentionally or Merely Incidentally Racist?" (*Slate*, September 11, 2014). Accessed June 18, 2015, from http://www.slate.com/articles/news_and_politics/jurisprudence/2014/09/voter_id_laws_analysis_shows_they_could_make_fraud_worse_and_disenfranchise.html; Adam Liptak, "Supreme Court Allows Texas to Use Strict Voter ID Law in Coming Election" (*The New York Times*, October 18, 2014). Accessed June 18, 2015, from http://www.nytimes.com/2014/10/19/us/supreme-court-upholds-texas-voter-id-law.html

51. Lyle Denniston, "Constitution Check: Have Voter ID Laws Survived A New Round of Challenges?" (National Constitution Center, March 24, 2015). Accessed June 18, 2015, from http://blog.constitutioncenter.org/2015/03/constitution-check-have-voter-id-laws-survived-a-new-round-of-challenges/; Brennan Center for Justice, "Fifth Circuit Should Uphold Ruling Striking Down Texas's Discriminatory Photo ID Law."

52. Denniston, "Constitution Check."

53. Ibid.

54. Brennan Center for Justice, "Fifth Circuit Should Uphold Ruling Striking Down Texas's Discriminatory Photo ID Law"; Denniston, "Constitution Check."

55. Denniston, "Constitution Check."

56. Richard Hasen, "DOJ's Silence on the Wisconsin Voter ID Case Before SCOTUS" (*Election Law Blog*, March 19, 2015). Accessed June 13, 2015, from http://electionlaw blog.org/?p=71116.

57. Richard Sobel, "Voter-ID Issues in Politics and Political Science" (*PS: Political Science & Politics*, Vol. 42, No. 1, January 2009), 81.

58. Ray Christensen and Thomas J. Schultz, "Identifying Election Fraud Using Orphan and Low Propensity Voters" (*American Politics Research*, Vol. 42, No. 2, 2014), 312.

59. Ibid., 313.

60. Hayley Munguia, "Voter ID Laws Are Now in 17 More States Than They Were in 2000" (*FiveThirtyEight*, October 31, 2014). Accessed June 13, 2015, from http://fivethirtyeight.com/datalab/voter-id-laws-are-now-in-17-more-states-than-they-were-in-2000/.

61. Zachary Roth, "The Voting Conversation Has Shifted. That's Good News for Dems" (*MSNBC*, June 5, 2015). Accessed June 13, 2015, from http://www.msnbc.com/msnbc/the-voting-conversation-has-shifted-thats-good-news-dems.

62. Weiser and Norden, "Voting Law Changes in 2012," 9.

CHAPTER 12

Women and Campaigns— Generation-Based Microtargeting and Tackling Stereotypes

*Susan A. MacManus**
With the assistance of Ashley Intartaglia

> *"There are plenty of subplots in the unfolding [2016] presidential election, but the gender fight is among the most interesting of them—and one that will be critical to the outcome."*
>
> Charlie Cook, *National Journal,* June 27, 2015[1]

"THE WOMEN'S VOTE WILL BE CRITICAL to our campaign's victory." This preelection declaration has become nearly universal, regardless of a candidate's gender, age, race/ethnicity, party affiliation, or office sought, including the presidency. Why? For years, women have made up a larger share of the electorate and turned out at higher rates, especially in presidential elections. What has fluctuated the most is the percentage of the female vote that is cast for specific candidates. Some have broader appeal and better voter outreach than others. But it is not always just about the candidates. Changes in the makeup of the electorate itself can alter voting patterns.

Generational differences, especially in racial and ethnic composition, political preferences, and news sources, have become a major focal point of today's campaigns. Analyses of the two "super generations," the Millennials and the Baby Boomers, have made it clear that successful campaigns need to microtarget women voters differently across generations, sometimes even within the same party.

*The author would like to gratefully acknowledge the work of University of South Florida student researchers Anthony Cilluffo, Alexandra Holliday, Victoria Pearce, and Georgia Pevy whose contributions were exceptional.

The growing presence of women in campaigns and as candidates has reformulated and redirected outreach efforts to female voters and has begun to turn the emphasis of campaign coverage to substance, rather than personal attributes (style). One recent study examining the evenness of the playing field among male and female candidates found "some evidence of generational differences in views of women candidates at the presidential level" and projected that over time gender stereotypes would disintegrate.[2] Supporting that observation was a June 2015 Gallup poll finding that 92 percent of those surveyed said they would vote for a woman for president. The same survey found younger voters (ages eighteen to twenty-nine) were more likely to say they would vote for a female candidate than would voters age sixty-five and older (96 percent vs. 88 percent).[3]

The primary theme of this chapter is that in order to devise more successful tactics to get out the critical female vote, campaigns must track changes in the composition, partisan identification, policy preferences, and media consumption patterns of different generations, paying close attention to the Millennials (born 1981–2001) and the Baby Boomers (born 1943–1964). The chapter also examines the presence of more age-diverse female professionals in the campaign and media worlds and their role in helping elevate the emphasis of substance over style in female candidates' campaigns and public appearances.

A Generational Look at Female Voters

Generations have played a key role in shaping gender perceptions about politics, culture, and values. Campaigns, parties, and independent political groups are now attuned to the preferences of different generations for both women and men. Registering women and then persuading them to vote are key goals of every campaign—from start to finish. Some groups are harder to mobilize than others. For example, older women turn out at higher rates than younger women. Poorer and less educated women turn out at lower rates than their more affluent, better-educated counterparts. And turnout rates among black women are higher than those of white, Hispanic, or Asian/Pacific Islander women. This means that a campaign's outreach strategies must be narrowly tailored (microtargeted) to different groups of female voters.

Women make up a much larger share of the older generations primarily because they live longer than men. But more than half (58 percent) of the adult female population are members of the Millennial generation and Generation X (born 1964–1981). Females in the two younger generations are much more racially/ethnically diverse than their elders. Millennials, especially minority females, tend to vote more solidly Democratic, while white Millennials are more evenly divided in their vote preference—females much more than males. Baby Boomer females are more politically divided than Millennials but less so than the oldest-generation

(Depression-era) females who tend to be more heavily Democratic. Many of these oldest women never worked outside the home. Without a pension, they are more dependent on Social Security and other government programs and are strong FDR (Franklin Delano Roosevelt) Democrats.

While it is true that "each generation has its story and no two generations are alike," the Millennials "differ markedly from past generations," having been shaped by "massive advancements in technology, unparalleled communication access, and more media exposure."[4]

While the women's vote has been more cohesive in some election years than others, it has never been monolithic. It is true that the women's vote in presidential election years has leaned more heavily Democratic in recent years (see Appendix, Table A.1) but has been more divided in midterm election years when turnout rates for young and minority voters plummet. For example, in the 2014 midterm election cycle, Republican female candidates fared better proportionately than Democratic female candidates in U.S. Senate and gubernatorial races.[5] Women voters in nonpresidential election years tend to be older and more conservative than women voters in presidential election years. *Thus, age-based methods and strategies utilized by candidates and political parties to target women voters often differ depending on whether the campaign is for a presidential or a midterm election.*

Women in Campaigns:
Less Emphasis on Style, More on Substance?

For years, the emphasis on female candidates has been more on style than substance. This is not the way female candidates in the twenty-first century want it to be. Female candidates desperately want media and voter attention to be focused on their issue stances and qualifications rather than their looks. Reaching this goal has been more difficult than anticipated.

The heightened role of visuals has increased attention on physical appearance as well as nonverbal behavior. In the words of one analyst, "Women in politics have it rough. Not only is it a merciless, dog-eat-dog, male-dominated field, but they also have to be incredibly meticulous with their appearance, much more so than their male counterparts, lest they look weak, inexperienced, or unprofessional."[6] As a former congressman pointed out, "You can tell how a female politician is faring by looking at the photographs of her in print media. . . . When things are going well, the photos accompanying stories are flattering. When things start to go south for a politician, so do the photos."[7] (He admitted this was not always true for male candidates.)

For many women, this overemphasis on appearance has tended to reinforce gender stereotypes. But for those heavily involved in campaigns, the misplaced emphasis is simply a reality of the technological times in which we live. Campaign managers have learned they must have proactive and reactive strategies in place. For example, in 2008, a YouTube video that made fun of Hillary Clinton's tears as she responded to a question of how she kept going through criticism prompted her campaign to quickly get her on the national airwaves and YouTube explaining her emotional response. Female support for her actually increased as more women saw the tears as a sign of compassion rather than as weakness. Knowing how to reach women voters allowed the campaign to turn bad coverage of Clinton into good. This transcends generations.

The Impact of Television on the Images of Women Candidates

Television remains a major source of political information for a majority of Americans. TV, along with online videos, is particularly challenging for women: "It's tough for women to come across as strong as men. Their voices are higher pitched, their features are softer, their mannerisms are not firm, and if they are, people are turned off because it's not feminine."[8] Yet voters pay closer attention to the physical attributes and mannerisms of female candidates than to those of their male counterparts, particularly when viewing television/video campaign ads.

Some attribute the media's and the public's overemphasis on female candidates' appearance to sexism, while others say it's because women have more choices affecting how they look. As one analyst put it: "A man decides to run for office: He plans the substance of his campaign and then buys a few black or navy suits and some red and blue ties. A woman decides to run for office: She does the same, and then has to consider hair, makeup, jewelry and shoes, in addition to her wardrobe."[9]

Hairstyle, hair length, and color are important decisions for both female and male candidates. The trick is to keep a consistent hairstyle that doesn't look out of date and is easy for the candidate to maintain without taking a personal hairstylist on the campaign trail.

Makeup should enhance facial features but never be garish. Minor lines and wrinkles, in men as well as women, can be erased by nonsurgical procedures such as Botox injections. Eyeglasses can be chosen to convey more intelligence (witness Rick Perry's adoption of black-rimmed spectacles in summer 2014),[10] while contacts convey youth. If voters are used to seeing a candidate wear glasses, switching to contacts for an ad can attract unwanted attention.

Clothes require a delicate balance between feminine and more masculine looks, bright and dark colors, and designer (expensive) and ready-to-wear fashions. Women also must take care in choosing clothing that won't show too much cleavage or leg. Accessories differ by age, region, and race/ethnicity. Florida congresswoman Frederica Wilson, for example, wears flamboyant hats as a nod to her Bahamian grandmother.

Stereotypes and Nonverbal Cues

Nonverbal behavior is often a more powerful voting cue than experience or issue stances. Political consultants advising female (and male) candidates tend to pay closest attention to the nonverbal behaviors/attributes that seem idiosyncratic or excessive, such as the following:

- Hand gestures. Women tend to use their hands to "talk" more than men. Some gesturing is good but not excessive flailing of hands. Gestures need to underscore a message.
- Eye contact. Direct contact with the camera and one's opponent or the moderator (in debates) is best.
- Facial expressions. Women generally smile more than men. In certain circumstances, that is good, but in others, it is less so (for example, when a situation calls for anger or disgust).
- Tears. While expected more from women, tears nearly always end up being the subject of negative news stories, particularly those written by male reporters. However, in certain circumstances, tears (if genuine) may be quite powerful—and positive.
- Laughs. Women are advised to "make sure your laugh is a laugh" rather than a giggle or a cackle.
- Voice volume and pitch. Women tend to speak more softly, are less emphatic, and have a higher-pitched voice than men. Women can retrain their voices for stump speaking and use anonymous narrators in their television spots, although some believe a soft voice makes it easier for a woman to run a negative ad than for a man.
- Hugs and kisses. Appropriate interactions between women and men candidates have evolved from handshakes (they're OK) to hugs. A kiss, however, is still not acceptable.
- In the past, some women candidates have been reluctant to feature their spouses and children in ads out of concern that they will seem less able to focus on public office. When a mother runs, voters of both genders often wonder "'Who will care for the children while she campaigns?'—a question for Pauline but not Paul."[11] Some refer to this phenomenon as the "mommy penalty."

The growing number of single women (never married) and single-parent moms running for office has prompted debates over how to handle marital status in ads, especially in the more traditional conservative areas of the South. Stereotypes regarding sexual preference and behavior must be anticipated. Some political consultants have advised single women to smile, use gestures, and picture young children as a way to deflect these biases. The elevated importance of children by Baby Boomer parents to their Millennials underscores this point. It's no coincidence these are the two most populated generations.

Many studies have found that overemphasis on style deters women from running for office, just as have "the toxicity of the political environment today, the gridlock in Congress and state legislatures, and the invasion of privacy that inevitably accompanies a campaign."[12] The danger to both female and male candidates is that such nonparticipatory attitudes may spill over into the female electorate.

Changing Times: Signs the Overemphasis on Style May be Waning Slightly

Signs indicate that the emphasis on style is fading, and women candidates are becoming more effective at combating gender stereotypes. First, more women are playing prominent roles as consultants—and not just for female candidates. Several Democratic presidential candidates have had female campaign managers, notably Hillary Clinton (Patti Solis Doyle, then Maggie Williams, 2008) and Martin O'Malley (Lis Smith, 2016). On the Republican side, the candidates with female campaign managers are Mike Huckabee (his daughter Sarah Huckabee Sanders, 2016) and Carly Fiorina (Sarah Isgur Flores, 2016).

Virtually every major campaign now has managers, strategists, pollsters, and consultants on board to ensure that female voters are targeted and mobilized. In the 2012 election cycle, 45 percent of all campaign workers involved in federal campaigns were female. Nearly 17 percent were women of color.[13] Many female campaign professionals are women talented at reaching other women. For example, each major political party uses female pollsters skilled at capturing the opinions of likely women voters (Kellyanne Conway and Kristen Soltis Anderson for the Republicans; Celinda Lake for the Democrats). In the 2016 race, a number of announced presidential candidates (Democrat Clinton and Republicans Rick Perry, Lindsey Graham, and Mike Huckabee) had female communication directors.

A second sign is the growing number of women, especially professional women, contributing to campaigns. Not long ago, just 27 percent of all donors to federal candidates and outside groups were female.[14] As of June 2015, however, more than 60 percent of Clinton's donors were women.[15] The Clinton campaign also targeted women who had not previously given to political campaigns—specifically, younger women thirty-five to forty years of age and minorities.[16] Small-scale fundraisers are also important: "They do more than bring in money. [Women] who give a small amount at the beginning of campaigns can be counted on to talk to their friends about why."[17] Because of the growing number of women contributors—and because women hold the purse strings in many households[18]—a number of the 2016 presidential candidates tapped women as their campaign finance directors. The candidates included Republicans Carly Fiorina, Rick Perry, Bobby Jindal, Lindsey

Graham, Ted Cruz, Ben Carson, Mike Huckabee, Jeb Bush, and Marco Rubio and Democrat Martin O'Malley. This counters the stereotypical view of generations past that women cannot be entrusted with managing money.

"Empowering women to serve on campaigns is essential in electing individuals who can reflect the changing demographics of today's voters."[19] The larger the campaign, the more diverse the female staff is likely to be, particularly in its age and racial/ethnic composition. Those two key demographics affect which issues female voters consider the highest priority. Age is also an important predictor of which type of media a female voter is most likely to access to get information about a particular candidate or issue.[20] Moreover, women of color can be invaluable in their "ability to initiate a dialogue on how race plays a factor in a candidate's viability to woo voters, which is equally as important as discussing the gender stereotypes they face on the campaign trail."[21]

Women Candidates' Efforts to Minimize Style, Maximize Substance

Female candidacies at all levels—federal, state, and local—are on the rise, even though female candidacy rates still lag behind male candidacy rates.[22] Contests in which women are running against women are also increasing. Savvy political party leaders and politically oriented special interest groups now actively recruit women to run, especially in open districts with no incumbents. They often conduct campaign schools designed just for female candidates. There are even political interest groups that specialize in fundraising for female candidates (EMILY's List for Democrats; the WISH List for Republicans).

Women running for office today are keenly aware of the style-versus-substance problem—but often more prepared to tackle it head-on. Here are four who have done just that.

Hillary Clinton (D) made light of her age while addressing the historic nature of a possible victory at the kickoff rally for her second run for the presidency. At sixty-nine, she would be the oldest president, after Ronald Reagan. But she noted: "I will be the youngest woman president in the history of the United States and the first grandmother as well."[23] She had already posted photos of herself and husband Bill with daughter Chelsea's new baby, saying that grandmother was her "most exciting title yet."[24] Clinton's photo with her daughter and granddaughter symbolizes the connection of generations from Baby Boomer (Clinton) to late Generation X (Chelsea Clinton) to Homeland (Charlotte Clinton Mezvinsky).

Clinton got in front of media comments about fashion choices and used humor to turn her trademark pantsuits into a positive symbol. Her first Instagram post showed a rack of pantsuits in red, white, and blue, labeled "hard choices." She said she didn't care what critics thought of her fashion choices, declaring that at her age she should be allowed to wear what she likes. She also joked about being a bottle blonde. "They are not going to see me turn white in the White House," as most presidents have, because "I've been coloring my hair for years."[25] It shows that Clinton, like many Boomers, is more interested in values than fashion statements.

She stressed her long public experience as a U.S. senator and U.S. secretary of state, while pushing for women's issues such as pay equity, reproductive rights, and paid family leave. In response to accusations of coming across as cold, she repeated her inspiration story about her mother, who was abandoned by her parents and had to work as a housemaid. "My mother taught me that everyone needs a chance and a champion. She knew what it's like not to have had either one." A video released in advance of her launch speech included a 1995 clip in which she said, "Human rights are women's rights, and women's rights are human rights, once and for all."

Carly Fiorina (R), who rose from being a secretary to CEO of a *Fortune* 500 company within fifty years, plunged into politics as the Republican Party's sole female candidate for president in 2016. Her campaign quickly focused on her unique position to launch attacks on Clinton, which male GOP (Grand Old Party) candidates could not do for fear of being regarded as sexist. That included a website designed to weaken Hillary's front-runner status—readytobeathillary.com.

In a major speech in June, Fiorina reflected on what it was like climbing the corporate ladder, being called the "token bimbo," and having to attend client meetings at a strip club. She added that a reporter asked whether a woman's hormones would prevent her from serving in the Oval Office. "Here's a question for you, ladies. Can you think of an example of when a man's judgment has been clouded by hormones—including in the Oval Office?" In addition to addressing the double standard, she hired more women than men on her campaign team and participated in women's events to establish a base with women voters.[26]

Unlike Minnesota congresswoman Michele Bachmann who refused to call herself a feminist in 2012, Fiorina said, "I consider myself a feminist Republican, and that's not an oxymoron." She also offered her own take on the term: "Feminism began as a rallying cry to empower women—to vote, to get an education, to enter the workplace. But over the years, feminism has devolved into a left-leaning political ideology where women are pitted against men and used as a political weapon to win elections."[27] She inferred that the devolution definition applied to Democrats, then proceeded to give her own definition of feminism: "A feminist is a woman who lives the life she chooses. . . . A woman may choose to have five children and home-school them. She may choose to become a CEO or run for President." Fiorina is the former CEO of Hewlett-Packard.

Elise Stefanik (R), from the North Country of New York, became the youngest woman ever elected to Congress in 2014 at age thirty. She had worked in a series of political jobs in Washington, D.C., including for the George W. Bush administration and the 2012 vice presidential campaign of Wisconsin congressman Paul Ryan. She considered Ryan a mentor, but the real inspiration came from Sheryl Sandberg, Facebook's chief operating officer and author of the best-selling *Lean In: Women, Work, and the Will to Lead.* Sometimes, Stefanik said, women like herself "hold themselves back from not seeking the next professional step, whether it's a promotion or whether it's running for office."[28]

She made the leap by challenging incumbent Democratic congressman Bill Owens in 2013, at age twenty-nine. Working in her family's plywood business by day, she crisscrossed the district in a Ford F-150 truck, systematically meeting with GOP leaders. At first, they were skeptical about her age and a possible perception of her as a Washington insider. Everything changed in January 2014, when Owens announced his retirement. Although a well-known Republican jumped into the race, Stefanik had already tied up the party's endorsement. With outside financial backing, she won the primary by twenty-two points. Going into the general election, she referred to herself as a Millennial associated with new ideas and a new generation of leadership in Washington. But when internal polling revealed scant support among seniors, especially women sixty-five and older, she proposed a modest reform in Social Security (raising the eligibility age but not for anyone older than fifty). Her advertising, linking seniors' aspirations for their grandchildren's future with Stefanik being in the same generation, helped her win with 55 percent of the vote.[29] Her victory, aided by the intergenerational approach, made her a rising GOP star.

Gwen Graham (D) won one of the most competitive elections for Congress in 2014 from a district where the ultraconservative Florida Panhandle sharply contrasted with liberal urban areas near the state universities. While her father, former governor and U.S. senator Bob Graham, was an obvious advantage, she emphasized her roles as "a wife and a working mom." She elaborated that image with family photos. On the campaign trail she held "Grilling with the Grahams" events that involved her husband, parents, children, and siblings.[30]

She defeated Republican U.S. representative Steve Southerland by using strategic timing (hitting the North Florida airwaves two months earlier), raising more money, and stressing local values ("The North Florida Way" slogan). When a male campaign strategist notified her father that she seemed to be wearing herself thin, Graham sent him a text message and made it very clear that he was not to "ever go to my dad and tell him I need a rest."[31] The comment got covered in local media.

Asked how being a woman in a male-dominated field affected her candidacy, she replied that it was the same way with "being a working mom, or when I was a PTA president, or when I was chief negotiator for our local school district: It drives me to always exceed expectations, with that little awareness in the back of my mind that someone, somewhere may be setting the bar just a tiny bit higher for me."[32]

Each of these female candidates tackled dominant stereotypes about women of her generation. Their proactive approaches caught the media's attention—and certainly that of women in the media covering their campaigns.

Women in the Campaign Media

Women are everywhere in media campaign coverage—as anchors, reporters, commentators, columnists, and bloggers. Virtually all the major news programs (network, public TV, and cable) have female anchors. These women vary in age, ranging from late twenties to early seventies, with a majority in their forties, and several are black or Hispanic.

The inclusion of more (and younger) females in top spots on politically focused cable television programs is designed to appeal to a wide range of voters in recognition of the expanding role of women in politics and the huge Millennial generation. The Fox News Channel's selection of Megyn Kelly as the host of a prime-time show "has not just given America's top-rated news channel its biggest new hit in 13 years; it has demonstrated an appeal to the younger and (slightly) more ideologically diverse demographic."[33] MSNBC's Rachel Maddow has attracted a loyal liberal audience. Initially, she garnered a disproportionately young audience. But according to a Pew Research Center study, her audience consists of about as many men as women (52 percent vs. 48 percent), and most viewers are older (57 percent are fifty years or older, and 25 percent are at least sixty-five).[34] As part of their media strategy, campaigns promote appearances of female candidates, party leaders, and surrogates with celebrity status (whether spouses,[35] family, friends, or Hollywood) on television programs. Democratic congresswoman Debbie Wasserman Schultz of Florida has appeared on national news programs, and Republican congresswoman Ileana Ros-Lehtinen, the first Cuban female elected to Congress, had a major media presence at her party's 2012 national convention.

Presidential candidates have increasingly appeared on late-night TV shows in recent years. In 2007, for example, Barack Obama and Hillary Clinton each took a turn on *Saturday Night Live*, and Arizona senator John McCain announced his candidacy on the *Late Show with David Letterman*. "The appearances have given the politicians opportunities to soften their images and show their humorous sides."[36] Their images are seen by an increasingly older audience that watches late-night shows live (age fifty-four for Jimmy Kimmel and fifty-seven for Jimmy Fallon), while younger viewers are watching them at a more convenient time via posted videos.[37] Popular daytime shows, such as *The Ellen DeGeneres Show* and *The View*, attract much larger female than male audiences under age fifty.

Use of female media figures, along with celebrities in Hollywood and the music world, is one of the most effective ways to reach female Millennials. According to one political consultant, "Engagement using celebrities has exploded using social media and the blog echo chamber. These female media figures have a strong, if not tribe-like following so when they approve of a particular candidate, they often bring their 'tribe' with them."[38]

One note of caution is in order: it is important to be cognizant of the ideological bent of different media personalities. While female hosts on some shows may try to build up the substance of their ideological soul sisters, they may be quick to tear down female candidates of a different political persuasion using the style critique. This is what some refer to as a triple standard—"women judged by men and women measured against other women."[39]

Developing Targeting Strategies: Perennial Questions

In every election cycle since 1992, the same question has emerged: "Will *this* be the 'Year of the Woman' again?" Although the 2014 election was slightly modified to the "Year of the Republican Woman," the intervening years saw related questions: (1) How cohesive is the women's vote? (2) Can female candidates raise as much money and get as many major media and celebrity endorsements as men and be invited to appear on major newsmagazine shows (e.g., NBC's *Meet the Press*)? (3) Do negative ads work as well for female candidates as for their male counterparts? (4) Will we ever have a female president?

When two women announced their candidacies for president in 2016— Democrat Hillary Clinton and Republican Carly Fiorina—several new questions were added to the perennial list: (1) Will the promise to break the gender barrier be a more powerful voting cue than positions on specific issues like reproductive rights or voter judgments of candidate trustworthiness and bipartisan decision making?[40] (2) Has the definition of *feminist* changed? Does it differ by generation or party affiliation? (3) What will be the role of family members in campaigns? What is the right balance? The implications are that women candidates still have more perceptive barriers to hurdle than male candidates do.

Techniques for Microtargeting Female Voters

Microtargeting as a mobilization (get-out-the-vote) strategy began in the 2004 presidential campaign and has escalated with every subsequent election. Treating all women voters the same can result in a candidate's defeat. As Democratic political strategist Donna Brazile has advised,[41] "To pull more women into the voting process—and to win votes—the two major parties should drop any idea of a one-size-fits-all approach to women. Instead, they should target their messages to diverse groups of women."

Today's campaigns use a wide variety of GOTFV (get-out-the-female-vote) tools—everything from text messages; online social networks; recorded (robo) phone calls from candidates and celebrities; and appearances by the candidates and high-profile surrogates in precisely targeted mail, radio spots, television, and online ads and videos on their websites and sites like YouTube. Campaigns use feedback and insights from focus groups and public opinion surveys (telephone and online) to craft the content, format, and placement of political ads to reach narrowly defined groups of potential female voters.

Issue-Based Targeting and the Timing of GOTFV

Issue-based targeting can be challenging across generations even on traditional women's issues. In the 2014 midterm election, Democrats heavily emphasized reproductive rights and the Republicans' "War on Women." Although that strategy had drawn women of all ages, notably younger women, to the polls in 2012, it did not have the same effect in 2014. Democratic strategists acknowledged they should have targeted younger women using more economic-oriented issues, like college loans and a higher minimum wage. Some women's issues appeal to all generations (pay equity, human trafficking, rape, domestic violence), while others are more age bound. But even within the same generation, women differ in their issue preferences by marital status, race/ethnicity, religion, ideology, and party preference. Marital status continues to be a key focus of both Democrats and Republicans because it is one of the strongest predictors of voter turnout and partisan support patterns. Republican voting women tend to be married, while unmarried women (widows, never-marrieds, and divorcées) lean heavily Democratic.[42]

Targeted ads also play a key role in informing women about how to vote early in person or how to cast an absentee ballot. These forms of voting are often more convenient to single parents, voters with disabilities, and women who work evening shifts. The timing of mobilizing women voters is often tricky. Historically, women have been late deciders—both in choosing a candidate and in deciding when to actually go vote. For some women, especially older women, direct mail is still the best approach. However, according to direct mail specialists, it has to happen between the time a person picks up a mailer and the time she reaches the first trash can. It's more likely to happen if the recipient can immediately see something of herself and her sentiments in the piece. That means compelling pictures and a simple, straightforward message. The timing of mail-outs is even more complicated in early voting states.

Millennials and GOTFV

Among Millennial females, television and the Internet (especially social networking sites and blogs) have proven effective. One recent Harvard University study concluded that "some of the most visible and creative users of social media in politics have been women."[43] For example, the author of *Mothers of Intention: How Women and Social Media Are Revolutionizing Politics in America* began her activism by creating a popular blog (PunditMom) aimed at progressive (liberal) mothers.[44] Social networking has been equally effective in mobilizing conservative women. Many stay-at-home mothers with young children used Twitter and other social networking platforms to connect conservative activists with the Tea Party movement and to spike turnout in the 2010 midterm elections.[45]

At the same time, political scientist Susan Carroll sees social media as "a mixed blessing for women" because "it lets people be more hostile, negative and vile. The normal social sanctions don't exist." She cautions that the vile factor "is worse on the blogosphere, more intense." It is here that crude Photoshopped images of women activists and candidates can take on a life of their own as they are shared with politically like-minded "friends." [46]

Among adults who go online, Millennials rely more heavily on social media for their political news than older generations. Among Millennials, 61 percent get political news via Facebook in a given week—by far the highest single source. The top source among Baby Boomer Internet users is local TV (60 percent).[47] Campaign strategists see Facebook as being "used to amplify all the offline activities of a campaign, whether it's paid media, organizing, persuasion, or fundraising," in order to "reach the right people with the right message at the right time."[48] They warn that the rapidity with which digital strategies are evolving means that the 2016 election will see groundbreaking approaches, most likely video based. Moreover, Nielsen (the TV ratings firm) has found that a greater percentage of women (28 percent) than men (25 percent) get more than half their news from social media sources.[49]

Campaign websites have become an important information source for prospective voters. Candidates have learned to craft website content, including photographs, to appeal to targeted voters. For example, Jeb Bush's bio, which began with a picture of him taking a selfie with several people, instantly appealed to a variety of demographics. The bio continued in first person and focused more on personal anecdotes, unlike those of other candidates. Interestingly, Hillary Clinton's bio mentioned husband Bill only once.

Many campaign websites also feature stores for supporters to buy shirts, bumper stickers, and other paraphernalia. Campaigns recognize that some of the most effective advertising is people-to-people within communities. Yard signs, bumper stickers, and candidate shirts can be extremely effective when used by community leaders or trusted friends. Similarly, college students like to wear candidate shirts on campus and are an important source of volunteers for campaigns. However, all campaign shops are not the same. Several candidates, including Marco Rubio and Rand Paul, feature "limited edition" designs intended to spur supporters to quick action. Bernie Sanders, keeping with his "everyman" persona, is selling shirts for significantly less than other candidates. Certain products are targeted to specific demographics as well. Clinton offers a variety of products, from shirts targeted to the LGBT (lesbian, gay, bisexual, and transgender) community to children's clothes targeted to parents. Candidates also appreciate the need for humor in campaign merchandise. Clinton debuted a line of summer products, including an apron with the words "Grillary Clinton" and a spatula with the campaign logo—both more likely to appeal to older women. Paul also features "fun" products: a shirt with the text "The NSA knows I bought this Rand Paul T-shirt"; an empty hard drive billed as Hillary Clinton's email server (a play on the Clinton email scandal); and iPhone cases targeted to young activists.

The best ways to market to Millennials include emphasizing uniqueness, offering a wide variety of colors and designs, selling modular pieces that can shift with an ever-evolving lifestyle and mood, making everything mobile accessible, pushing merchandise through a blog or Instagram videos, and shunning long-term brand names as ineffective.[50]

Looking Ahead

Gender will continue to play a critical role in election campaigns. The possibility of a cohesive women's vote, however, is highly unlikely. Women will continue to differ by their age, race/ethnicity, socioeconomic status, culture, and politics—across and within generations. Demographic, societal, and technological changes will force campaigns and candidates to constantly reevaluate the best ways to reach women voters.

We already see changes in the degree to which beauty trumps brains. Yesterday's YouTube trend that tended to overemphasize a woman's looks is waning and deterring fewer women from running for office. Among younger generations, especially Millennials, more women than men are graduating from college and heading to law school. The impact of visuals may decline as more women play active roles on the campaign trail and the novelty of a female candidate, consultant, or media star wears off.

The proliferation of more politically homogeneous online communities may help minimize the style factor and increase the focus on substance. Until then, appearance and nonverbal behavior will continue to matter more to the successes of female candidates than to those of male contenders. It makes the job of political consultants considerably more difficult, the need for female voices among their ranks more critical, and the effectiveness of microtargeting the female electorate more essential.

Whether the candidate is a female or a male, the 2016 election cycle will find younger voters—the Millennials—wielding an "immense influence" over how parties and candidates get out the critical female vote. This "supersized generation" will be writing much of the political commentary about the 2016 election, posting it on social media, and "working the rooms where candidates tap donors for campaign funds."[51] It will be responsible for much of the work of grassroots organizing, including how to mobilize the other supersized generation—the Baby Boomers—along with the oldest generations heavily composed of vital female voters.

Appendix

TABLE A.1   Voting Patterns by Gender in Recent Presidential Elections: Race/Ethnicity and Marital Status Differences

Category	2000		2004		2008		2012	
	Bush (R)	*Gore (D)*	*Bush (R)*	*Kerry (D)*	*McCain (R)*	*Obama (D)*	*Romney (R)*	*Obama (D)*
Gender								
Men	54	43	55	44	48	49	53	45
Women	44	54	48	51	43	56	44	55
Marital Status by Gender								
Married men					53	46	60	38
Married women					51	47	53	46
Unmarried men					38	58	40	56
Unmarried women					29	70	31	67

Source: National presidential exit polls from the Voter News Service 2000–2012.

Notes

1. Charlie Cook, "The Gender Subplot" (*National Journal,* June 27, 2015).
2. Deborah Jordan Brooks, *He Runs, She Runs: Why Gender Stereotypes Do Not Harm Women Candidates* (Princeton, NJ: Princeton University Press, 2013), 14.
3. Gallup Poll (June 2–7, 2015). For a continual updating of public opinion polls on electing a woman president, go to Center for American Women in Politics, "Presidential Gender Watch 2016." Available at http://presidentialgenderwatch.org/polls/a-woman-president/.
4. Torus Marketing, "Move Over Boomers, Here Come the Millennials" (July 28, 2014), citing Pew Research Center research.

5. Alana Abramson, "Election 2014: How Female Candidates Fared in the Midterms" (*ABC News*, November 5, 2014). Utah elected Mia Love, the nation's first African American female Republican elected to Congress, and New York elected Republican Elise Stefanik (District 21), the youngest woman ever elected to Congress.

6. Anonymous, "Power Hair" (Television Tropes & Idioms). Accessed on February 27, 2010, from http://tvtropes.org/pmwiki/pmwiki.php/Main/PowerHair.

7. Martin Frost, "The Politics of Photos" (*Politico*, July 17, 2011).

8. Milena Thomas quoted by Monica O'Brien, "How to Become a Leader When You're a Woman" (December 5, 2009). Accessed on February 27, 2010, from http://blog.monicaobrien.com/category/lifestyle/women-lifestyle.

9. Theodora Blanchfield, "Superficial Significance: Tailoring the Perfect Female Candidate" (*Campaigns & Elections*, January 2007), 35.

10. "In Defence of Rick Perry's Eyeglasses" (*The Economist,* June 5, 2015). Accessed October 17, 2015, from http://www.economist.com/blogs/democracyinamerica/2015/06/republican-field.

11. Swanee Hunt, "Women, Start Your Campaigns" (*The Boston Globe*, January 28, 2010). Accessed on February 27, 2010, from www.boston.com/bostonglobe/editorial_opinion/oped/articles/2010/01/28/women

12. Naureen Khan, "Galvanizing Women Candidates" (*National Journal*, March 31, 2011).

13. Statistics generated by the New Organizing Institute and reported by Tonia Bui, "When Diverse Women Shape American Politics by Working on Political Campaigns" (*Montgomery Community Media*, February 17, 2015).

14. Matea Gold, "Why So Many Women Are Raising Money for Hillary Clinton" (*The Washington Post*, June 7, 2015). Outside groups are organizations that can receive unlimited funds for the purposes of making independent expenditures or electioneering communications (Super PACs, 501(c)(4)s, 527s)—quoting Kelly Dittmar, *Money in Politics with a Gender Lens* (The National Council for Research on Women, the Center for American Women and Politics at Rutgers University's Eagleton Institute of Politics, and the Center for Responsive Politics, January 2014).

15. Ibid.

16. Anna Palmer and Tarini Parti, "Clinton Aims to Cash in with Female Donors" (*Politico*, June 7, 2015).

17. Anthony Man, "Echoing Obama Playbook, Clinton Musters Volunteer Army in Florida" (*Sun Sentinel*, June 11, 2015).

18. One study has projected that within the next ten years, women are expected to take control of as much as two-thirds of U.S. personal wealth. Elizabeth Dilts and Svea Herbst-Bayliss, "Now Hiring Women and Millennials: Executives" (Reuters, June 10, 2015).

19. Tonia Bui, "When Diverse Women Shape American Politics by Working on Political Campaigns" (*Montgomery Community Media*, February 17, 2015).

20. Aaron Smith, *The Internet and Campaign 2010* (Pew Research Center, March 17, 2011). Accessed on October 17, 2015, from http://pewinternet.org/Reports/2011/The-Internet-and-Campaign-2010.aspx.

21. Bui, "When Diverse Women Shape American Politics by Working on Political Campaigns."

22. Reasons for the lower candidacy rates are wide-ranging and include a lack of confidence in women's ability to be competitive with males in raising money, securing party help or endorsements, and winning; family responsibilities, especially young children at home; and fear of the media—intense scrutiny and negative stereotyping of female candidates. See Julie Anne Dolan, Melissa M. Deckman, and Michele L. Swers, *Women and Politics: Paths to Power and Political Influence*, 2nd ed. (New York: Longman, 2010); Jennifer L. Lawless and Richard L. Fox, *It Takes a Candidate: Why Women Don't Run for Office*, revised ed. (New York: Cambridge University Press, 2010).

23. RealClearPolitics, "Hillary: 'I May Not Be the Youngest Candidate in This Race, but I Will Be the Youngest Woman President'" (Video, June 15, 2015). Accessed on October 17, 2015, from http://www.realclearpolitics.com/video/2015/06/15/hillary_i_may_not_be_the_youngest_candidate_in_this_race_but_i_will_be_the_youngest_woman_president.html.

24. NBC News, "Bill and Hillary Post Pictures of Chelsea Clinton's New Baby" (September 27, 2014). Accessed on October 17, 2015, from http://www.nbcnews.com/news/us-news/bill-hillary-post-pictures-chelsea-clintons-new-baby-n213166.

25. Real Clear Politics, "Hillary."

26. Maggie Gallagher, "Carly Fiorina Has Earned the Right to Run as a Woman" (*National Review*, June 12, 2015). Accessed on October 17, 2015, from http://www.nationalreview.com/article/419684/carly-woman-hear-her-roar-maggie-gallagher.

27. Teresa Berenson, "Here's How Carly Fiorina Wants to Redefine Feminism" (*Time*, June 11, 2015). Accessed on October 17, 2015, from http://time.com/3918014/carly-fiorina-feminism/.

28. Alan He, "Facebook COO's Influence on New Member of Congress, Elise Stefanik" (*CBS News*, January 6, 2015). Accessed on October 17, 2015, from http://www.cbsnews.com/news/facebook-coos-influence-on-new-member-of-congress/.

29. The name of the ad was "Commitment." She also ran an earlier ad on protecting and preserving programs for seniors ready to retire or already retired ("Protect"). Matthew Hamilton, "Woolf, Stefanik Release New TV Ads" (*Capitol Confidential*, September 9, 2014). Accessed on October 17, 2015, from http://blog.timesunion.com/capitol/archives/220174/woolf-stefanik-release-new-tv-ads/.

30. The grilling events (an e-day tour) were primarily held in rural areas of the Panhandle. Eric Conrad, "Grilling with the Grahams Sneak Peek" (Blog Post, Graham for U.S. Congress, 2014). Accessed on October 17, 2015, from http://www.gwengraham.com/grilling-with-the-grahams-sneak-peek/.

31. Alex Leary, "How Gwen Graham Won" (*Tampa Bay Times*, November 6, 2014). Accessed on October 17, 2015, from http://www.tampabay.com/blogs/the-buzz-florida-politics/how-gwen-graham-won/2205464.

32. Anna Brand, "'30 in 30': Women Candidates to Watch in 2014—Gwen Graham" (*MSNBC*, August 29, 2014). Accessed on October 17, 2015, from http://www.msnbc.com/msnbc/women-candidates-watch-2014-gwen-graham.

33. Jim Rutenberg, "The Megyn Kelly Moment" (*The New York Times Magazine*, January 21, 2015). Accessed on October 17, 2015, from http://www.nytimes.com/2015/01/25/magazine/the-megyn-kelly-moment.html?_r=0.

34. Pew Research Center, "Demographics and Political Views of News Audiences" (September 27, 2012). Accessed on October 17, 2015, from http://www.people-press.org/2012/09/27/section-4-demographics-and-political-views-of-news-audiences/.

35. For an overview of the historical role of presidential wives on the campaign trail, see Susan A. MacManus and Andrew F. Quecan, "Spouses as Campaign Surrogates: Strategic Appearances by Presidential and Vice Presidential Candidates' Wives in the 2004 Election" (*PS: Political Science and Politics*, April 2008), 337–348.

36. George E. Condon Jr. "Obama Not the First to Hit Talk Shows" (*National Journal*, Oct. 25, 2011). Accessed October 17, 2015, from http://news.yahoo.com/obama-not-first-hit-talk-shows-123421776.html.

37. Justin Bachman, "The Old Watch Late-Night Shows; the Young Watch DVRs" (*Bloomberg Business*, April 4, 2014). Accessed October 17, 2015, from http://www.bloomberg.com/bw/articles/2014-04-04/replacing-david-letterman-in-late-night-landscape-old-people-watch-live-shows-young-viewers-watch-dvrs.

38. Correspondence with Nicholas M. Hansen, Principal, PoliSolutions Consulting (St. Petersburg, FL, July 14, 2015).

39. Hadas Gold, "Meghan McCain: A Triple Standard" (*Politico*, October 22, 2014).

40. For a good review of this literature, see Kelly Ditmar, *Navigating Gendered Terrain: Stereotypes and Strategy in Political Campaigns* (Philadelphia, PA: Temple University Press, 2015).

41. "Energize the Women's Vote in 2004" (*Women's eNews*, July 3, 2004).

42. Stanley Greenberg and Erica Seifert, "Why Unmarried Women Are the Key to 2014" (*Politico*, April 15, 2014).

43. Alexis Gelber, "Digital Divas: Women, Politics, and the Social Network" (Cambridge, MA: Harvard University John F. Kennedy School of Government, Joan Shorenstein Center on the Press, Politics, and Public Policy Discussion Paper Series, #D-63, June 2011).

44. Joanne Bamberger (Ed.), *Mothers of Intention: How Women and Social Media Are Revolutionizing Politics in America* (Houston, TX: Bright Sky Press, 2011).

45. Gelber, "Digital Divas," 2.

46. Susan Carroll, quoted in Gelber, "Digital Divas," 27.

47. Amy Mitchell, "Millennials and Political News: Social Media—The Local TV for the Next Generation?" (Pew Research Center, June 1, 2015).

48. Anna Brand, "The Women Bridging Tech and Politics in the 2016 Election" (*MSNBC*, June 29, 2015).

49. Nielsen Corporation, "The Female/Male Digital Divide" (March 5, 2014). Accessed October 17, 2015, from http://www.nielsen.com/us/en/insights/news/2014/the-female-male-digital-divide.html.

50. Emma Fitzpatrick, "5 Tips and Tricks to Market Your Brand to Millennials" (Multibriefs.com, August 19, 2014).

51. Julian Zelizer, "Who Will Grab the Millennial Vote?" (CNN.com, February 23, 2015). Accessed October 17, 2015, from http://www.cnn.com/2015/02/23/opinion/zelizer-millennials-politics/.

CHAPTER 13

Minority Candidates and the New Landscape of Campaigns in the Twenty-First Century

Atiya Kai Stokes-Brown

THE INCREASING POPULATION of racial and ethnic minorities, particularly Latinos and Asian Americans, is transforming the U.S. political landscape in a dramatic way. Furthermore, the elections of Barack Obama to the presidency and congressional candidates including Mia Love and Alex Mooney highlight how candidates of color are gaining increased access to positions of political power, ascending to the highest levels of political leadership. The success of these candidates today has been attributed to the manner in which they run their campaigns—some choosing to employ electoral strategies designed to encourage greater support among white voters while maintaining electoral backing in minority communities, while others adopt strategies that appeal to overwhelmingly conservative communities. In addition to using traditional communication methods such as television and radio advertisements and more traditional elements of outreach and fieldwork (e.g., targeted mobilization, direct mailing, door knocking, phone banking, get-out-the-vote [GOTV] activities), these candidates also adopt a new style of political campaigning that takes advantage of the latest technologies. In this chapter, we will explore the various ways in which minority candidates are using these technologies to influence elections. Following a brief discussion of the role of race and ethnicity in elections, we focus on the transformative character of campaign experiences for minorities and implications they have for the future.

The Changing Face of the United States and Its Impact on U.S. Politics

The demographic transformation of the United States has become a popular topic of discussion for social scientists, recognizing that who we are as a people has significant implications for the manner in which we live our lives. Shifts in the populace can reshape the electoral map in a district or state and have national implications, influencing what individuals and what party will ultimately hold office.

The United States will be more racially and ethnically diverse by 2060, and non-Hispanic whites are expected to become a minority group over the next three decades.[1] Reports of the declining growth rate and aging of the white population and the growth of the non-white population generally mirror demographic trends in voting. Between 1996 and 2012, African American, Asian, and Latino shares of the eligible electorate and the voting population increased while the white share of these groups decreased. Voting rates for African Americans, in particular, have steadily increased since 1996 and were higher than those for whites in 2012.[2] While gains in Asian and Latino voting have not been as consistent as those for African Americans, there have been relatively steady increases in minority vote rates. Should efforts to increase minority voter mobilization and registration continue, increases in the voting population in future elections will most likely be attributed to minority voters.

Minority Campaigns and Candidate Behavior

Changes in the country's demographic makeup have important implications for representation and officeholding. Group identities significantly inform political behavior and decision making, including how often and for whom individuals vote. Furthermore, the increasing presence of minority candidates in the political pool and in political office is positively associated with greater participation. While candidates of color in general are severely underrepresented in U.S. politics, their numbers have been increasing in recent years. African Americans hold more than 10,000 elected offices.[3] Latinos hold 5,850 elected offices nationwide, a 53 percent increase in the total number of Latinos serving in elected office in 1996.[4] Asian Americans hold over 4,000 elected offices in thirty-nine states and in the federal government.[5] The rising number of elected minorities is largely a result of the creation of majority-minority districts where these groups (together or singularly) make up a majority of the population in the district. These districts have played a central role in creating opportunities for African American candidates and, to a lesser extent, Latino and Asian American candidates.

Many African Americans and Latinos in Congress today represent these types of districts. For example, Democrat Hakeem Jeffries won New York's eighth congressional seat in 2012. The majority–African American district in Brooklyn and Queens had been represented by Representative Edolphus Towns for thirty years before his decision to retire at the end of his fifteenth term. Democrat Michelle Lujan Grisham, elected in 2012, won New Mexico's majority-minority first congressional district where Latinos make up approximately half of the district's population. In 2014, Brenda Lawrence won Michigan's fourteenth congressional district where African Americans make up 57 percent of the district's population.

This is in stark contrast to the electoral realities of Asian American elected officials who have mostly emerged from districts where Asians do not constitute a majority of the population and are therefore "most likely among all minority groups to be elected by another racial group."[6] This was the case for Democrats Ted Lieu, who won the 2014 election in California's thirty-third congressional district, and Ami Bera, who won the 2012 election in the state's seventh congressional district, becoming the third Indian American to be elected to the U.S. House of Representatives. In each district, Asian Americans make up approximately 14 percent of the population. However, it must be noted that dramatic shifts in the country's population and subsequent redistricting have created additional opportunities for Asian American candidates. Similarly, Democrat Mazie Hirono was elected to the U.S. Senate from the state of Hawaii in 2012, becoming the first Asian American woman elected to the Senate from the state (as well as the first elected female senator). Hirono won with 62 percent of the vote in a state where Asian Americans make up 38 percent of the state population.

While the number of majority-minority districts has increased since 1982 due in large part to population shifts (specifically increases in the non-white share of the nation's population) and subsequent efforts to redraw electoral district boundaries, a growing number of minority candidates have in recent years run for office and won outside of predominantly minority districts. Elected in 2014, Democrat Bonnie Watson Coleman is the first African American woman to represent the state of New Jersey in Congress. She won the state's majority-white twelfth congressional district where African Americans make up 15 percent of the population. Democrat Nellie Gorbea also achieved a significant "first," becoming the first Latina to serve in statewide office in the New England region in a state where Latinos make up 14 percent of the population. The success of these candidates and others like them has been attributed to candidates' use of electoral strategies designed to build a successful electoral coalition. As part of a strategy designed to appeal to a broad array of voters, deracializing candidates project a nonthreatening image, avoid employing direct racial appeals, and avoid emphasizing a racially specific issue agenda.[7] Another perspective suggests the use of multiple strategies— a "mainstream" strategy to appeal to white voters and simultaneous appeals to minority constituencies through political surrogates and tailored messages in racial and ethnic media.

While theories of minority campaign strategies have primarily focused on Democrats, recent elections demonstrate how these strategies can also be useful for Republican candidates. Most notably, Ted Cruz won the 2012 election to replace retiring Texas senator Kay Bailey Hutchison, becoming the first Latino to be elected to the Senate from the state. Republicans Mia Love and Alex Mooney also won seats in the 2014 midterm elections, becoming respectively the first African American Republican woman elected to Congress and the first Latino elected to Congress from the state.

Campaign Activities of Minority Candidates

Traditionally, minority campaigns have adopted tactics to mitigate electoral disadvantages often attributed to the racial conservatism of some white voters and to mobilize enthusiasm and support in minority communities. Increasingly, as minority candidates run outside of districts and states with large minority populations, some of the campaigns have focused primarily on attracting white and socially conservative voters and make little to no effort to mobilize minority communities. While minority candidates' overarching strategies to build a successful electoral coalition may differ, all of their campaigns rely on a wide range of tactics. Most rely primarily on traditional campaign methods and communication strategies that include television, radio, and print and mobilization tools including GOTV drives and phone banking. But like their white counterparts, minority candidates are also using new technologies such as Facebook, Myspace, and Twitter to make targeted contacts with individual voters and rally supporters and are using cutting-edge fundraising techniques to pursue their electoral goals.

Traditional Media

Communication is a key component of any political campaign. Candidates rely heavily on paid mass media advertising to communicate their messages to voters for several reasons. Television is quite popular, as the average American watches approximately three hours of television every day.[8] Candidates are also likely to use this medium (in addition to radio) because it attracts a good deal of media attention and can help drive the media narrative.[9] Finally, it is worth noting that despite the rise of the digital era, not everyone is on the Internet. Older voters in particular, who are more likely to vote than younger voters, may be less familiar with technology and rely on television for political information.[10] Like their white counterparts, minority candidates take a more conventional approach to mass media, spending a significant portion of their funds on television and (to a lesser extent) radio advertising.

Ad spending for federal candidates in 2014 surpassed $1 billion, with overall increases in airings from U.S. Senate races and interest groups.[11] In Florida's 2010 competitive twenty-second congressional race between incumbent Democrat Ron Klein and his Republican challenger Allen West, West allocated $3,066,000 (approximately 50 percent of his budget) for television ads.[12] West went on to win the election, becoming the first African American Republican congressman from Florida since Reconstruction. In his 2012 bid for reelection against Democrat Patrick Murphy, West allocated $13.8 million (approximately 74 percent of his spending budget) for television ads and mailers.[13] Despite outspending his opponent roughly five to one, West lost the election with 49.7 percent of the vote. Candidates can also benefit from outside spending on ads. In 2012, the National Republican Congressional Committee spent $1.7 million to help Mia Love win Utah's fourth congressional seat.[14] In 2013, the race was added the committee's "On the Radar" list, but the committee spent considerably less in 2014 at the request of Love's campaign manager.[15]

The Internet

In recent years, the Internet has become a more central part of the campaign environment. Voters are embracing the Internet to engage in political decision making, and candidates are using the Internet as a more efficient means of communicating. The Internet also helps candidates establish online communities of supporters, which ultimately enhance their grassroots campaigns. The most prominent example of the role that new media can play in elections is that of then-candidate Barack Obama, who in 2008 became the first African American president of the United States. Obama's success in the 2008 presidential election has been linked to his use of information technology. Since 2008, the Internet and online tools have become the centerpiece of national political campaigns. Thus, the need to master changing communications technology is often seen as vital to communicate campaign messages and target various voter bases.

Campaign Websites

Campaign websites have become more common each election cycle as candidates realize their potential for giving them an almost unlimited ability to introduce themselves and their issue positions to voters. Controlling both the content of the site and how users interact with it, candidates use websites to provide information on as many issues and in as much detail as they choose. As a result, most candidates, regardless of level of office, have personal websites that serve as the core of their digital political messaging.

Seeking to strengthen support from traditional voting blocs including racial and ethnic minorities, the 2012 Obama campaign revamped the campaign website and launched several group-oriented webpages as part of a larger program called "Operation Vote."[16] The program, designed to push targeted messages online and through the media to specific constituency groups, encouraged Internet users to join one of eighteen specific constituency groups and receive information targeted to that group.[17] The 2012 election also marked an important change in digital campaign communications in presidential elections, as efforts to localize information and limit the role of the mainstream press via online communications were more prevalent. Whereas the Romney website featured (positive) mainstream media reports about the candidate, the "news" section of the Obama website only featured news directly from the campaign itself.[18]

Social Networks

Unlike websites, social networks connect people in online communities, and allow users to contribute to content and to initiate contact with other users. Facebook allows candidates to set up pages where they can post information about themselves, photos, and information about upcoming and past events, and has a section for people to donate to the campaign and/or volunteer. It also allows others to form groups in support of candidates. The 2008 Obama campaign encouraged supporters to build their own sites, and more than 900,000 people joined the "One Million Strong for Barack Obama" group on Facebook.[19] In 2012, the campaign strengthened the president's Facebook presence, increasing the number of followers and "likes" to more than 31 million on Election Day.[20] In 2010, Hansen Clarke used Facebook to connect with voters in Michigan's thirteenth congressional district to defeat seven-term incumbent Carolyn Cheeks Kilpatrick in the Democratic primary and Republican John Hauler in the general election, becoming the first Bangladeshi American elected to Congress. Similarly, Tulsi Gabbard was able to connect with voters in Hawaii's second congressional district, winning the open seat vacated by Mazie Hirono to become the first Hindu American elected to the House in 2012.

The rise of Twitter has also altered the media landscape. Twitter allows users to send and receive short messages called tweets on a variety of topics to and from the people they follow. Obama's 2008 Twitter site had more than 10 million followers, who receive updates from Obama's town hall meetings and links to his website. His number of followers has since increased to more than 60 million. By some accounts, the 2012 election was the most tweeted political event in history, and the candidates not only made efforts to communicate using Twitter but analyzed Twitter conversations to identify potential supporters. Using sophisticated tools to monitor the tone and tenor of political conversations, Obama's campaign identified and asked Twitter followers to take various actions on behalf of the campaign.[21] Yet it is important to note that neither campaign made an effort to retweet comments from individuals outside the campaign.[22] In the 2014 race in New Hampshire's second congressional district, Republican Marilinda Garcia used Twitter to encourage voting and on Election Day tweeted pictures of herself voting and shaking hands with supporters.[23] Garcia, a relatively young (thirty-one) rising star in the Republican Party, lost her bid to unseat incumbent Annie Kuster.

Minority candidates' campaigns also benefit from the popularity of social media sites like YouTube, a site where users share videos on the Internet by uploading or downloading video clips to and from websites, mobile devices, blogs, and email. Using YouTube, candidates are able to reach segments of the population, including young people, with minimal costs and attract mainstream media attention. Yet the site was somewhat less prominent during the 2012 presidential campaign, as the number of posts and viewership of those posts decreased.[24]

YouTube was particularly useful for Allen West in 2010 and Mia Love in 2014, both of whom we discussed earlier. West first ran for office in 2008 against Democrat Ron Klein and lost by ten percentage points. His success against Klein in 2010 has been attributed in some part to a YouTube video of him delivering what amounted to a conservative call to arms before a Florida Tea Party audience. Viewed more than 2 million times, the video became an Internet sensation, helping him secure the backing of high-profile antiestablishment conservatives including former Alaska governor Sarah Palin.[25] Online videos from former soldiers praising West's leadership were also attributed to helping him circumvent allegations of misconduct during his time of service in the military when he was stationed in Iraq.[26] Love first ran for office in 2012 and was chosen to speak at the 2012 Republican National Convention in Tampa, Florida. Her speech garnered her national attention and was one of the most watched political speeches on YouTube, cementing her image as a rising Republican star. Love narrowly lost the race to incumbent Jim Matheson but continued to use YouTube to spread her campaign message and highlight endorsements. Love ran again and won the seat in the 2014 election.

Political Blogs

Minority candidates also use political blogs to inspire supporters through open discussion and inspire them to get engaged in the campaign. Some blogs tend to be somewhat controlled by the campaign whereas others give visitors to the blog unrestricted access to post comments. In addition to creating and maintaining blogs, campaigns also coordinate with grassroots supporters who have created their own blogs. Official candidate blogs, in addition to other forms of media, also help candidates keep supporters updated about the campaign in real time. In the 2014 New Hampshire congressional race between Republican Marilinda Garcia and Democrat Annie Kuster, Garcia, who lost the election, featured a news blog on her campaign website that provided information about upcoming events and featured citizen content. Supporters were encouraged to share their support for the candidate and her stance on political issues.

Finally, in an effort to mobilize communities of color, social media can also be used by minority candidates for targeted mobilization. Despite the breakdown of formal barriers to participation, racial/ethnic gaps in voting still persist. High-minority voting has been shown to be crucial for candidates of color. Alienating African American voters and failing to stimulate turnout are often cited as a few of the reasons why several African American gubernatorial candidates lost their elections.[27] Mindful of this, the 2008 Obama campaign created profiles on influential social networks for minorities including AsianAve.com, MiGente.com, and BlackPlanet.com, blogging about important issues of concern and sending carefully honed messages to specific communities.[28] The campaign employed the same strategy in 2012. Similarly, in his campaign to become the first Vietnamese American member of the California State Assembly in 2004, Van Tran distributed press releases to Vietnamese radio, print, and online media focused on mobilizing by discussion of issues relevant to Vietnam and the power of ethnic unity.[29] Information released to white, mainstream media made no mention of these issues.

Email and Texting

Emailing and texting have also become part of most political campaigns. Emails are relatively cheaper to circulate, are easier to initiate, and can reach people faster than traditional mail. Candidates use email to inform supporters about upcoming events, solicit donations, organize volunteers, publicize press releases, and mobilize their GOTV efforts. In addition to email, minority candidates rely on additional new approaches such as robocalls and text messaging.

Former Alaska governor Sarah Palin recorded robocalls urging Republicans in South Carolina to vote for Nikki Haley in the state's GOP gubernatorial primary.[30] Haley won the election, becoming the first woman to serve as governor in the state and the second Indian American to serve as governor in the country. Running in a 2013 special election for New Jersey's U.S. Senate seat, Democrat Cory Booker benefited from robocalls made by the Hudson County Democratic Organization.[31] Booker won, and won reelection in 2014. Minority candidates have also become savvy about using mobile devices to communicate with potential supporters. Text messaging is a relatively cheap and effective tool that offers an opportunity to reach supporters directly at any place and time.

Fundraising

In addition to communications, the Internet has been used most powerfully by candidates to facilitate fundraising. The Internet has, in many ways, reinvented campaign fundraising, shifting it from a few big donors to countless small donors. Obama's campaign website, my.barackobama.com, helped him set records. In the first month of the nomination contest, Obama raised $32 million, $27 million of which came from online supporters who gave less than $50.[32] Deval Patrick also successfully leveraged online marketing tools to bring in more donations to his

2006 campaign for governor in Massachusetts. His Internet donations made up about 15 percent of the $1.6 million he raised from donors.[33] During the 2010 U.S. Senate race in Arizona, Democratic primary candidate Randy Parraz raised most of his campaign funds online.[34] In the 2012 campaign, Obama raised approximately $690 million from online contributions, up from about $500 million in 2008.[35] Most of this amount was raised from donors who gave $200 or less through email, social media, and the website.[36] The campaign (along with the Romney campaign) also became the first campaign to raise contributions via text messages.[37]

Minority candidates, like their white counterparts, also rely heavily on interest groups for funds. Interest group support proved vital for candidates like Bonnie Watson Coleman. While Watson Coleman received monetary support from a wide range of groups, women's political action committees played a significant role in her campaign and in Brenda Lawrence's campaigns. Watson Coleman received $7,050 from EMILY's List contributors, and Lawrence received $38,104.[38] Tim Scott also benefited from campaign contributions from prominent elected officials in his 2010 election to represent South Carolina's first congressional district. Scott, the first African American Republican elected to the House from the state since Reconstruction, received campaign contributions from Karl Rove, a top adviser to former president George W. Bush, and House Republican leaders including Representatives Eric Cantor of Virginia and Kevin McCarthy of California. He also received more than $100,000 from the antitax Club for Growth.[39] Mazie Hirono also benefited greatly from donor group contributions, receiving donations from EMILY's List ($215,640), Planned Parenthood ($12,700), the League of Conservation Voters ($12,341), and law firms. [40]

Voter Mobilization of Minorities, Part I—Microtargeting

Campaigns have the task of determining which voters to communicate with and what messages to send. Targeting helps campaigns preserve scarce resources while maximizing their impact. Microtargeting is a technique that makes use of commercial data mining and large-scale polls to do this more precisely. Microtargeting involves using voter files that overlay previous election results with individuals' voter turnout histories, contact information, and detailed demographic and consumer information that is correlated with political preferences.[41] Campaigns often use new technology to collect some demographic and consumer information. Enabling candidates to concentrate their efforts on supporters or persuadable voters, these sophisticated databases of voter information can then be used for multiple purposes including guiding direct mail programs, media purchases, and voter drives designed to register and mobilize segments of the electorate. Microtargeting can also be used to understand more advanced voter behavior so that campaigns can send highly specialized messages to voters. The Obama campaigns used this technique to identify crucial constituencies of voters and likely supporters, which helped put states once considered unwinnable by a Democratic candidate into play.[42] The 2012 election was the most microtargeted election in history, with millions spent on online advertising and other efforts to reach slices of the electorate.[43] Microtargeting is also credited for Watson Coleman's congressional victory in New Jersey. She was projected to lose the primary election to state senator Linda Greenstein. Using Obama-style techniques, Watson Coleman's campaign focused on a narrow communications and voter contact program informed by a microtargeting voter model, helping her win the primary.[44]

Voter Mobilization of Minorities, Part II—Get-Out-the-Vote

As discussed earlier, campaigns are giving renewed attention to "the ground game" and are increasingly using the Internet as a cost-effective tool to target and mobilize supporters. Much like Obama, Deval Patrick received national attention for employing a grassroots election strategy that made use of new media technologies in his 2006 (and 2010) gubernatorial campaigns. Using social media primarily for organizing and messaging in 2006, the campaign's email list numbered over 40,000, each of whom sent messages to at least 10 others, thereby reaching an estimated 400,000 field volunteers, supporters, and potential supporters who turned out in high numbers for "Meet Deval" events all over the state.[45] Using cell phones and email to get-out-the-vote among young people, the Obama campaign turned over its voter lists to volunteers who then used their personal laptops and cell phones to contact people from the lists.[46] In 2013, Cory Booker hired a consulting firm run by Obama's former battleground states director and national field director that trained thousands of volunteers across New Jersey, made nearly one million door knocks and phone calls to targeted voters, and put together a strong volunteer-led field program, relying on many of the key organizing strategies honed on Obama presidential campaigns.[47]

More than ever, campaigns are expected to use modern technology given that racial and ethnic minorities (particularly African Americans and Latinos) are more likely than the general population to access the Internet by cellular phones, and use their phones more often to do more things.[48] However, racial and ethnic differences in rates of computer and Internet use make it likely that most candidates will also rely on traditional models of targeting voters. Obama aggressively courted Latino voters using radio, television, and mail.[49] Deval Patrick also had a strong traditional GOTV effort, using door-to-door canvassing and town hall meetings.[50] Hansen Clarke's 2010 campaign lacked resources for a television campaign and relied heavily on door-to-door canvassing and town hall meetings in soup kitchens, churches, and polling places.[51] Brenda Lawrence's 2014 campaign in the same district also relied heavily on door-to-door canvassing and GOTV events.[52]

Challenges for Minority Candidates in 2016 and Beyond

While the changing demography of the United States is transforming the political landscape, it also poses unique challenges for minority candidates looking to run in districts where one racial or ethnic group is a dominant majority. Some districts that were once heavily African American are now pluralities. This increases the chances that minority candidates will run against each other as legislative seats become available. This was the case in 2007 in California's thirty-seventh congressional district's special election. The Democratic primary pitted Laura Richardson, who is African American, against Jenny Oropeza, who is Latina, in a district where Latinos and African Americans make up 43 percent and 25 percent of the population, respectively. Richardson won the primary, garnering 38 percent of the vote compared to Oropeza's 31 percent of the vote, and won the general election.[53] The last three members of Congress representing the district have been African American; however, the growth and engagement of the Latino population could raise social and political tensions in the district should the political dynamics in the district change. This not only impacts the district but has implications for the racial and ethnic composition of Congress.

Several elections in majority-minority districts also highlight the way in which modern political campaigning can impact the racial and ethnic composition of Congress. In 2009, Judy Chu used websites and social media to defeat Gil Cedillo in California's thirty-second, majority-Latino (62 percent) congressional district. Chu became the first Chinese American woman elected to Congress, winning a seat that had exclusively sent Latino members to Congress.[54] Similarly, using traditional and new media to promote his knowledge of national security, Will Hurd narrowly defeated incumbent Pete Gallego in 2014, becoming the first African American Republican from Texas elected to Congress since Reconstruction. The competitive seat in Texas' twenty-third, majority-Latino (70 percent) congressional district had been held exclusively by a Latino representative since 1985.[55]

While personal contacts are often viewed as the most influential form of voter mobilization, social media is a critical component of an effective minority outreach strategy. Minority candidates may seek to use social media to maximize minority turnout while simultaneously appealing to races and ethnicities beyond their own; however, their ability to run a dual campaign may be limited given the accessibility of technology. Candidates' ability to convey different messages to distinct constituencies is strongly influenced by the degree to which race-conscious messages can be confined to the appropriate audience so that there is minimal risk of alienating out-group voters. Advances in mobile technology make it possible for almost anyone to capture candidates on video and post the video on the Internet. Furthermore, campaigns often employ workers to search for comments (and actions) that can be used to discredit their opponents.

Knowing that opposition researchers routinely search for evidence to disqualify their opponents, minority candidates may have to turn primarily to surrogates to target and mobilize minority voters. This was the case for Democrat Harold Ford Jr. who, in the 2006 Tennessee Senate election, used African American clergy, labor activists, students from black colleges and universities, and Democratic Party functionaries to discuss racial policies and issues.[56] Yet the degree to which alternative ethnic and racial media are segregated from mainstream media will also influence the usefulness of this approach.

And, like their white counterparts, minority candidates and their campaigns will also have to invest time and energy in learning how to use modern campaign tools effectively and with caution. Whereas the earliest candidate websites were often word-for-word copies of traditional campaign literature, most Internet users expect a high level of sophistication, anticipating that websites and social media sites will be interactive, engaging, and comprehensive. Campaigns that choose to take advantage of the web's ability to offer interactive content will also have to monitor sites to prevent potentially damaging information or inappropriate comments or videos from appearing on them.

Finally, recent challenges to the Voting Rights Act (VRA) of 1965 and the process of redistricting may also pose unique challenges for minority candidates in future elections. In June 2013, the Supreme Court struck down a key part of the VRA (section 4) that required nine states with a history of African American voter discrimination to receive federal approval to change their election laws.[57] By invalidating this section of the law and thereby rendering other sections (particularly section 5) meaningless, the Court's ruling may lessen the pressure states feel to create majority-minority districts during the redistricting process. Yet it is also possible that the geographic concentration of minorities in various communities, coupled with redistricting formal and informal criteria—including compactness, contiguity, and partisanship—will minimize the impact.[58]

In June 2015, the Supreme Court also agreed to hear arguments in a case that challenges how congressional districts are created. The Constitution requires congressional seats to be reapportioned among the states after each decennial census, and the Court since the 1960s has mandated that each district have an equal number of people. The case, *Evenwel v. Abbott*, challenges the standing position that districts be drawn using total population figures, and argues instead that districts should be drawn with equal numbers of eligible voters.[59] Latinos have lower rates of voter registration in part because a significant portion of the population is foreign born and without U.S. citizenship. Should the Court adopt this new standard, it is possible that largely Latino districts would be redrawn to include more whites and Republicans to increase the eligible-voter population.[60] Thus, the outcome of the case could have major implications for Latino candidates (most of whom run in majority-Latino districts) and Latino representation.

Conclusion

While the election of President Barack Obama is often cited by political commentators as a defining moment in which the nation transcended racial and ethnic politics, race and ethnicity undoubtedly remain central cleavages in U.S. politics. How, then, can we come to understand the relevance of race and ethnicity as we look to historic "color-blind" or "postracial" victories of minority candidates? Focusing on the campaigns of minority candidates, this chapter suggests that these recent successes are due in some part to minority candidates' adoption of a new style of political campaigning. Thus, the development and adoption of new technologies can facilitate the mainstreaming of minority candidates, enabling them to transcend their minority status and reducing the likelihood that their candidacies will be marginalized.

Future minority campaigns will be characterized by diverse campaign strategies and communication methods to win elective office in districts and states across the country. This will be due, in large part, to a shift in perspective among individuals, who will care more about how a candidate is going to represent his or her issues and concerns than about who the candidate is. Thus, the future of minority campaigns is the enduring tradition of minority candidates working to solidify their bases but also working toward building multiracial electoral coalitions.

Notes

1. U.S. Census Bureau, "U.S. Census Bureau Projections Show a Slower Growing, Older, More Diverse Nation a Half Century from Now" (December 12, 2012). Accessed on April 1, 2015, from https://www.census.gov/newsroom/releases/archives/population/cb12-243.html.

2. Thom File, "The Diversifying Electorate—Voting Rates by Race and Hispanic Origin in 2012 (and Other Recent Elections)" (U.S. Census Bureau, May 2013). Accessed on April 21, 2015, from https://www.census.gov/prod/2013pubs/p20-568.pdf.

3. Joint Center for Political and Economic Studies, "History of the Joint Center for Political and Economic Studies" (March 31, 2014). Accessed on October 18, 2015, from http://jointcenter.org/about/history-joint-center-political-and-economic-studies.

4. National Directory of Latino Elected Officials, http://www.naleo.org/.

5. *National Asian Pacific American Political Almanac*, 15th ed., edited by Don T. Nakanishi and James Lai (Los Angeles, CA: UCLA Asian American Studies Center Press, 2014).

6. James S. Lai, Wendy K. Tam Cho, Thomas P. Kim, and Okiyoshi Takeda, "Asian Pacific-American Campaigns, Elections, and Elected Officials" (*PS: Political Science and Politics*, 2001), 611.

7. See Christian Collet, "Minority Candidates, Alternative Media and Multiethnic America: Deracialization or Toggling?" (*Perspectives on Politics*, Vol. 6, 2008).

8. Bureau of Labor Statistics, "American Time Use Survey Summary—2014 Results" (June 24, 2015). Accessed on June 27, 2015, from http://www.bls.gov/news.release/atus.nr0.html.

9. Travis N. Ridout and Glen R. Smith, "Free Advertising: How the Media Amplify Campaign Messages" (*Political Research Quarterly,* Vol. 61, 2008), 598–608.

10. Travis Ridout, "Campaign Microtargeting and the Relevance of the Televised Political Ad" (*The Forum,* Vol. 7, 2009), 11.

11. Wesleyan Media Project, "Ad Spending in 2014 Elections Poised to Break $1 Billion" (October 14, 2014). Accessed on May 1, 2015, from http://mediaproject.wesleyan.edu/releases/ad-spending-in-2014-elections-poised-to-break-1-billion.

12. Compiled from data provided by Political Money Line (www.politicalmoneyline.com).

13. Melissa E. Holsman and Jonathan Mattise, "MSNBC, Murphy Calling District 18 Race for Murphy with All Precincts Reporting" (*TCPalm,* November 6, 2012). Accessed on May 3, 2015, from http://www.tcpalm.com/news/us-house-representatives-district-18-2012.

14. Kate Nocera, "Mia Love–Jim Matheson Race Puts Utah District on Map" (*Politico,* October 2, 2012). Accessed on April 24, 2015, from http://www.politico.com/news/stories/1012/81938.html.

15. Bob Bernick, "National GOP Figures to Stay Away from Utah in 2014" (*Utah Policy,* August 12, 2014). Accessed on April 1, 2015, from http://utahpolicy.com/index.php/features/today-at-utah-policy/3218-national-gop-figures-to-stay-away-from-utah-in-2014.

16. Peter Wallsten, "Obama 2012 Campaign's Operation Vote Focuses on Ethnic Minorities, Core Liberals" (*The Washington Post,* September 24, 2011). Accessed on April 10, 2015, from http://www.washingtonpost.com/politics/obama-2012-campaigns-operation-vote-focuses-on-ethnic-minorities-core-liberals/2011/09/23/gIQA-lY7JuK_story.html.

17. Pew Research Center for Journalism and Media, "How the Presidential Candidates Use the Web and Social Media" (August 12, 2012). Accessed on March 15, 2015, from http://www.journalism.org/2012/08/15/how-presidential-candidates-use-web-and-social-media/.

18. Ibid.

19. Zachary A. Goldfarb, "Facebook Flexes Political Might" (*The Washington Post,* February 3, 2007).

20. Julianna Goldman, "Obama Winning Social Media, If #Hashtagwars Really Matter" (*Bloomberg Business,* October 22, 2012). Accessed on April 22, 2015, from http://www.bloomberg.com/news/articles/2012-10-22/obama-winning-social-media-if-hashtagwars-really-matter.

21. Sarah Lai Stirland, "Was Twitter the TV of 2012? How Barack Obama Tracked Your Tweets" (*Personal Democracy Media,* December 3, 2012). Accessed on May 1, 2015, from http://techpresident.com/news/23210/how-barack-obamas-2012-campaign-used-twitter-monitor-and-influence-politics.

22. Pew Research Center for Journalism and Media, "How the Presidential Candidates Use the Web and Social Media."

23. Suzanne Gamboa, "On Election Day, Latino Candidates, Groups Busy on Social Media" (*NBC News,* November 4, 2014). Accessed on April 2, 2015, from http://www.nbcnews.com/news/latino/election-day-latino-candidates-groups-busy-social-media-n240906.

24. Pew Research Center for Journalism and Media, "How the Presidential Candidates Use the Web and Social Media."

25. Alex Isenstadt, "Florida Challenger Raising Cash Fast" (*Politico*, August 13, 2010). Accessed on April 2, 2011, from http://www.politico.com/news/stories/0810/41028 .html.

26. Michael M. Philips, "A Colorful, Costly Dogfight Takes Shape in House Race" (*The Wall Street Journal*, October 12, 2010). Accessed on May 1, 2011, from http://online .wsj.com/article/SB10001424052748703927504575540330106432228.html.

27. Jack Citrin, Donald Philip Green, and David O. Sears, "White Reactions to Black Candidates: When Does Race Matter?" *Public Opinion Quarterly*, Vol. 54, 1990), 74–96; Carol A. Pierannunzi and John D. Hutcheson, "The Rise and Fall of Deracialization: Andrew Young as Mayor and Gubernatorial Candidate," in *Race, Politics, and Governance in the United States*, edited by Huey L. Perry (Gainesville: University Press of Florida, 1996).

28. Daniel M. Shea and Michael John Burton, *Campaign Craft: The Strategies, Tactics, and Art of Political Campaign Management*, 3rd ed. (Westport, CT: Praeger, 2006).

29. Christian Collet, "Minority Candidates, Alternative Media and Multiethnic America: Deracialization or Toggling?" (*Perspectives on Politics*, Vol. 6, 2008), 716–717.

30. Peter Hamby, "Palin Records Robocall for Nikki Haley" (*CNN*, June 3, 2010). Accessed on May 1, 2011, from http://politicalticker.blogs.cnn.com/2010/06/03/palin-records-robocall-for-nikki-haley/.

31. PolitikerNJ, "Hudson Dems Blanket County with 11th Hour Robocalls for Booker" (October 16, 2013). Accessed on May 5, 2015, from http://politickernj.com/2013/10/hudson-dems-blanket-county-with-11th-hour-robocalls-for-booker/.

32. Dewey M. Clayton, *The Presidential Campaign of Barack Obama: A Critical Analysis of a Racially Transcendent Strategy* (New York: Routledge, 2009), 147.

33. Frank Philips, "Patrick Campaign Says Online Giving Generates $240,000. Aide Says System Boosts Number of New Supporters" (*The Boston Globe*, December 21, 2005).

34. Teresa Puente, "If Randy Parraz Wins Arizona Democratic Primary for U.S. Senate, He Could Face John McCain" (*Chicanisima*, August 24, 2010). Accessed on March 25, 2011, from http://www.chicagonow.com/blogs/chicanisima/2010/08/if-randy-parraz-wins-arizona-democratic-primary-for-us-senate-he-could-face-john-mccain.html#ixzz1Nwz5u3TQ.

35. Michael Scherer, "Exclusive: Obama's 2012 Digital Fundraising Outperformed 2008" (*Time*, November 15, 2012). Accessed on May 2, 2015, from http://swampland.time .com/2012/11/15/exclusive-obamas-2012-digital-fundraising-outperformed-2008/.

36. Center for Responsive Politics. Accessed on October 18, 2015, from opensecrets.org.

37. Alina Selyukh, "Donations via Text Approved for Obama, Romney Campaigns" (*The Christian Science Monitor*, June 13, 2012). Accessed on April 5, 2015, from http://www.csmonitor.com/Business/Latest-News-Wires/2012/0613/Donations-via-text-approved-for-Obama-Romney-campaigns.

38. Center for Responsive Politics.

39. Patrick O'Connor, "Tim Scott, Black Republican, Nominated for House Seat" (*Businessweek*, June 22, 2010). Accessed on March 20, 2011, from http://www .businessweek.com/news/2010-06-22/tim-scott-black-republican-nominated-for-house-seat.html.

40. Center for Responsive Politics.

41. Paul S. Herrnson, *Congressional Elections: Campaigning at Home and in Washington* (Washington DC: CQ Press, 2008), 110.

42. Leslie Wayne, "Democrats Take Page from Their Rival's Playbook" (*The New York Times*, October 21, 2008). Accessed on June 10, 2011, from http://www.nytimes .com/2008/11/01/us/politics/01target.html.

43. Dan Eggan, "Obama Campaign Puts Bo on the Trail" (*The Washington Post*, April 30, 2012). Accessed on May 1, 2015, from http://www.washingtonpost.com/politics/ obama-campaign-puts-bo-on-the-trail/2012/04/30/gIQAgZrYsT_story.html.

44. Sherrie Preische, "Obama-Style Modeling Down the Ballot" (*Campaigns and Elections*, October 13, 2014). Accessed on April 8, 2015 from http://campaignsandelections.com/ campaign-insider/2341/obama-style-modeling-down-the-ballot.

45. Christine B. Williams, "Government, the Permanent Campaign, and e-Democracy: Massachusetts Governor Deval Patrick's Interactive Web Site" (May 1, 2009). Accessed on May 2, 2011, from http://ssrn.com/abstract=1397686.

46. Dewey M. Clayton, *The Presidential Campaign of Barack Obama: A Critical Analysis of a Racially Transcendent Strategy* (New York: Routledge, 2009), 108.

47. Alexandra Jaffe, "Booker Hires Obama Campaign Veterans; Pallone Staffs Up for Senate Bid" (*The Hill*, June 14, 2013). Accessed on April 2, 2015, from http://thehill .com/blogs/ballot-box/senate-races/305701-booker-hires-obama-campaign- veterans-for-senate-bid; 270 Strategies. Accessed October 18, 2015, from https://www .270strategies.com.

48. Jesse Washington, "For Minorities, New 'Digital Divide' Seen" (*MSNBC*, January 11, 2011). Accessed on April 20, 2011, from http://www.msnbc.msn.com/id/41023900/ns/ us_news-life/t/minorities-new-digital-divide-seen/.

49. Alicia Menendez, "Margin of Error: How McCain Lost Latinos—and What Obama Must Do to Keep Them" (*Campaigns and Elections Magazine*, January 1, 2009). Accessed on May 1, 2011, from http://www.campaignsandelections.com/publications/ campaign-election/2009/january-2008/margin-of-error.

50. Angela K. Lewis, "Between Generations: Devel Patrick's Election as Massachusetts' First Black Governor," in *Whose Black Politics? Cases in Post-Racial Black Leadership*, edited by Andra Gillespie (New York: Routledge), 177.

51. Reddiff News, "Hansen Clarke's Amazing Story Continues" (September 8, 2010.) Accessed on April 4, 2015, from http://news.rediff.com/slide-show/2010/sep/08/slide- show-1-hansen-clarkes-amazing-story-continues.htm.

52. Michael McGuinness, "Reminder: Brenda Lawrence for Congress Events Today, Tomorrow" (*MichiganLiberal.com*, August 1, 2014). Accessed October 18, 2015, from http://www.michiganliberal.com/tag/Brenda%20Lawrence; Michael McGuinness, "Brenda Lawrence for Congress Events August 1st and 2nd" (*MichiganLiberal.com*, July 31, 2014). Accessed October 18, 2015, from http://www.michiganliberal.com/ diary/21617/brenda-lawrence-for-congress-events-august-1st-and-2nd.

53. Josh Kraushaar, "Black Candidate Wins Disputed District" (*Politico*, June 27, 2007). Accessed on May 30, 2011, from http://www.politico.com/news/stories/0607/4693 .html.

54. Josh Kraushaar, "Will Chu Change 32nd?" (*Politico*, May 14, 2009). Accessed on June 10, 2011, from http://www.politico.com/news/stories/0509/22492.html.

55. Kevin Robillard, "The Best Little House Race in Texas" (*Politico*, November 3, 2014). Accessed on April 10, 2015, from http://www.politico.com/story/2014/11/2014-texas-elections-pete-gallego-will-hurd-112424_Page2.html.

56. Sekou Franklin, "Situational Deracialization, Harold Ford, and the 2006 Senate Race in Tennessee," in *Whose Black Politics? Cases in Post-Racial Black Leadership,* edited by Andra Gillespie (New York: Routledge), 222.

57. Adam Liptak, "*Supreme Court Invalidates Key Part of Voting Rights Act*" (*The New York Times,* June 25, 2013). Accessed on April 1, 2015, from http://www.nytimes.com/2013/06/26/us/supreme-court-ruling.html.

58. Nate Silver, "Geography, Not Voting Rights Act, Accounts for Most Majority-Minority Districts" (*The New York Times*, June 25, 2013). Accessed on April 2, 2015, from http://nyti.ms/1aISAHE.

59. Drew DeSilver, "Supreme Court Could Reshape Voting Districts, with Big Impact on Hispanics" (Pew Research Center, June 3, 2015). Accessed on June 4, 2015, from http://pewrsr.ch/1Q7fvm.

60. Ibid.

CHAPTER 14

Political Campaigns and Democracy

Dick Simpson

WHEN HE WAS A STATE LEGISLATOR IN ILLINOIS, Abraham Lincoln said there are three basic tasks in a political campaign: canvass the district, identify your voters, and get them to the polls. At one level, nothing much has changed, except for the technology. To win elections, you still have to talk to the voters, find out who supports your candidate, and get them to vote on Election Day. The fact that we use computers, email, websites, paid media ads, public opinion polls, voter analytics, microtargeting, "robo" phone calls, and direct mail appeals does not change the fundamentals of campaigning. Yet technology in cutting-edge political campaigns does make a huge difference. On the one hand, it provides the opportunity to increase democratic participation in elections. On the other, it also provides Orwellian opportunities to manipulate voters and citizens.

The authors of this book, who are both academics and practitioners, discuss trends in cutting-edge campaigns. Today there is a convergence, such that traditional methods in contacting voters since the days of Abraham Lincoln are being integrated with voter analytics, social media, fundraising, and the Internet to produce powerful campaigns, but they also have the potential to undermine voter privacy. Just as National Security Agency (NSA) data mining undermines civil liberties in the name of national security, campaigns can now learn too much personal data about voters.

In addition to privacy issues, the challenge of raising enormous sums of money to run for public office; the presence of "dark money" from unknown donors; and millions of dollars spent by businesses, labor unions, wealthy individuals, and interest groups are changing who can run for public office and the outcomes of elections. Today, campaigns are no longer just candidate-centered but donor-centered and group-centered in ways that make keeping public officials accountable to the voters more difficult.

In a continuing trend, media coverage of campaigns is filterless and more likely to be superficial, emphasizing personality, rumor, and infotainment. Paid advertising, social media, and the Internet, along with cutbacks in the number of investigative reporters, have further weakened the mass media.

Finally, while women and minorities continue to make gains in electing more candidates and provide critical swing votes to determine election outcomes, they are still underrepresented.

Cutting-edge campaigns are marvels to behold, but they challenge democracy in at least six ways: (1) money in campaigns buys influence and elections; (2) the "selling" of candidates with false images and communications can trick voters into supporting less well-qualified candidates; (3) analytics provide too much information on voters, some of which should remain private; (4) parties and interest groups in elections can convince voters to support candidates against their own or the public interest; (5) the discrimination against women and minority candidates continues to keep them from being fully incorporated into the political process; and (6) citizen participation, despite barriers and some voter disaffection, has increased with the last two presidential elections—2008 and 2012—providing the highest voter turnout since 1964, but it has to be maintained.

Money in Campaigns

Because of new technology and the cost of staff and campaign consultants, political campaigns have gotten very expensive. In local campaigns for city council in large cities as well as for county board, state legislature, and citywide offices in smaller towns or suburbs, there are usually at least three paid staff members. There is also the need to buy paid campaign ads on at least cable TV, on radio, and in local newspapers. Direct mail and phone campaigns and a candidate website in addition to the traditional precinct operations add to expenses. Often, local campaigns for even a city council seat in a larger city now cost from $100,000 to $250,000. In congressional, statewide, and presidential elections, the cost of elections is astronomical. Techniques and methods once confined to presidential campaigns are now employed in nearly all successful elections except for the very, very local.

In 2008, only two presidential election cycles ago, state candidates and political action committees (PACs) spent $2.7 billion. By 2012, federal elections alone cost approximately $6 billion. In the most expensive states like California, the average cost of winning a state assembly seat has been $769,000, winning a state senate seat cost $1,098,000, and the cost keeps escalating each election cycle.[1]

A large congressional campaign will require as many as five or six paid staff members; paid public relations, advertising, and campaign consultants; and outside services like servers to host websites and the software and data to do "big data" analysis. Television ads are still among the highest costs despite increased use of

Internet advertising and social media. Successful congressional campaigns in competitive districts now cost an average of $1.5 million to run.[2] Hotly contested races cost $3 million or more.[3] Campaigns for statewide office, at least in the larger states, cost more than $10 million with the average U.S. Senate seat costing $8.5 million.[4]

Presidential campaigns cost more than $1 billion with more than $100 million raised before the first primary or caucus vote is cast. This early fundraising is the so-called money primary that determines who will be a competitive candidate in the later primary elections, which are expensive and happen in quick succession. Estimates on the final cost of all 2016 presidential campaigns are that they will be as much as $6 billion with certainly more than $1 billion coming from outside money being spent by Super PACs and 501(c)(4) committees.

These expensive campaigns can no longer be funded just by the candidate, a few modestly wealthy friends, excited volunteers, and small donors. Professional fundraising and larger campaign contributions by interest groups, political parties, and PACs are required along with the parallel expenditures of the Super PACs and 501(c)(4) groups, which do not even report their donors. The Center for Responsive Politics reports that 1 percent of the richest 1 percent (some 32,000 donors) accounted for $1.18 billion in disclosed political contributions at the federal level alone in the midterm 2014 elections.[5] In short, campaigns do not just cost more, but the funding is being provided to an ever-greater extent by fewer donors who have an agenda for giving. This is a challenge to our democracy when the few control the outcome of elections with their money. These huge sums of money escalate the cost of campaigns and affect their outcomes. As Robert G. Boatright points out in Chapter 2 on fundraising, "the sorts of groups that have come to dominate politics rely on small numbers of large contributions; in many cases, these are not really contributions at all, but expenditures made, unprompted, by wealthy individuals seeking to change the political system."[6]

In short, high-tech, candidate-centered, multimedia, new technology campaigns are too expensive for just a good candidate running on good issues to win regularly. The high cost of these campaigns undermines democracy because it is often the candidates with the most money, not the best character and the best ideas, who win. Candidates without personal wealth or the ability to raise large campaign donations are eliminated. Under the current rulings of the Supreme Court, individuals and highly partisan interest groups intervene in campaigns with few restraints.

James Madison, one of the authors and advocates of the U.S. Constitution, famously warned about the need to provide "checks and balances" to prevent "factions" or interest groups motivated by ideology or self-interest. He argued that if they were unchecked they could undermine representative democracy. Certainly, factions and wealthy individuals affect election outcomes when they get involved.

According to Nina Therese Kasniunas, Mark J. Rozell, and Charles N. W. Keckler in Chapter 8, 527 organizations or Super PACs in the 2012 election after the *Citizens United* decision spent more than $609 million. They are expected to spend more than $1 billion in the 2016 election. Not only have the limits on spending by interest groups been eliminated, but their donors remain secret. Their involvement in elections has tended to make elections much more ideological, negative, and vitriolic. This finding is echoed by Peter L. Francia, Wesley Joe, and Clyde Wilcox in Chapter 10, who say that the *Citizens United* decision fostered the growth of outside associations and groups spending on elections and a lessening of contributor accountability and transparency. As Francia et al. indicate, the only solutions to big money polluting our politics are a greater dependence upon small donors and what is called small donor democracy.

Thus, there is a cure for the problems of big money and dark money, but it will require new campaign finance disclosure and, ultimately, public funding, and small donor democracy legislation to be adopted.

The Selling of the Candidate

In any campaign, a candidate's image is important. In the 2008 presidential campaign, Barack Obama projected the image of a young, "new" candidate who stood for change. His famous slogan, "Yes, we can," was meant to signify that we could end the Iraq War, incorporate minorities into the political process, and solve our domestic problems at home. By 2012, he argued that he needed more time in office to deliver on the promise of change. He ran on the theme "Forward," promising policies like Obamacare and immigration reform, which the Republicans opposed.

In contrast, Obama's opponent in the 2012 election, Republican Mitt Romney, was defined first by his Republican primary opponents and then by the Obama campaign as one of the richest 1 percent of Americans. His opponents told voters that Romney's Bain Capital had sold off U.S. manufacturing companies in a way that cost thousands of U.S. workers their jobs. When a secretly recorded video of a campaign fundraiser was released showing Romney saying that many Americans were welfare and tax cheats, the image of him as part of the out-of-touch rich folks who don't care about average Americans was cemented. In the battle of images, Obama won and went on to win the election.

Successful Image Building

Even before the issues of the campaign are joined, a positive image for the candidate must be created. Shaping that image is the task of the candidate, the campaign manager, and public relations consultants. Allowing an opponent's portrayal of the candidate to go unanswered will surely lose the election.

In the new cutting-edge campaign era of polling and focus groups, a candidate's persona can be altered more than in the past when many voters knew at least local political candidates personally. Public opinion polls allow characteristics of the candidate and campaign issues to be constantly followed by tracking polls so that sophisticated media advisers can better manipulate the candidate's image. This has been known as far back as Joe McGinniss's book, *The Selling of the President 1968*, which told the story of Richard Nixon's successful campaign makeover.[7]

Susan A. MacManus points out in Chapter 12 that women especially are stereotyped by image—such as the clothes, hair, and makeup they use. The presence of more successful women candidates has, however, "begun to turn the emphasis of campaign coverage of female candidates to substance, rather than their personal attributes." MacManus shows as well that women candidates are viewed differently by different generations of voters. Still all candidates, men and women, whites and minorities, must pay careful attention to how they present themselves in public and in the media.

Image Building and the Use of Campaign Polls

For decades, campaign polls and focus groups have been used to determine the most positive image of candidates and which negative attack ads best discredit their opponents. They are also used to research their own candidates to determine their weaknesses and to plan responses to any attacks that may come from opponents. With this information, campaigns can choose the most effective media to deliver their messages, which have been sharpened by polls and focus groups, forcefully. These techniques, so highly developed in presidential campaigns, are now available to any candidate for state, local, and congressional office with the money to pay for the consultants and experts who know how to use them.

The changes in techniques for public opinion polling and focus groups, from random digit dialing to calling from voter files, and now to online Internet surveys, do not change the basic use of polls and focus groups. Pollsters are having to overcome new problems like the expanded use of cell phones that are unlisted and whose geographical location is uncertain. Also, many voters are no longer willing to participate in surveys, polls, and focus groups. Nonetheless, however conducted and whatever the limitations, polls and focus groups are still used to determine the views of potential voters on issues as well as the candidate's image, and to test both positive and negative advertising.

Polling is no longer just a one-shot poll to provide a snapshot of opinion. Cutting-edge campaigns begin with a benchmark survey followed by focus groups to sharpen issue stands, candidate image, and the campaign message. This is followed by trend surveys and tracking or rolling polls to gauge changes in voter attitudes during the campaign. These may be supplemented by dial meter, mall testing, and more focus groups to fine-tune final campaign ads.[8]

Of course, campaign polling provides useful information to candidates, media, and public officials whether obtained by phone interviews, Internet surveys, or focus groups as Candice J. Nelson points out in Chapter 5. Unfortunately, it also has the potential to undermine the campaign process by creating a false persona for a candidate, an untrue stand on issues, or an inaccurate portrayal of one's opponent. Democracy works only if the voters have accurate information on which to make a decision on the best person to be elected. Image manipulation is too often used to deny voters the chance to make an honest choice between candidates.

Analytics and Privacy

One of the biggest changes in campaigns has been the change from developing a general message of the campaign to appeal to groups of voters to personalized messaging for individual voters. Voter analytics and "big data" allow for microtargeting and nanotargeting. On the one hand, voters now receive a specific appeal from the candidate, which allows them to see their self-interest in the election more clearly and can motivate greater voter participation. On the other hand, "big data" or analytics utilize personal information about voters such as their voting history in past elections; their response to workers in previous campaigns; their party identity; and their consumer purchases, including the home they rent or own, their car, and their credit card activity. These data are made available to every phone caller or precinct worker who contacts the voter and help him or her tailor his or her pitch to each individual. The privacy of the voter is violated in the process.

Of course, political campaigns take advantage of all available voter data in order to win. We cannot ban voter analytics or the use of "big data." The best we can strive for is to create standards for the use of analytics.[9]

Campaigns have embraced analytics because it has made targeting voters easier and getting messages to them less costly. It behooves us now to limit the possible drawbacks of these techniques. Adopting and publicizing standards for analytics use in political campaigns is probably better than passing new laws or regulations at this stage. But it is essential that steps be taken to ensure privacy of data on individuals to the extent possible. This may well require legislation in the future.

On the Internet

For a number of campaign cycles now, candidates have been using websites as a means to communicate with voters—to help them win elections. Since most Americans are on the Internet, many on their phones and tablets, the Internet cannot be ignored by any modern campaign. Beyond previous Internet tools, social media on platforms like Facebook, Twitter, Instagram, and YouTube have played an ever-larger role in campaigns. Cutting-edge campaigns are now working to maximize cell phones and tablets and developing their own aps to deliver campaign messages. But some key adjustments are now necessary to utilize all these tools effectively.

Campaign websites must be developed with the smaller mobile device screens and download times in mind. Campaign email blasts have to be recrafted without larger graphics and lengthy text. Since both Facebook and Twitter target the mobile audience, campaign photographs from events are often loaded directly onto the campaign's Facebook page. Finally, candidate campaigns and political parties are investing in customized applications for mobile devices.[10]

In its various forms, the Internet on computers, laptops, or mobile devices can be used to recruit and coordinate volunteers, provide background campaign information to media reporters and bloggers, raise significant sums of money, reach important opinion and community leaders, and, of course, convince voters to vote for a certain candidate. Direct mail fundraising costs forty cents for every dollar raised, while Internet appeals cost less than a penny for every dollar a campaign receives in contributions.

Virtually all congressional candidates now have websites, as do all seated congressmen and city council and county board members in many places. Among the latest techniques are videos posted on sites like YouTube and Facebook and photos posted on Facebook, Twitter, and Instagram. The most famous YouTube videos thus far are the defeated senator George Allen's "macaca" comment, Barack Obama's "Obama Girl," and Hillary and Bill Clinton's "Sopranos" ad.[11] In the 2008 presidential campaign, CNN sponsored the first presidential debate at which Democratic candidates at the Citadel in Charleston, South Carolina, answered questions submitted by video on YouTube. The videotaped questions were selected from 3,000 entries. Several of the presidential candidates in the 2016 election announced their candidacies with posts on the Internet such as emails to their supporters and the media with accompanying videos.

In addition to websites and YouTube videos, many state and local candidates coordinate their volunteers by email lists that allow the campaign staff to send email letters to all volunteers at once at no cost. These can now be received instantly on mobile phones either as emails or as text messages. Campaigns use email and tweets in addition to the candidate's webpage to which constituents, supporters, and potential supporters can be referred. Today, there is clearly a convergence of traditional and digital methods in winning campaigns.

Like all other communications methods, it takes money and expertise to set up campaign websites, Internet, and social media operations. Campaign offices are supplemented with powerful mobile apps, tablets, and smartphones that make supporters an office unto themselves. These tools are used to empower fundraising volunteers to contact potential donors instantly. Precinct workers are able to report petition signatures gathered, neighbors registered to vote, or voters canvassed for support instantly to secure campaign websites.

Of course, emails, text messages, videos, and websites have to be updated as often as several times a day, which requires staff and candidate time. Campaign funds are also spent advertising on the Internet as that is where more and more voters will be. As Atiya Kai Stokes-Brown points out in Chapter 13, minority candidates are increasingly using new media to reach their constituents as well. Nearly all campaigns have had to add these new communications technologies to their campaign tool kits with all the costs and expertise they require.

Perils of Internet Technology

There is also danger in the use of Internet technology. As Philip Howard describes it, "[P]olitical campaigns in the United States are increasingly manipulative, as managers find new ways to distribute propaganda, mine data, mark political interests, and mislead people unfamiliar with computing technologies."[12] Yet there is also a democratizing potential to the Internet. It costs less to use than expensive mass media advertising. It can mobilize large numbers of citizens to participate in the election. It allows hundreds—or thousands—of small financial contributors to become more significant to a campaign than a few wealthy individual or powerful interest groups, freeing elected officials to represent "the people" rather than special interests. Anyone can support a candidate by email, by a Facebook post, by writing a blog, or by sending a text message to friends to build the buzz for a candidate and the momentum of a campaign. The danger is that just as easily Internet technology can be used to misinform voters in ways that are hard to counter.

Media Coverage

All political campaigns from president to school board member still depend heavily on press coverage. Several disturbing trends have occurred in the mass media since the famous Kennedy/Nixon debates of 1960. As Jeremy D. Mayer, Richard J. Semiatin, and Joseph Graf say in Chapter 9 on press coverage, "Sound bites that played on the news for sixty seconds in 1968 have been reduced to seven seconds or less today."[13] Thus, politicians' comments are often reduced to extreme, colorful, short sound bites such as when Barack Obama and Hillary Clinton went at it in the South Carolina primary debate in 2008. Obama stated that he was a community organizer while "you were on the corporate board of Wal-Mart." Clinton retorted that while she was fighting Republicans, "you were representing your contributor Rezko in his slum landlord business."[14] Tony Rezko was under indictment at this time. The chapter shows us how campaigns have now come full-circle. The partisan press of the early 1800s has returned in the cloak of Internet bloggers and "reporters" who masquerade as journalists reporting innuendo as fact but who are really surrogates or partisans.

Issues that are immensely important and complex are reduced to simple slogans or character attacks. So, for instance, some politicians pledge they will support "no new taxes," which may not allow for decisions that have to be made when future conditions may require them. Slogans and character attacks made by politicians can box them into a corner before they take office.

Try an experiment for yourself. Think about any major foreign policy such as wars overseas or any domestic issues like tax policies in the United States. Time yourself on your watch or stopwatch and try to convey what you know about the subject or what you believe in seven seconds, without notes and speaking aloud. This effort will convince you how much our discussion of issues has truncated from the several-hour debates between Abraham Lincoln and Stephen A. Douglas before the Civil War and how unlikely we are to make good decisions about candidates or policies based on seven-second sound bites.

The second mass media trend that is troubling is the new rhythm of media coverage. With cable TV and the Internet, the news cycle is 24/7. Ever since the Bill Clinton campaigns of the 1990s invented the war room, major political campaigns have had instant response teams ready to respond to the actions, rumors, events, and charges by the other side almost as soon as they occur. No reflection, no discussion; only a quick counter thrust. The truth is likely to be the victim under these pressures.

Finally, the evolution of the media—especially cable TV, Internet websites, blogs, Internet ads, and directed email blasts—have increased the opportunity for "narrowcasting" in addition to "broadcasting." This means that campaigns can buy cable TV ads now only for the viewers in a particular district or neighborhood, on shows covering sports or news, or on liberal or conservative talk shows. This allows campaigns to tailor their messages for particular groups rather than the general public. Other than the fear of being caught by their opponents or the mass media, campaigns can take more extreme positions on issues and even different positions for different voter audiences in order to win votes and get elected. With nanotargeting, it is also possible to buy Internet ads that appeal to specific Internet users. Thus, those who buy particular products see ads about repealing automobile or gas taxes while veterans see only ads about a candidate's stand on increasing veteran benefits. Narrowcasting and nanotargeting undermine the ability of voters to know candidates' real stands on issues.

As press and media coverage of campaigns evolves to only "headline news coverage" as we get more of our news coverage on mobile devices such as smartphones and tablets, the news coverage inevitably becomes more superficial. Like the amount you can say in a seven-second sound bite, the amount of detail you can provide on a smartphone screen is very limited. Along with that, the attention to scandals and the constant surveillance of candidates increases "the emphasis on personality, appearance, and character, and further lessen[s] the importance of parties, platform and issues."[15] This is a threat to our democracy.

Campaigns will continue to invest much of their money and staff time in mass media press coverage and the Internet, but these imperfectly serve us, the voters. Sound bite and headline news coverage does not provide adequate information for us to choose the best candidate or the best public policies. Narrowcasting and nanotargeting Internet ads rather than broadcasting limits debate and biases the information voters receive. The new rhythm of 24/7 media and the need for candidate immediate responses to smears and misinformation do not encourage reasoned debate. Media coverage is still essential in elections, but the collapse of newspapers and the changes in press coverage of campaigns place limits on what is possible and what is good for the democratic process.

Personal Voter Contact Still Matters

Candidate image can be greatly influenced by media. Yet from precinct to state to national level, voter contact still matters—a lot. Staffing a field operation with trained workers able to carry out petition and voter registration drives, a door-to-door canvass, and poll watching on Election Day is still the secret to winning most state and local elections. And voter contact is a major component of national campaigns, including presidential campaigns. Precinct work provides a much more personal and less expensive way to carry out Abe Lincoln's electioneering advice to canvass the district, identify your voters, and get them to the polls. It is also key for effective get-out-the-vote at the state and national levels.

In high-tech, candidate-centered, modern campaigns, sometimes money, professional political consultants, and paid advertising, along with specialized direct mail and phone campaigns, can defeat precinct work campaigns. It is harder and harder in an economy that demands that everyone work, often at more than one job, to find enough people to volunteer to cover all the precincts and reach all the voters in statewide, congressional, and presidential campaigns. In the larger districts, precinct work by itself will not be sufficient. It also has to be adapted to changes such as the fact that states like Oregon, Florida, and Washington now have a substantial percentage of their voters vote before Election Day—in some cases more than half. This is a problem for all campaigns to adapt their precinct work and marketing strategies to influence these early voters.

Voter Registration

We are gradually moving to universal voter registration. In many states, we now have electronic voter registration. The opposite attempt in some states to require strict voter identification to be able to vote is unlikely to succeed in the long run. It can severely affect election outcomes at the moment, however.

For several decades now, we have had voters register to vote when they obtain their driver's licenses. This is likely to be made automatic for all drivers in the next decade or so. But it would also be possible to have every American automatically registered to vote at birth or when he or she obtains a Social Security number.

Longer earlier voting periods are also very popular and make voting easier in states where it is an option. Universal voter registration and easier methods of voting, without yet moving to Internet voting, are positive steps we can take to encourage voting participation.

However, better voter registration or easier voting methods do not automatically lead to higher rates of voter participation. For instance, when the voting age was lowered to eighteen, youth voting did not reach the level of participation of the rest of the population. Less than half (45 percent) of those from eighteen to twenty-nine years old voted in the 2012 presidential election, and only 21.5 percent voted in the 2014 elections.[16]

Voter Mobilization

To win elections and to increase voter participation, voter mobilization is required, and that is achieved by political campaigns, political parties, and interest groups.

Precinct work is only one form of voter mobilization, but it is very important. In the high-tech new campaigns of the twenty-first century, microtargeting, direct mail, phone campaigns, Internet advertising, and email voting reminders are all part of the process for recruiting volunteers, identifying supporters, and getting them to vote on Election Day. By 2006, both the Republicans and the Democrats had developed sophisticated seventy-two-hour plans using political parties, interest groups, and volunteers to deliver "their" voters to the polls. Blogs, emails, and websites are pressed into service creating a "virtual community" and an online campaign to supplement the traditional precinct worker ground wars reaching voters. Yet, as Semiatin reports in Chapter 6, precinct work is still the most powerful technique yielding one vote for every fourteen contacts in comparison with, say, phone bank calls, which yield one vote for every thirty-five calls. Thus, all mobilization methods are critical in close campaigns.

Some modern voter mobilization techniques pose disturbing problems for our democracy. Again, consumer and lifestyle orientation in addition to demographic information and voter profiles from electronic databases can be used to microtarget voters in ways that undermine a citizen's right to privacy. Political parties and campaigns are gaining access to information that was private, and using that information for political purposes. What if the information fell into the hands of an individual who would misuse that against voters? For instance, a malicious campaign worker could let neighbors know that particular voters were gay, belonged to a minority, or owed a large debt to a bank or credit card company. While microtargeting and data collection have not yet reached the intrusive level of "Big Brother," the brave new political world has the potential for campaign workers and political officials gaining too much private information about individuals.

From Candidate-Centered to Interest Group– and Donor-Centered Campaigns

For at least the last fifty years, elections have been changing from party-centered to candidate-centered. Candidates have had to raise more of their own money, define the issues on which they are running, and deliver their message to the voters with less and less help from the political parties. As Tari Renner points out in Chapter 7, political parties remain important as central service providers. But as Kasniunas et al. spell out in their chapter, interest groups both in their traditional forms and as 527 committees are having an ever-greater impact on campaign fundraising, issue advocacy, endorsements, and voter mobilizations. Their campaign contributions through PACs are critical to all major campaigns.

Political campaigns, which were for decades candidate-centered, are being more and more influenced by interest groups and big donors. Interest group and wealthy donor support may determine who has sufficient resources and who controls the dialogue in an election contest—and that can be dangerous.

Interest groups are invaluable in articulating the concerns of their members and in mobilizing voters on Election Day. Yet interest group–controlled campaigns are also a threat to democracy. As James Madison warned in *Federalist* No. 10, interest groups, which he called factions, promote the self-interest and ideological passions of some citizens over the rights of other citizens and the public interest. Interest group mobilization is good because it organizes individuals and gives a voice to their concerns. It amplifies their voices so that they are heard in government decision making. But interest groups also pose a threat. Wealthy donors may well pose an even greater threat because they may only espouse policies and elect officials who support laws that favor only the wealthy, lower their taxes, and destroy the middle-class, which is the backbone of our democracy.

While interest articulation is important, society also requires interest aggregation. While interest groups or movements like the Tea Party can further polarize political decision making in government, there is a need for the party-in-government function to organize different interests and factions and to bring about compromise in lawmaking. This is best done by political parties, which first of all bring together different interests and force groups to compromise in order to create a single political platform that will be supported by a majority of voters. Interest groups do not play this critical function. If interest group and wealthy donor campaigns become stronger, political parties may become too weak to play their role successfully.

Leave No Group Behind

Not only are campaign techniques changing, but the electorate is changing in fundamental ways. In 2008, nearly one in four voters was a racial minority, and minority voters increase with each election cycle. Whites still made up 76 percent of the 131 million people who voted in 2008, but blacks were 12 percent, Latinos 7 percent, and Asians 2.5 percent.[17] In the 2010 election, 6.6 million Latinos voted, again representing 7 percent of the voters, but they cast more than 12 million ballots in 2012.[18] Latinos continue to increase more rapidly than any other segment of society.

This has important political implications for while 52 percent of white voters identify Republican and only 39 percent identify Democratic, minorities remain steadfastly Democratic. Eighty-six percent of African Americans and 64 percent of Latino voters are Democrats or continue to identify as Democrats.[19]

The big story, however, is the population changes that will occur. For example, Chicago, which was previously largely populated with white ethnic groups and African Americans, looks very different today. The Latino population has been growing steadily in the city and is a growing political force. While Latinos are only 29 percent of Chicago's population now, 41 percent of the Chicago children under eighteen years of age are Latino.[20] As they become eligible to vote, Latinos are going to become a major political force, not only in Chicago but in the suburbs and the country at large.

Under these population changes, we have no choice but to develop multiracial and multicultural campaigns.

While it is heartening that more women and minorities are being elected to office with more than 10,000 African Americans, 5,850 Latinos, and 4,000 Asians now holding some of the 540,000 elected positions, the simple change of gender or race of those holding public office does not automatically guarantee better government. Despite having an African American president, we have not yet reached a nonracial or deracialized politics. Nor does "symbolic representation" of different racial representatives guarantee a political incorporation that creates policies in their best interests. Minorities and women have been as guilty of public corruption and bad decisions as white men. But cutting-edge campaigns in statewide and federal elections have to do a better job of promoting minority and women candidates and in appealing to minority and women voters.

Citizen Participation Despite Obstacles

One good sign has been citizen voter participation in elections in spite of obstacles state and local governments have tried to erect. While states have initiated voter ID laws to deter turnout, the fact is that voter turnout in the last two presidential elections is up. As Jeffrey Crouch notes in Chapter 11, voter ID laws have created tremendous controversy. That controversy has been played up in the media such as on the Spanish-language network Univision. Univision showed long lines of minorities queuing up to "early" vote in Florida in 2012 despite the state restricting early voting. Yet these voters were determined to vote and waited hours on their days off to do so. While the intent has been to restrict voting, it has mostly backfired.

Winning Elections and the Democratic Process

Campaigns for elected office are exciting, demanding, and rewarding. They are essential to democracy. New campaign techniques, for the most part, simply modernize the basic campaign strategies articulated by Abraham Lincoln. The cutting-edge campaigns with new campaign technologies have the potential to allow "the little guy" to participate more effectively and to better inform the electorate. However, they also have a dark side: the possibility of manipulation, disinformation, and unfair negative tactics, which defeat good candidates and create greater voter apathy and antipathy. They have the potential of invading our privacy to microtarget us as potential supporters for a candidate for whom we would not otherwise vote.

The ideal model of election communication is a debate in which the voters can hear all the candidates at the same time and weigh carefully the strengths and weaknesses of the candidates themselves and their stands on issues. We can come closer to achieving this ideal with new laws creating public financing of elections, requiring greater transparency especially of financial donors, and providing better privacy protections. All of these changes contribute to the debate standard in which candidates are better able to communicate to voters, must disclose their financial contributors, and are less able to use microtargeting to manipulate voters.

In the end, however, modern campaign techniques will not be controlled by new laws alone. Nor can the potential evils of political campaigns be curbed by protests by political scientists and editorial writers. These new cutting-edge campaigns with their modern technology can be made to serve and not to subvert democracy only if the public uses the additional information and Internet possibilities to elect the best possible candidates. Voters must reject candidates who misuse new technology to spread disinformation about themselves or their opponents.

If the democratic ideal remains a public debate, then all candidates must have the opportunity to present themselves and their messages as unfiltered as possible to the public. With public financing, full campaign contribution disclosure, and guaranteed voter privacy, candidates will have an equal chance to present their cases to the voters without undue microtargeting and media manipulation. With greater candidate information presented by cable television and the Internet, careful campaign scrutiny by political reporters and bloggers, and neutral voter information pamphlets published by the government, voters will have the opportunity to cast informed votes that best reflect their beliefs and best promote the public interest. Finally, automatic registration of all legal voters and easier access to the voting booth by extending periods of early voting and deadlines for mail-in ballots can increase voter registration and participation so that an actual majority of citizens vote. All of these changes need to occur if we are to have fair elections in the twenty-first century.

New cutting-edge political campaigns using advanced technology and new methods have the prospect of either promoting or undermining democracy. To make sure that democracy is promoted, we need new campaign laws. Most of all, however, we need an aware and informed electorate that will elect those candidates who use the new techniques to increase democracy and defeat those who would subvert it.

Notes

1. Dennis Johnson, *Campaigning in the Twenty-First Century* (New York: Routledge, 2011), 45–46.
2. Johnson, *Campaigning in the Twenty-First Century,* 44.
3. Center for Responsive Politics. Accessed on July 1, 2015, from http://www.opensecrets.org.
4. Johnson, *Campaigning in the Twenty-First Century,* 45.
5. Center for Responsive Politics.
6. See pages 22–23 of this volume.
7. Joe McGinniss, *The Selling of the President 1968* (New York: Simon and Schuster, 1969).
8. Johnson, *Campaigning in the Twenty-First Century,* 67; Dennis Johnson, No Place for Amateurs: How Political Consultants Are Reshaping American Democracy, 2nd ed. (New York: Routledge, 2007), Chapter 5.
9. Paul M. Schwartz, "Privacy, Ethics, and Analytics" (*Privacy Interests,* The IEEE Computer and Reliable Societies, 2011), 67–68. Accessed on July 1, 2015, from http://www.paulschwartz.net/pdf/pschwartz_privacy-eth-analytics%20IEEE%20P-%20Sec%20%282011%29.pdf. Among his recommendations are develop organizational policies that govern information management, training, and oversight; implement appropriate safeguards to protect the security of information; and avoid collecting certain kinds of information.
10. Steve Pearson and Ford O'Connell, "Down Home Digital" (*Campaigns and Elections,* June 2011), 49. See also Averill Peasin, "Consultant to Consultant," a paid insert in the same issue.
11. Richard Auxier and Alex Tyson, "Uploading Democracy: Candidates Field YouTube Questions" (Pew Research Center Publications, July 24, 2007).
12. Philip N. Howard, *New Media Campaigns and the Managed Citizen* (Cambridge University Press, 2006), 3.
13. See page 128 of this volume.

14. Kathy Kiely, "Clinton, Obama Step Up Attacks at South Carolina Debate" (*USA Today*, January 21, 2008). Accessed on September 2, 2011, from usatoday.com.

15. Joseph Graf and Jeremy D. Mayer, "Campaign Press Coverage—Instantaneous" in *Campaigns on the Cutting Edge* (2nd ed.), edited by Richard J. Semiatin. Los Angeles, CA: SAGE, 2013. 153.

16. "UPDATE—21.5% Youth Turnout" (The Center for Information and Research on Civil Learning and Engagement). Accessed on July 1, 2015, from http://www.civicyouth.org/21-3youth-turnout.

17. Mark Hugo Lopez and Paul Taylor, "Dissecting the 2008 Electorate: Most Diverse in U.S. History" (Pew Research Center, April 30, 2009). Accessed on July 1, 2015, from http/pewresearch.org/pubs/1209/racial-ethnic-voters-presidential elections.

18. Rick Person, "Latino Vote Projected to Hit Record in 2012" (*Chicago Tribune,* June 23, 2011).

19. "GOP Makes Big Gains among White Voters" (Pew Research Center, July 22, 2011). Accessed on October 18, 2015, from http://pewresearch.org/pubs/2067/2012-elecdtorate-partisan-affliations-gop-gains-white-voters.

20. Latino Policy Forum, "2010 Census Update" (August 8, 2011).

INDEX

CQ Press, an imprint of SAGE, is the leading publisher of books, periodicals, and electronic products on American government and international affairs. CQ Press consistently ranks among the top commercial publishers in terms of quality, as evidenced by the numerous awards its products have won over the years. CQ Press owes its existence to Nelson Poynter, former publisher of the *St. Petersburg Times*, and his wife Henrietta, with whom he founded Congressional Quarterly in 1945. Poynter established CQ with the mission of promoting democracy through education and in 1975 founded the Modern Media Institute, renamed The Poynter Institute for Media Studies after his death. The Poynter Institute (*www.poynter.org*) is a nonprofit organization dedicated to training journalists and media leaders.

In 2008, CQ Press was acquired by SAGE, a leading international publisher of journals, books, and electronic media for academic, educational, and professional markets. Since 1965, SAGE has helped inform and educate a global community of scholars, practitioners, researchers, and students spanning a wide range of subject areas, including business, humanities, social sciences, and science, technology, and medicine. A privately owned corporation, SAGE has offices in Los Angeles, London, New Delhi, and Singapore, in addition to the Washington, DC, office of CQ Press.